THE CUP
THEY
COULDN'T
LOSE

Also by Shane Ryan

Slaying the Tiger:
A Year Inside the Ropes on the New PGA Tour

THE CUP
THEY
COULDN'T
LOSE

AMERICA, THE RYDER CUP, AND THE LONG
ROAD TO WHISTLING STRAITS

SHANE RYAN

New York

Hachette Books
Hachette Book Group
1290 Avenue of the Americas
New York, NY 10104
HachetteBooks.com
Twitter.com/HachetteBooks
Instagram.com/HachetteBooks

First Edition: May 2022

Published by Hachette Books, an imprint of Perseus Books, LLC, a subsidiary of Hachette Book Group, Inc. The Hachette Books name and logo is a trademark of the Hachette Book Group.

The Hachette Speakers Bureau provides a wide range of authors for speaking events.
To find out more, go to www.hachettespeakersbureau.com or call (866) 376-6591.

The publisher is not responsible for websites (or their content) that are not owned by the publisher.

ISBNs: 978-0-306-87441-3 (hardcover), 978-0-306-87439-0 (ebook)

Library of Congress Control Number: 2022932466

Printed in the United States of America

LSC-C

Printing 1, 2022

To Harold, for the past, and to Emily,

Sutton, and Alden, for the future.

CONTENTS

A SHORT PRIMER

The Ryder Cup is a three-day competition pitting the best golfers from the United States against the best from Europe. It has been staged every two years since 1927, with a lapse from 1937 to 1947 for World War II. It was delayed by a year in 2001 after the September 11 attacks, putting the Cup on even years, and is now back in odd years after another one-year delay in 2020 for the COVID-19 pandemic.

Each team fields twelve players, a mixture of automatic qualifiers and captain's picks, the balance of which has changed over time. The event uses the match play format, in which the score is kept by holes won and usually listed in reference to the winning team. As an example, if the American team wins holes one through three, they are 3-up, and if Europe wins the fourth hole, the US falls to 2-up. The match ends when one team has established a lead that is greater than the number of remaining holes. Thus, if a team wins by the score of 3&2, it means they were 3-up with two holes to play; it was no longer possible for the other team to beat or tie them.

On Friday, the first day of competition, there are four two-on-two matches of four-ball (each player plays his own ball, and the best score wins the hole for his team) and four two-on-two matches of foursomes (teammates alternate shots). Each match is worth 1 point. If a match is tied after eighteen holes, the match is "halved," and each team receives half a point. The home captain has the right to choose which session is played in the morning and which is played in the afternoon, and it's also up to each captain to choose which eight players compete in each session, and which four sit out. This format repeats on Saturday, and on

Sunday, all twelve players from each team square off in a singles match. In total, 28 points are at stake—16 from pairs matches, 12 from singles. The team that holds the Cup needs to win half of these points, 14, to retain the trophy, while the team trying to take the Cup back must win 14.5 points.

The Ryder Cup venue rotates every two years between the United States and Europe. It is organized in the United States by the PGA of America, which is distinct from the PGA Tour, and in Europe by the European Tour. The 2021 Ryder Cup took place in late September at Whistling Straits Golf Course on the western shore of Lake Michigan, a few miles north of Sheboygan, Wisconsin.

After a blowout win in Paris in 2018, the Cup was in European hands. The Americans had to win it back.

"You've probably heard this in press conferences, where losing captains and players will say, 'Well, the other guys just played better.' Can you imagine if someone said that in the defense world? The general has to go and explain why he lost the war, and he says, 'Well, the other guys just fought better.' Or in the business world, the CEO has to explain why he lost a million dollars and he says, 'Oh, the other guy just sold more widgets.' I got tired of hearing it. Yes, there's variance in results. Yes, there's unpredictability. But the Ryder Cup fundamentally is an organizational and a management challenge. It's a collective action problem. How do you channel the talents and abilities of a large group of people into a common goal? The reality is that winning Ryder Cups is making lots and lots of right decisions enough times to increase your chances of winning."

—Jason Aquino, founder of Scouts Consulting Group,
Team USA's strategic analysts

PROLOGUE

The Weight of History

Kevin, Stewart, and the Big Problem

"You know, if I could put my finger on it, we would have changed this shit a long time ago."

—Jim Furyk

On Saturday at the 2021 BMW Championship in Maryland, another merciless scorcher of a day in a long, hot August, I sat on a stone wall by the clubhouse and waited for Kevin Kisner to finish his round.

I'd alerted the PGA Tour's media officials that I wanted to speak with him, but I was dreading it, and they weren't thrilled about having to ask. Two weeks earlier, Kisner had won the Wyndham Championship in Greensboro, reviving his hopes of making the Ryder Cup team for the first time. The great irony of Kisner's career is that he is one of America's best match play golfers, but has never made a Ryder Cup team. He checks all the boxes—smart, combative, and with the kind of relentless game that wears his opponents down. He holds a 16-6-2 career match play singles record, with a win at the 2019 WGC Match Play and a second-place finish a year earlier, and a 2-0-2 mark the one time he played a Presidents Cup. His list of conquests reads like a who's who of great match play golfers: Matt Kuchar, Francesco Molinari, Louis Oosthuizen, Tony Finau, Dustin Johnson, Patrick Reed, and Ian Poulter.

But he's never managed to play well enough to qualify for the Ryder Cup at the right time, and though he's seemingly in the discussion every year, he's also failed to earn a captain's pick. If he were European, it's possible he'd be a Poulter-like figure, because his skill and résumé would have landed him on several European teams, and their captains tend to value match play as a distinct discipline. In America, he has been lost in the depth of talent and the inability of captains to see his value.

History seemed to be repeating itself in 2021. A few days after his win in Greensboro, I was the only media member to show up for his virtual press conference, which clearly annoyed him—"Thanks for valuing my time," he grumbled—and almost as quickly as the Kisner Ryder Cup buzz grew, it seemed to fade. He missed the cut at The Northern Trust the next week to start the PGA Tour's playoffs, and while I waited for him by the clubhouse at the BMW, he was on his way to finishing in a tie for dead last.

We didn't yet know that Steve Stricker, the US captain, was focused on players that fit the profile of Whistling Straits, which rewarded length, and that Kisner, a shorter hitter, wasn't on his radar. But the writing was on the wall, and it was another piece of sad irony—in this case, Stricker was smart in his thinking, but in 2018, when Kisner's profile fit Le Golf National to perfection, captain Jim Furyk used his picks on long hitters who spent the week flailing around in the thick Paris rough. Always, it seemed, Kisner was on the wrong end of Ryder Cup fortune. (Later, Furyk recognized that Kisner was exactly the kind of player he'd needed in Paris.)

I liked Kisner—he was generous with his time in 2019 when I picked his brain on the art of match play, and he's funny in an aggressive, bust-your-balls way. When we spoke at Bay Hill that year, he told me to meet him during the Wednesday pro-am, and when I caught up to him on the course, he turned and flashed an angry glare.

"What the *hell* are you doing here?" he hissed.

My stomach sank, and I thought of a thousand ways to explain myself and apologize, but in the end I just stared at him dumbly. He broke out laughing—this was his idea of a good joke. Later, in the middle of our interview, he spotted a friend near the ropes and shouted a greeting in his South Carolina drawl: "What's up, pencil dick?" And when our interview entered the ninth minute, he groaned. "*God*, are you writing a fucking novel?"

But in the midst of that banter, he gave me the best schooling I've had in what makes match play so different from stroke play. He spoke of how it benefits people like him who have a cutthroat mentality when it comes to one-on-one competition, and how that mentality is underused in golf, where the vast majority of tournaments are one-man-against-the-field stroke play; how being a shorter hitter, a liability in stroke play, can become an advantage when the shorter player hits his approach first and puts pressure on the opponent (I watched Ian Poulter drive Rory McIlroy out of his mind doing this over and over in a 6&5 victory at the 2021 WGC Match Play); how the tension on every single hole rewards grinders who aren't afraid of the heat; how a sense of momentum is critical; and how the ability to do something unexpected, like chipping in from off the green, can devastate an opponent who isn't mentally prepared.

At the end of our conversation, he gave me the best description I've ever heard of the difference between match play and stroke play.

"It's like having a ten-footer to win on the last hole of a stroke play event six times per round," he said. "You feel like this has to happen *right now*."

If there was one player I wanted to see in the Ryder Cup, it was Kisner. But that Saturday at the BMW, as I tracked his increasingly mediocre round on my phone, I got the distinct sense that I was about to see his dark side up close. And for what? To pile on, and remind him that he wasn't going to make the Ryder Cup team?

In a moment that contained both wisdom and cowardice, I went back to the Tour media official and called an audible: Stewart Cink was also in Kisner's group, and if possible, I'd like to speak with him instead.

A few minutes later, Cink ambled over. He had shocked the golf world by winning the RBC Heritage at Hilton Head earlier in the spring at age forty-seven, with his son caddying, and now he was making his deepest playoff run in a very long time. More importantly for my purposes, he had played in five Ryder Cups, losing all but one of them, and though he seemed like an obvious choice for a future captaincy, he was clearly outside the clique that now dominated the US order of succession. It was almost certain that he'd never get his chance.

"You and I are both on the same part of the pipeline," he admitted a bit ruefully. "I think if convention had stayed the same as it was fifteen or twenty years ago, I probably would have been in line. I played a lot of Ryder Cups, I won a major championship. But when the task force came about, conventions started to break down. It's not necessarily a bad thing. But it's a bad thing for me."

The one Ryder Cup his team won came in 2008, when Paul Azinger instituted his famous "pod" system, taking a page from the US Navy SEALs by placing his players in smaller units of four to foster camaraderie. The philosophy turned out to be a stroke of genius, effective and empowering, and every player on that team still brims with good memories of how they crushed Nick Faldo and the Europeans that weekend in Kentucky . . . especially after being crushed themselves in the three preceding Ryder Cups. Cink was no different, and after he finished listing the virtues of Azinger's approach, I asked a question that had been bothering me for a long time.

"Does it ever seem strange to you," I asked, "that you lose three in a row coming into this, Azinger does this new thing, it works perfectly . . . Does it seem strange that you don't just keep doing it?"

He paused, and I got the sense that I had asked the right question. The silence lingered, and he shook his head like someone who had thought of this question many times, but never the answer.

"It's one of the strangest things in my whole career."

* * *

A month later, in the media center before the start of the 2021 Ryder Cup in Wisconsin, a lot of very smart people were ignoring the facts on the ground. The American team assembled for Whistling Straits was superior on paper; it was already obvious that Steve Stricker was at least competent as a captain—perhaps much better than competent—and the home team had the advantage of a partisan crowd that, thanks to the pandemic, would be almost bereft of European supporters. Every factor pointed to an American win, and to analyze the problem objectively was to arrive at the inevitable conclusion that it probably wouldn't be close.

Clear as the outcome may have seemed, it was impossible for many to believe. There was an underlying sense that Europe would find a way, for the simple fact that they *always* found a way, and the Americans would implode because they *always* implode. I predicted the US blowout on the record, but the minute that prediction was published, I was consumed with doubt—I had missed something, I was sure, and was setting myself up to look like an idiot.

Why were we all so scared? Why was Team Europe in our heads?

If you ask that question, you might as well ask a few others: In the eighteen Ryder Cups between 1983—the start of the modern competitive era—and 2018, why did Europe win twelve Ryder Cups to just six for the Americans? Why did they amass a 158.5-129.5 edge in pairs matches, while the singles were almost dead even, with America leading by a single point, 108.5-107.5?

If America routinely has the advantage in terms of talent, tournament wins, world rankings, and success in the majors, how have they only *just* managed to eke out a .500 record in singles, and how are they routinely pounded into submission in pairs matches?

The answer is as simple—and complicated—as history.

* * *

It can be hard to remember today, but for the first fifty-six years of the Ryder Cup, America dominated. By the time the United States won in 1983 at PGA National in Florida, their record was a gaudy 21-3-1. The talent deficit was massive, and so were the margins.

None of it was surprising, considering the superior state of American golf. The only remarkable fact about those early days was that the Ryder Cup survived at all. Had this relentless slaughter taken place in the modern era, when sporting events depend for their lives on ad revenue and TV viewership, and top professional golfers are loaded with lucrative opportunities that eat up their time and energy, an unpaid exhibition without a hint of competitive balance would have died a swift death.

Instead, the Ryder Cup seemed bound for a very slow death, and the fifty-year anniversary found the event in a state of near ruin. Those who saw the problem most clearly had some tricks up their sleeves, like adding Irish golfers to the British team and decreasing the number of matches to create parity, but nothing worked. Americans became increasingly indifferent, and the British governing bodies became increasingly desperate. Finally, the Great Britain and Ireland team expanded to all of Europe, incorporating nations like Spain and Germany, who were entering the global golf conversation with emerging superstars like Seve Ballesteros and Bernhard Langer.

Their high hopes sputtered out. Continental Europe didn't have enough to offer, at least not yet, and at the start of the 1981 Cup, the British golfer Howard Clark was shocked to overhear his captain, John Jacobs, asking the Americans to "go easy on us." Confidence was non-existent. By the early 1980s, the British PGA lost its principal sponsor, top American players were pulling out for dubious reasons—a sure sign that whatever prestige the event retained was leaking away fast—and the Ryder Cup was on death's door. The modern era was rearing its head, and it didn't have space for a lopsided exhibition that couldn't make anyone rich.

What happened next was one of the greatest turnaround stories in the history of sport. A new sponsor gave the Europeans a short lifeline, and they chose a thirty-eight-year-old English golfer named Tony Jacklin as Europe's next captain. They needed the situation to change fast, and somehow, it did. Jacklin delivered so quickly, in fact, that the results are mind-boggling to review today. In 1983, he led his team to America, where no foreign Ryder Cup team had ever won, and lost by a single point. In 1985, at the Belfry in England, his team won for the first time in twenty-eight years. In 1987, they went back to America and accomplished the unthinkable, winning in the belly of the beast.

By 1991 in Kiawah Island, the tension was so high, and the two teams loathed each other to such a degree, that the Ryder Cup became irresistible. After a dramatic and controversial Sunday that included the first really passionate gallery of American Ryder Cup fans, the United States won back the trophy.

You might expect that an era of parity would ensue. Instead, the pattern of utter domination reasserted itself, but with the two teams flipped. Between Jacklin's first victory in 1985 and the 2018 romp at Le Golf National in Paris, Team Europe won twelve Ryder Cups out of seventeen. How do you go from 3-22 over the first fifty-six years to 12-5 over the next thirty-three? How do you stun the world's greatest players so thoroughly that it takes them literal *decades* to recover?

How do you stop history in its tracks, and then reverse it?

It's a question that has been endlessly debated, analyzed, and picked apart. The one constant is that most Americans with any influence tend to get the answer wrong, and the ones who get it right are treated like heretics. Meanwhile, decades pass, superstars come and go, and the losses mount.

All of it, inevitably, leads to another question that every American captain must face. It's a question that becomes more urgent with time, and one that landed with particular force on the narrow shoulders of Steve Stricker:

How do you reverse history again?

Welcome to the mystery of the Ryder Cup. Welcome to the forty-year story that culminates on the western shores of Lake Michigan, and a course called Whistling Straits.

CHAPTER ONE

December 2019, Melbourne, Australia

Fires down under ... the great escape ...
the end of the legend of Patrick Reed

We knew Australia was burning. We could smell it in the air.

As omens go, it was almost too good, and certainly better than we deserved—the unseen fires, closer all the time, heralded by the faint odor of smoke ... the vapors of the coming wrath. A better thinker, one more in tune with the apocalyptic thunderclaps arriving by the minute, might have seen the shape of what was hurtling toward us down the doomsday pipeline. Not me. I had just survived the miserable cramped plane ride from Los Angeles, fifteen godforsaken hours, and the only selfish concern in my head was that they'd hold off the flames long enough to stage the Presidents Cup.

In Sydney, the capital, where the Australian Open golf tournament had been played a week earlier, the effect from the bushfires was so bad that just breathing the city air for a day was the equivalent of smoking two packs of cigarettes. On the course, the players coughed through the smoke, eyes burning, and couldn't see where their balls landed through the haze. Farther south, in Melbourne, there was talk that the more famous Australian Open, the tennis tournament, would have to be canceled in January as the fires raged toward the coast.

In those days of ignorance, we still thought that the Ryder Cup would be played in ten months in Wisconsin, and that Australia would be a preview. We'd learn a little about the team, the captains, and whether their collective psyche had recovered from the drubbing handed to them by the Europeans in Paris at the 2018 Ryder Cup—a loss so bad that it called into question every bit of progress they were supposed to have made since 2014, through the "task force" that emerged in the aftermath of the previous drubbing in Scotland.

You often hear that Ryder Cup season begins at the Presidents Cup, and it's probably true. First off, everything that comes before—the choice of captain, the one-year-to-go pressers—is interesting but still vague. It's impossible to tell what kind of leader Steve Stricker or Pádraig Harrington will become based on a few remarks made at a presser in gray Wisconsin a year before anyone hits an actual shot. And if you *could* tell, it would mean one of them had said something remarkably stupid, which even the really legendary flops manage to avoid.

The Presidents Cup, though, gives us the first chance to see the Americans in action at a team match play event that's almost identical in format to the Ryder Cup. It's where they take on the International Team, the long-suffering kid brother that includes the entire rest of the world minus Europe. Many of the American players are the same, the US Ryder Cup captain is usually on site, and whether they admit it or not, many see it as a tune-up for the big show.

Tiger Woods would serve as playing captain for the Americans in Melbourne, but my eyes were on his assistant, Stricker, the man set to take center stage in Wisconsin. We knew that Stricker was "nice"—so nice that he had never won a major, which made him the first American captain in that category—but in terms of his leadership style, and whether he was the right man for the job, we were clueless. All you could say, back then, was that the choice wasn't exactly inspiring, at least if masculine charisma and career accomplishments are your criteria. Was there anything *to* the man, so slight, so nervous? We didn't know.

And there was something else we didn't know. Five thousand miles to the northwest, in a Chinese provincial capital called Wuhan, a handful of otherwise healthy people were coming down with pneumonia, and nobody knew why. By the time they figured it out, it was already too late—the entire world was about to be shattered, and the effects would trickle down everywhere. Even to golf, and even to the Ryder Cup.

That week in Melbourne, we were living in the last days of the pre-COVID era, when all we had to worry about were jet lag, an inscrutable captain, and the ominous fires just out of sight, forecasting our grim future.

* * *

"He doesn't know it's a damn show! He thinks it's a damn fight!"
—Duke the trainer, just as Rocky begins to beat the
hell out of Apollo Creed

The one near guarantee in Melbourne was that the Americans would win. Prior to 2019, in twelve Presidents Cups, the US won ten and tied another. The Americans hadn't lost in twenty-one years, and on paper they were miles better than the International Team captained by Ernie Els, who would arrive at Royal Melbourne Golf Club with a motley crew that included seven rookies.

There was no reason to suspect trouble, and history made the Americans oblivious. They had no clue what Els had planned for them: that for the first time, an International Team captain was taking the Presidents Cup very seriously, and thinking not just of victory in Australia, but of the future—of turning the International Team into an institution that could actually compete. Els and his unlikely team were on the verge of making the 2019 Presidents Cup a shocking, unqualified success, and seriously rattling the cages of the complacent Americans.

Unaware of the trap awaiting them, the Americans came in woefully unprepared. On Monday night, on the banks of the Yarra River in

Melbourne's business district, I watched Tiger Woods, Justin Thomas, and Xander Schauffele take the stage at a promotional event just hours after emerging from the charter plane that had taken all twelve of them from Tiger's Hero World Challenge in the Bahamas. Exhaustion painted their faces, and a bleary-eyed Thomas barely had the energy to crack a joke about his fatigue. Their travel experience was more luxurious than mine by a factor of about a thousand, but I recognized my own raw mental state in them. Call it Trans-Pacific Travel Dread—a mixture of confusion, anxiety, and comprehensive weariness that comes from spending a full day in the air and landing in a strange land where winter has become summer and you've skipped ahead a full day.

Not an auspicious start. And amid the fatigue, the ugly specter of American dysfunction was already raising its head. This was the week when Patrick Reed managed to finally, and emphatically, kill his viability as a captain's pick.

* * *

Reed and I were old friends, dating back to 2015, when I wrote about his college career, and the bad news is that we have to revisit that history now. He'd been kicked out of Georgia after a year for two alcohol violations, the second of which he tried to hide from his coach, and before that he'd been accused by his teammates of cheating during a qualifying event. Then he went to Augusta State, where he turned the entire team against him almost immediately, and once again he was accused of cheating, this time by shaving strokes in two straight qualifying events. His teammates held a meeting and voted to kick him off the team, but Augusta State coach Josh Gregory reduced it to a two-match suspension. Reed went on to lead them to two national titles, the second in a championship showdown against Georgia. In the final match of his career, against Georgia's Harris English, Reed's Augusta State teammates approached *English* before the match to wish him luck. He had none—Reed won in a match that one onlooker called "the death of karma."

When the ugly details came out, Reed set to work blundering his way into deeper trouble, which was the start of a PR strategy that he's doggedly stuck to ever since. He went on the Golf Channel, produced a couple of vague statements from his coaches, and generally took the path of full denial. The end result was that Reed's teammates who had previously been silent came out of the woodwork to crucify him further, confirming the old details and adding new ones. *Deadspin* summed it up in a headline: "Patrick Reed Takes a Swing at Defending Himself, Slices into the Woods."

And life moved on. Just as in 2014, Reed was a Ryder Cup hero in 2016, going 3-1-1 and winning an electric match against Rory McIlroy in Sunday singles. McIlroy had never lost a Ryder Cup singles match before, and he had plenty of fireworks for Reed on the front nine, but the American had all the answers. After a legendary exchange of long birdie putts on the eighth hole that sent the Minnesota crowd into hysterics, Reed spent the back nine handing McIlroy his first loss.

That win was the height of his match play reputation—he was Captain America, and whatever his history, nobody could deny his greatness.

Things got better from there, and then a whole lot worse. He achieved golf immortality in 2018 by winning the Masters, but every time his Ryder Cup and Masters performances threatened to swing the narrative in his favor, he'd backslide. The stories never stopped: he'd carp to a rules official, saying, "I guess my name needs to be Jordan Spieth," after an unfavorable ruling, or huff off after a bad round and snub the media, or yell at a cameraman for jingling change in his pockets, or publicly complain to the PGA Tour because the seats they got him at Fenway Park weren't good enough. As Joel Beall at *Golf Digest* reported, someone on his team even seemed to be using a burner Twitter account to attack his fellow pros. By the end of 2018, the general feeling of the golf world reflected an old quote by Kisner about Reed: "I don't know that they'd piss on him if he was on fire."

Then came Paris and the 2018 Ryder Cup, where Reed was a walking disaster, hacking his way to two losses on the first two days and putting the first dent in his Captain America image. After the team loss, he made the bizarre choice to unleash on Jim Furyk in a phone call to his anointed media confessor, the *New York Times*' Karen Crouse. He said he felt "blindsided" when Furyk didn't pair him with Spieth, his old reliable partner. "The issue's obviously with Jordan not wanting to play with me," he said, and went on to decry the "buddy system" that left him out in the cold. (On this, sources have told me he was right—Spieth called Furyk before the Ryder Cup and asked not to be paired with Reed.) He concluded with great irony by blaming the American failure on the fact that they couldn't leave their egos at the door.

It was a shocking attempt at mutiny. Reed seemed to believe that going to the media would earn him sympathy from teammates or fans. "I was looking at him [Furyk] like I was about to light the room up like Phil in '14," he said, a reference to Mickelson's rebellion against Tom Watson that led to the task force and radically changed the way the Americans approach the Ryder Cup. The difference is that Mickelson had the stature to make a bold move, and he picked the perfect moment to obliterate Watson in public . . . and even then, he did so with reluctance. Reed, in contrast, lacked any social capital, and the fact that he expected a positive outcome from attacking a respected figure like Furyk showed a level of delusion that was almost unbelievable.

Which is a lot of backstory to get to this: it was a shock when Tiger Woods selected Reed as a captain's pick for Melbourne. Reed had apparently "cleared the air" with Tiger and his American teammates, but to take someone like Reed for a team event is to take a big risk—to balance his incredible skill at match play with the decent chance that he could become a fully malignant clubhouse cancer.

If nothing else, it was clear that Reed had one more chance to ingratiate himself with his team and to behave like someone who could be trusted. Tiger's confidence gave him a new lease on life as a captain's pick, and all he had to do was make sure he didn't do something stupid. He needed only a temporary pause in the ongoing debacle that is the Patrick Reed Show, just long enough to get the hell out of Australia.

And then came the Incident.

* * *

It happened the week before, while Reed and everyone else on the US team except Dustin Johnson were playing in the invite-only Hero World Classic hosted by Tiger in the Bahamas. Reed found himself in a waste area that looked indistinguishable from a sand trap. The rules, though, are different: in the waste area, a player is allowed to ground his club. Which is exactly what Reed did, but then he proceeded to drag the club backward, sweeping away the sand in front of his ball. Then he resettled the club and did it again.

This is blatantly illegal, and nothing about it was ambiguous. Reed had improved his lie by clearing the path to his ball, and when the first effort wasn't satisfactory, he did it again. The TV cameras caught him red-handed, and Golf.com's Dylan Dethier, on the scene, heard Rickie Fowler say, "I don't even know what you have to review." On the telecast, Paul Azinger was similarly unimpressed. "If that's not improving your lie, I don't know what is," he said. "He knows better."

Reed was assessed a two-stroke penalty when the round was over, but the bigger problem was the hit to his reputation. Before long, someone dug up a clip of him doing the same exact thing at a 2015 tournament, and for a guy whose credibility was already in the mud, who had been accused of cheating in the past, it was like throwing gas on the flames. He was skewered.

At the Golf Channel, Brandel Chamblee came out firing on Monday. "Deep down in the marrow of this team, they will be affected by this controversy," he said. "Their DNA as a team has been altered. There's just no two ways about it. To defend what Patrick Reed did is to defend cheating."

Chamblee went so far as to say that when Tiger added Reed to the team, he "made a deal with the devil." By forcing the Americans to defend him, Reed put them in an impossible situation and forced them to greet an obvious violation—one that would have horrified most of them to commit, in a sport where players frequently call penalties on themselves even when the cameras aren't running—with silence, putting their own integrity on the line.

On that front, the only player on the International Team who spoke out unapologetically was Cameron Smith, the twenty-six-year-old Aussie. While everyone else was giving the standard "We've moved on" quotes, Smith unloaded both barrels. "To give a bit of a bullshit response like the camera angle," he said, "that's pretty up there . . . I don't have any sympathy for anyone that cheats. I hope the crowd absolutely gives it to not only him, but everyone [on the US team] next week."

When Reed went out for his practice round in Australia, he was greeted on the first tee by a fan taking on the role of volunteer PA announcer: "On the first tee, from the United States . . . the excavator!"

Coupled with the exhausting travel, it would further burden a team that was already in trouble. This was the definition of the dreaded distraction, but it put the most pressure on Reed. Making a deal with the devil is useful only if the devil can give you something important in exchange, and everyone was watching . . . especially Steve Stricker.

* * *

Royal Melbourne is the kind of golf club that gets the diehards salivating, and with good reason: in the baked summer climate of southern Australia, it stands out as a beautiful, temperamental piece of architecture, a true product of its geography. Clusters of low, gnarled tea trees with peeling bark crowd the fairways, sharing space with the flowering gums and the purple blooms of the jacaranda. Monterey cypress trees like those found on Pebble Beach are one of the few nonnative species on the course, but they work exceptionally well in the arid climate, their high, jagged crowns framing most holes—and the course itself—in a stark and imposing tableau. The Bermuda grass fairways remain a resplendent green with the aid of sulfate fertilizer and perhaps a bit of transnatural art, but when it gives way to the dry heathland, the wallaby grass, stipa, and sword sedge take over.

A northerly wind blew on Monday, picking up heat from the Outback, driving temperatures into triple digits and bringing the dreaded *musca vetustissima*, the "bush fly" that is attracted to human bodily fluids and wreaks havoc on anyone deranged enough to step outside. By Tuesday, the wind had changed, coming from the south and leading to far cooler temperatures and fewer flies. It stayed that way for the remainder of the week, a small blessing for Americans journeying from winter conditions.

The matches for the first four-ball session were announced on Wednesday night, and the most interesting pick of the session came almost immediately, when Tiger selected himself and Justin Thomas to face Marc Leishman and Joaquín Niemann. It's no surprise that Tiger chose Thomas as his partner. With his friend Jordan Spieth out of the action after a tough year, Thomas was the man everyone wanted on his team. The twenty-six-year-old from Louisville had already emerged as one of the great team match play golfers on the American side—in one Presidents Cup and one Ryder Cup, he'd amassed a 7-2-1 record—and depending on how things went in Melbourne, he'd have a chance to stake his claim as the "real" Captain America. He was popular among his teammates and well liked generally, which made him an irresistible choice for Tiger.

He and Tiger won that opening match, 4&3, but it would be the only match the Americans won on Thursday. Elsewhere, it was a shocking call to arms for the Internationals, who took a 4-1 lead on the strength of Els's master plan. Mixing veterans with rookies and relying on statistics to find the best pairings within that framework, Els dialed the right numbers up and down the board.

I followed Patrick Reed that morning to see how the Australian fans would treat him in his match with Webb Simpson against C. T. Pan and Hideki Matsuyama. Under gray skies and a mist so light it barely deserved the name, Reed emerged from the crowd and strode onto the first tee. When the music died, the time had come to unleash hell on the American.

"Are you going to make your caddie carry fourteen clubs and a shovel?" shouted one.

"Improve your lie off the tee!" screamed another.

The insults got less clever from there, with a few cries of "Sand wedge!" and "Tell me where the bunkers are!" and the extremely blunt, unfriendly "Cheater!"

Reed, impassive in the face of the barrage, stepped up to hit his first drive, and because life has a sense of humor, it rolled into the greenside bunker. When it disappeared over the ledge on the big screen, the crowd roared its appreciation, and one of the Aussies sent him off with a warning: "Patrick, there's cameras out there too!"

So it began. He marched on in that hostile land, finding the sand on each of the first three holes. Reed and Simpson could have staved off the broader American disaster with even a half point, but instead they lost 1-up, and it gave the Internationals a 4-1 lead—not just the first lead they'd had after the first session since 2005, but the best lead they'd *ever* had at that point.

* * *

Friday brought with it the first alternate shot session, and late in the afternoon, things were proceeding so badly for the Americans that an 8-2 score felt downright realistic. With a margin like that, and only 15.5 points needed to secure the Cup, it's no exaggeration to say that the event would have been effectively over before the weekend.

Instead, still tired and confused, the Americans managed to shake off their fatigue to produce some very late magic. Call it a rearguard action, highlighted by Patrick Cantlay and Xander Schauffele making a critical birdie on hole eighteen to beat Joaquín Niemann and Adam Hadwin. In the most iconic moment of the day, Justin Thomas rose to the occasion yet again for the Americans, burying a fifteen footer for the win on the eighteenth hole. When the ball went down, he turned to his partner Tiger, stomped his feet dramatically on the green, and shouted,

"I love me some me!" (Long story, but Thomas borrowed the line from an old Terrell Owens video that had been making the rounds among the team.)

Miraculously, the Americans were trailing by just 3 points overall.

On Saturday, after Reed and Simpson suffered another loss, an incredible bit of news began to circulate in the media center: Kessler Karain, Reed's caddie, had apparently fought a fan. Barstool Sports came out with the first statement from Karain, who wrote, "I had had enough . . . riding on the cart, guy was about 3 feet from Patrick and said, 'You fucking suck.' I got off the cart and shoved him, said a couple things, probably a few expletives. Security came and I got back in the cart and left . . . unless his bones break like Mr. Glass, the most harm done was a little spilled beer, which I'm more than happy to reimburse him for."

It figured that the first time anyone on Reed's team had been honest and open with the media, it would be a caddie admitting he'd shoved a fan. PGA Tour commissioner Jay Monahan set up a meeting with Karain and quickly did the only thing he could do, which was to ban him from Sunday singles.

At that point, the American embarrassment felt well and truly complete. All that remained was to complete the disaster on the course, slink back to America, and ponder what it all meant for the next year.

Justin Thomas simply refused. He kept them alive again on Saturday, dragging the Internationals back to earth over and over in a lonely and stubborn act until reinforcements could arrive. The score by day's end was just 10-8 to the Internationals. The American team was finally awake, and their superior talent was about to become decisive.

* * *

Sunday singles is where narratives go to die. For three days, Els had taken a lesser team and dominated. Despite the fact that he was facing an opponent with players from the same country who all spoke the same language, he'd somehow built a more cohesive unit. In terms of tactics, he'd run circles around Tiger Woods, and it was only due to bad luck that his team wasn't leading by an insurmountable margin.

Once the players hit the course on Sunday, though, the captain's influence dwindles to almost nothing. It was time for the players to take over, and the Americans shone brighter from the start.

The story that sticks with me most from that final session came at the fifth hole, with Xander Schauffele 1-up on Adam Scott. This was an incredibly important match for Scott—not only was Presidents Cup pride at stake, but he was playing in front of his home crowd, and his team was relying on him to deliver a point. Els, his captain, was standing on the tee at the par-3 fifth, and though Scott wanted to hit a 9-iron, Els advised him to use an 8-iron instead to cut through the wind. Scott eventually relented, and his 8-iron went directly at the flag . . . and over the green. His lie was so bad that he had to take a drop, and by the time it was over, he had handed Schauffele the hole and a 2-up lead.

The walk to the fourth tee was a long one, and while observing Scott, Schauffele realized exactly how angry he was at Els's intervention. He turned to his caddie, Austin Kaiser, and conveyed a simple message: *he's pissed off, and it's time to take advantage.* The attitude was aggressive—press when you sense weakness—but later, Schauffele explained that there was a more practical side too. On the back nine, he was sure Scott would make a run, propelled by the crowd, and a slim lead wasn't going to be enough. Now was the time to run up the score and prepare for the onslaught.

With Scott mired in frustration, Schauffele won the next two holes to go 4-up, and by the time Scott recovered and made his predicted late charge, he couldn't get closer than 2-up and wound up losing 2&1. With that win against one of the game's great veterans, Schauffele showed a remarkable sense of match play psychology—a surprising trait in someone so young, and one that would show up again at Whistling Straits.

The International dream ended slowly but inexorably. Tiger exchanged blows with Ancer in the first match, but he never trailed, and on the back he hit the gas and put him away on the sixteenth. Haotong Li, the black sheep of the International Team, was eaten alive by Dustin Johnson. Cant-lay throttled Niemann, Schauffele took down the ice-cold Adam Scott in front of his home crowd, and both young Americans finished 3-2 in their first major Cup competition.

I followed Reed again, and that day on the course, it was run-of-the-mill savagery, delivered in the piercing native twang. Armed police followed him around the course, confronting the fans whose voices stood out against the crowd, entering the stands when necessary, and threatening to throw them off the course. The hecklers were incredulous and not very cowed—they didn't seem to accept a world in which yelling at an athlete had become a crime.

"I didn't even say anything *personal!*" one Aussie complained after calling Reed a "cheater" and a "disgrace."

Overall, Reed looked muted, perhaps even tired. The screeching crows, the warbling magpies, the jeering fans—these were the sounds of the match. But the American wanted only to put his head down and plow toward the mercy of the finish line.

He won, as he almost always does in singles, and it was a critical point—for a little while, it looked like the Internationals might still force at least a tie. Cam Smith came away with a late win against Justin Thomas, who had run completely out of steam. That left Oosthuizen and Leishman, Els's two most reliable veterans, facing Kuchar and Fowler, respectively. Both would have to win, but despite holding a 2-up lead after thirteen, Oosthuizen let it slip. When Kuchar drilled his approach on seventeen to five feet and knocked in for a birdie to go 1-up, the Cup was over—the Americans had won 16-14.

* * *

During the celebrations, I found Steve Stricker standing by himself. He looked thoughtful and, as always, a little lonely, a little isolated. I asked him whether he felt more joy or relief, and his answer was both. We spoke for a few minutes as the team walked back to the clubhouse. He told me about taking notes all week for Ryder Cup purposes, but he wasn't giving much away. In fact, I couldn't tell if he was happy or sad, worried or ecstatic. If anything, I thought, he was already deep into his Ryder Cup captaincy, obsessed and burdened by the task that lay before him.

What we would find out, though it would take a year longer than expected, is that Steve Stricker was a different kind of American captain. He was the kind who learned from *everything*, especially the mistakes, and Royal Melbourne had a few lessons for him. First, the importance of planning, an element that was almost entirely absent in that US side. Second, the importance of using advanced statistics to form a team and plan pairings. Els used them, Tiger didn't, and it started the Americans out at a massive deficit. Finally, he learned what it might mean to spend a captain's pick on Patrick Reed. None of those lessons escaped him.

Nor was he suffering from any illusions on the big topic, and this, I guessed, was what was on Stricker's mind that day—if the Americans prepared this way, behaved this way, and *played* this way in Whistling Straits, the Europeans would beat them like a drum.

Yet even in the aftermath of that near disaster, there was a flip side to that equation. What would happen if this team, which managed to win on foreign soil by force of sheer talent and willpower, had a good leader? What if they had a *great* one? It was a question that hadn't been answered in forty years, but Stricker was about to put it to the test.

CHAPTER TWO

1977–1983, the United Kingdom

*The four meetings . . . Jack's vision . . .
the great Jacklin . . . the birth of a new
Ryder Cup*

*"For months I went door to door like a brush salesman, try-
ing to sell someone—anyone—the Ryder Cup . . . eventually
we had a meeting of the Ryder Cup committee, and I had to
report that in six months the only offer I'd had was £80,000
in cigarette coupons which could be redeemed for cash."*
—Colin Snape, executive director of the British PGA,
in Robin McMillan's *Us Against Them*

The First Meeting: Fall 1977, Royal Lytham and St. Anne's: Jack Nicklaus and Lord Derby

In the fall of 1977, American Tom Weiskopf made the decision to skip the Ryder Cup because he wanted to hunt for bighorn sheep in Canada. Viewed from the present day, this seems like the smallest possible footnote in golf history. So does the fact that on the Thursday of that Ryder Cup, at Royal Lytham and St. Anne's, Jack Nicklaus became annoyed during a foursomes match against Thomas Horton and Mark James. It wasn't because of the outcome—he and Tom Watson won in a typical blowout, 5&4—but because of how slow their opponents played on a cold day. That frustration, combined with Weiskopf's abandonment, irritated Nicklaus so much that he decided to have a conversation with a man named Edward John Stanley, 18th Earl of Derby. Lord Derby was cousin to Queen Elizabeth and—more importantly—head of the British PGA. Nicklaus was on a first-name basis with him, and true to form, he wasn't afraid to speak his mind.

"I said, 'John, you know that for everyone on the American Team it's a great honor to make the team and it's a great honor to play in these matches,'" Nicklaus later told the *Boston Globe*. "But frankly, when the matches start, there isn't much competition. We win every year. And I don't think that's right."

Nicklaus knew the British PGA had close ties with the fledgling European Tour, and he had a vision of a Ryder Cup that pitted the Americans against all of Europe. Lord Derby agreed with him, and though Nicklaus's push was crucial, it was no secret that *something* had to be done. Far from a footnote, Weiskopf's choice to go hunting was seen around the golf world as a seriously bad sign of things to come and perhaps just the tip of the iceberg in a story that could end with the demise of the Ryder Cup. Nicklaus loved the event enough to want to save it, and though there were some traditionalists who opposed the expansion—Peter Aliss on the British side, Dow Finsterwald on the American side—and other radicals who thought it should be expanded to America versus the entire world, in general the proposal was widely popular.

As for the British, they were smart enough to recognize that buried in Nicklaus's "proposal" was a threat—not a direct threat from Nicklaus himself, necessarily, but a threat about the future of the event. If they didn't change things fast, and if they ignored a figure as esteemed as the Golden Bear, it wouldn't be long before they had a dozen Weiskopfs on their hands. The British PGA's finances were always a little dicey, and even though they weren't making a ton of money from the Ryder Cup, they envisioned a future where the event was far more competitive and yielded enormous profits. If it ceased to exist, where would they be? (This question, by the way, remains pertinent today—the Ryder Cup is by far the greatest moneymaker for the European Tour, and essentially props up the rest of their calendar. Unlike the PGA Tour in the United States, which attracts far more revenue in sponsorships and TV rights, the European Tour actually loses money in years when the Ryder Cup isn't played.)

There was another incentive for Lord Derby and the Brits. A young, charismatic Spanish golfer named Seve Ballesteros had become a huge star in Europe. He led Spain to World Cup titles in 1976 and 1977, captured a handful of European Tour wins, and even won a PGA Tour event in Greensboro in 1978—at that time, a rare feat for a European golfer. Within two years, he'd capture his first Open Championship. They wanted him on the team.

Lord Derby asked Nicklaus to send him a formal letter with his arguments, Nicklaus obliged, and by May 1978, Lord Derby had pushed it through the British PGA. Starting in 1979, the Americans would no longer be taking on a collection of the best golfers from Great Britain and Ireland—they'd be facing the whole continent of Europe.

* * *

The Second Meeting: December 1982, Perth, Scotland

The addition of Team Europe, which people like Derby and Nicklaus hoped would be a cure-all for the sorry competitive state of the Ryder Cup, did nothing to alter the status quo—at least at first.

In 1979, at the Greenbrier in West Virginia, Seve Ballesteros and Antonio Garrido of Spain became the first players from continental Europe to play in a Ryder Cup match. They played all four pairs matches together, including the first match out on Friday morning, and had the bad fortune to face Lanny Wadkins and Larry Nelson in three of them. They lost all three. Ballesteros met Nelson once more in singles, and lost again. (Nelson went 5-0 that week, a feat that wouldn't be repeated in the Ryder Cup until Francesco Molinari pulled it off in 2018.)

Just like that, the reigning Open Champion was off to a 1-4 start to his Ryder Cup career. There was no indication, when that weekend came to a close with a 17-11 American victory, that the Spaniard who had been obliterated in almost every match would go on to become the driving heart of the European team, and one of the greatest Ryder Cup golfers ever.

Nor would anyone have a reason to suspect that another player on that losing team, the thirty-five-year-old Englishman Tony Jacklin—past his prime and playing poorly in his final Ryder Cup—would emerge in four short years to take the captaincy and change everything. There were wolves within Team Europe that weekend at the Greenbrier, but they were very much in sheep's clothing.

Today, 1979 is best remembered not for Seve's debut, but for the behavior of two of Europe's players, Ken Brown and Mark James. From the start, they seemed hell-bent on playing the role of passive rebels. They wouldn't wear the team uniform, chatted during the national anthem, covered their faces for team photos, and generally ignored their teammates—even during competition. When James was asked to sign a program for a priest, he wrote his name and then the words *son of a bitch* underneath. He had to be yelled at to attend the opening ceremonies because he preferred to stay in his room and eat cheeseburgers, and after one match, he claimed a suspect injury and didn't play again. When the team returned to Europe, they were fined—£2,000, according to Tony Jacklin, a massive figure at the time—and Ken Brown was banned for a year from international play.

It's an interesting Ryder Cup footnote, because the two of them would go on to become reliable stalwarts of European teams, and James would even be awarded the captaincy in 1999. Whatever the reason for their conduct in West Virginia that year—Jacklin said they behaved "abominably" and "like felons"—it can be seen as another symptom of the endless losing that plagued the British. If the American response to the routine blowouts was real indifference, this was one of the man-ifestations of wounded British pride—a show of rebellion designed to take the sting out of the inevitable outcome. It was the dark side of an inferiority complex, prevalent among the British and European teams, that Jacklin called "bravado."

"It wasn't real confidence," he said. "You *wouldn't* be confident. It was more, 'We can do it!' But nothing really happened to make you believe it was true. It was superficial bravado, like, 'We can beat these buggers.' But when you've got the real confidence required, it comes from inside. It's not something you brag about, it's something you *do*. We stood on the first tee, and we were 2-down before we ever hit a bloody ball."

Though it was hard to imagine, things were about to get worse in 1981 at Walton Heath Golf Club in England. There, Jacklin finished thirteenth in the order of merit, and he expected to be one of two captain's picks selected for the team. He had good reason—eleventh on the list was Mark James, who had let down the entire team in West Virginia. Not only that, but John Jacobs, the captain in 1979, was back for his second turn and would keenly remember what happened in West Virginia. Amazingly, though, Jacobs picked James over Jacklin. When he offered Jacklin a vice captaincy, Jacklin told Jacobs and the rest of the establishment to "stick it in their ear."

Leaving Jacklin off the team was one thing—he was past his best days and hadn't qualified automatically. But the Europeans made an even bigger mistake by leaving off Seve Ballesteros.

Since West Virginia, Ballesteros's profile had only grown. He captured five European Tour titles in two years, and in 1980, he became the first European ever to win the Masters. Around that time, he first requested appearance fees of around £50,000 per event, and for good reason—Jacklin estimates that an appearance by someone with Seve's skill and charisma would increase the gate by up to 50 percent. In some places, he got those fees, but then the European Tour decided they wanted to put a complete and permanent stop to the practice. One problem: they kept paying Americans. That enraged Seve further, who responded by playing most of the summer of 1981 in America. When it came time to decide whether or not to make him a captain's pick, Jacobs wanted him on the team. Neil Coles, the chairman of the European Tour's board of directors, disagreed, so the two of them went to Bernhard Langer for a tiebreaking vote. He said no, and Seve was out.

Into this cauldron of dysfunction, add the fact that America came to England with one of its best teams ever, and the result was predictable: the US went 15-5 over the last two days, and in the end, it was a worse blowout than the Greenbrier.

All of which left the Ryder Cup in a sorry state. Following the nightmare of 1981, the Sun Alliance Insurance Company pulled out as a sponsor, which sent Colin Snape, the executive director of the British PGA, on a desperate hunt for new money. Not since World War II had the Cup faced such an existential threat, and though it was a spirit of restoration that kept it alive then, in 1982 very few parties seemed interested in playing savior. More than a year after the 1981 Ryder Cup, Snape had nothing on the sponsorship side beyond an offer for redeemable cigarette coupons. At a meeting with the PGA of America in the summer of 1982, the British PGA had been forced to admit to their American counterpart that if the search continued to bear no fruit, they wouldn't be able to send a team.

Months passed. On a tip from a friend, Snape met with Raymond Miquel of Bell's Scotch Whisky in Perth in December 1982. Miraculously, Miquel didn't just want to sponsor the home Ryder Cup, but was hoping to expand his business into America and saw the 1983 Cup in Florida as a great marketing opportunity. He convinced his board of directors to sponsor the 1983 and 1985 Cups for £300,000 pounds, a total that was beyond Snape's wildest dreams. His last obstacle was to convince the PGA of America to allow the Bell's Scotch Whisky name to be affiliated with the Ryder Cup, but his position was somewhat strengthened by the fact that if they said no, the entire event would go bust.

They said yes.

* * *

The Third Meeting: May 1983, the Driving Range at Sand Moor Golf Club, Leeds

Tony Jacklin is one of the most underrated players in the history of professional golf, and emphasis here goes on the word *player*. Before he ever thought of becoming a Ryder Cup captain, he was a pioneer on the course.

The early history of major championship golf was dominated by the British, and that's no surprise—the game was invented there. The Open Championship, sometimes called the British Open in America (to the great consternation of the Brits) began in 1860, and for thirty-five years it stood alone among the tournaments we consider majors today. As you'd guess, there are no Americans on the winner's list in those early years. The US Open began in 1895, and for seventeen years, it too was won exclusively by English and Scottish golfers. Things began to change slowly in the 1910s with the emergence of American champions like John McDermott, Francis Ouimet, and Walter Hagen, but when World War I hit, it was like a switch had been flipped. After the war, the Americans were everywhere. Hagen became the first American-born player to win the Open Championship in 1922, Gene Sarazen and Bobby Jones began collecting professional and amateur titles, and in 1926, for the first time ever, the five biggest events of the year—the Open Championship, US Open, PGA Championship, British Amateur, and US Amateur— were all won by Americans.

Once the tide shifted, it only got worse for the British. World War II wasn't any kinder, and though players like Bobby Locke, Peter Thomson, and Gary Player emerged from Australia and South Africa to challenge American hegemony, soon the British were being completely shut out. By the late 1960s, no British golfer had won the Open Championship for almost twenty years, much less a US Open or PGA Championship. As for the Masters, which began in 1934, it would be fifty-four years before a British golfer, Sandy Lyle, won a green jacket. For decades, players from the "home of golf" were nowhere to be found.

Tony Jacklin is the man who changed all that. He was the pioneer who replanted the British flag in global golf, and proved it was possible to compete with the Americans. His influence wasn't limited to his home nation, either; the effect was felt all over Europe.

Jacklin was an only child, born at the tail end of the war in 1944 in Scunthorpe, England. Scunthorpe was an industrial town, and his father was very much a product of the place—a truck driver and a factory worker in the steelworks. His mother worked weekends at the local market, and when he was young, Jacklin helped her load vans and ran his own paper route. Money was a constant problem for the Jacklins, and in his story we see something that is far more common overseas than it is in America: a poor kid taking up golf and becoming a great professional.

His father began playing when Tony was eight, and he allowed his son to tag along. By age thirteen, the boy was winning local championships against older teenagers, and doing it with a certain amount of flair. Jacklin was good-looking, self-taught, and brazenly confident, verging on cocky—he was so sure he would become famous that he'd often practice his autograph.

He quit school at age fifteen and spent a year at the steelworks, but he never stopped playing golf, and he never stopped seeing the sport as his ticket out of the working-class life. He continued on the local circuits and turned professional at eighteen. Success was almost immediate—he made the cut at the 1963 Open Championship at Royal Lytham and St. Anne's, and by 1964 and 1965, he was winning small events like the Coombe Hill Assistants' Tournament and the Gor-Ray Cup, which were affiliated with the British PGA or the fledgling precursor to the European Tour. He had a taste for the finer things—he'd often be seen wearing gold lamé pants and lavender cashmere sweaters—and he knew early on that the staid life of British golf wasn't big enough for him. He met his wife, Vivien, in Northern Ireland in 1965, and for the next three years, they traveled across the world, with Jacklin playing events in Australia, New Zealand, South Africa, and Asia, and winning plenty.

At that point, Jacklin made what might have been one of the most consequential decisions of his life, which was to play in America. That wasn't easy at the time. For one thing, the competition was far stiffer than anything in Europe. For another, the rules made it tough to go full-time on the PGA Tour. (As late as 1986, Dean Beman and Seve Ballesteros were locked in a bitter feud over eligibility rules for European players.) Finally, the reception wasn't very warm—early in Jacklin's career, a player named Dave Hill stood a few feet away from him and opined loudly that foreign players shouldn't be allowed on the American tour.

But Jacklin's ambition was so great that nothing short of competing against and beating the best players in the world would gratify him. Those ambitions were personal, but also national—British golf had been so far behind, for so long, that any attempt to crack the spell of US dominance was almost patriotic by default.

Jacklin knew that to become the best, he had to beat Jack Nicklaus, Arnold Palmer, and Lee Trevino. And to do that, he had to be in America. He got his PGA Tour card in 1967, and soon discovered that part of the secret of American success was their more complete technical knowledge.

"I had played with all the best players we had in Britain," he told Golf.com, "but they didn't know as much about the golf swing, particularly the importance of the lower body, the legs. We were compromised by the weather and the links courses; it wasn't about making swings, it was about playing shots, you know? But in America, I had the opportunity to work on technique."

It's a stunning admission—British golf lagged so far behind that they were literally not swinging the club correctly—but Jacklin rose to the occasion. In 1968, he won the Jacksonville Open Invitational. That might seem like a pretty pedestrian accomplishment today, but when you look at the history, it stands out as spectacular. Since the 1920s, when the PGA Tour looked far different than it did decades later, no European player had won a Tour event. Jacklin was the first ever, and he did it paired in the final round with Arnold Palmer.

"Playing in front of Arnie's Army was like playing with Jesus Christ," he said. "I mean, they didn't give a damn about what you were doing. And despite that, I got it done. I had to be tough playing over here, because there were a bunch of guys who resented any foreign player in those days. Fifty years is a long time ago—the attitudes were a bit different then. It was a battle to survive. When I stepped on the golf course, the softest thing about me was my teeth."

He was twenty-four years old, and he had already planted his flag as a pioneer. In the near future, things only got better. Bolstered by the confidence of his American breakthrough, he won the Open Championship in 1969, breaking the eighteen-year British drought, and then, in 1970, he won perhaps the greatest title of his life when he was the only player to post a score under par at the US Open. The runner-up in that event, in a bit of poetic justice, was Dave Hill.

It was the first victory for a British player at the US Open since 1924, and it's impossible to overstate what it did for the British and European game. Like a defibrillator, it revived an entire continent, and everyone who came next, from Ballesteros to Langer to England's greatest champion, Nick Faldo, owed him a debt. As late as 2013, when Justin Rose won the US Open, he made sure to thank Tony Jacklin. It might have been the most historically resonant win in the history of British golf.

Throughout this period, Jacklin was also playing in Ryder Cups. The most memorable came in 1969 at Royal Birkdale, when Jacklin led his team with 3.5 points over the pairs sessions. Heading into singles, the score was knotted at 8-8, which was remarkable all on its own for a British team that hadn't even sniffed victory in a decade. It was also a strange Ryder Cup for the sheer tension. The British captain, Eric Brown, went so far as to tell his players not to help the Americans find missing balls, and the American team was loaded with players like Dave Hill and Dan Sikes—a "miserable bastard," to quote Jacklin—who had extremely provincial attitudes. On Saturday, things got so bad that a fistfight nearly broke out. It was a toxic combination of American exceptionalism and

British defensiveness, made worse by the fact that the Brits actually had a chance to win.

There were two singles sessions on the final day that year, and in the first, Jacklin anchored his team by defeating the American rookie Jack Nicklaus 4&3. Britain held a 13-11 advantage heading into afternoon singles, but then, as so often happened in this era, the Americans began to exert control. Hill, Sikes, Miller Barber, and Gene Littler all won, and by the time Brian Huggett and Billy Casper halved the second-to-last match, it was tied at 15 points with just a single match left on the course. Yet again, it was down to Nicklaus and Jacklin.

It was an unlikely setting for what would become one of the legendary moments of sportsmanship, not just in golf, but in any sport, and even more so because Jacklin found himself 1-down on the seventeenth. He needed a miracle—halving the match for a 16-16 tie would allow the Americans to retain the Cup, which is essentially a victory—and he got it when he buried a fifty-foot eagle to win the hole. They went to the eighteenth all square, and despite Jacklin's efforts to dash away after his tee shot, Nicklaus caught up and threw an arm around him.

"Are you nervous?" he asked.

"I'm bloody petrified," Jacklin responded.

"Me too."

They both reached the green in regulation, both were about thirty feet away, and Jacklin hit his putt to two feet. His instinct was to watch Nicklaus putt close, concede each other's putts, and exit the pressure cooker. But Nicklaus, a Ryder Cup rookie, did something uncharacteristic, sending his putt four feet past the hole. It forced Jacklin to make him attempt the putt—his team still had a chance to win.

Nicklaus made it. And then, with the eyes of his team and the entire golf world on him, he picked up Jacklin's marker and conceded the last putt.

"I don't think you would have missed it," he said, "but I never would have given you the opportunity in these circumstances."

Today, this is called "the concession," it's almost universally praised, and it can be easy to forget what a big deal it was at the time—and how angry Nicklaus's teammates were in the aftermath. Yes, they retained the Cup, but their loathing for their British opponents was so deep that they wanted the outright victory. Sam Snead, the captain, was particularly furious, and years later still called it "ridiculous." Others, like Billy Casper, would understand the importance of the gesture only with time. In the moment, Casper, Tommy Aaron, and many others were shocked and upset.

In that atmosphere, for Nicklaus to even think of saving Jacklin from potential humiliation—as a rookie, no less, and at the end of a bitter competition—shows an astounding sense of the moment and an even more astounding sense of empathy. Jacklin sent him a letter thanking him for the gesture, and it's easy to wonder now if at that moment, the two men became tied together, bound by fate to meet again in this format, at this event.

As a player, that's the only Ryder Cup that Jacklin came close to winning. He played seven total, and none of the rest were close. His playing career was also at a peak. There were no world rankings at that time, but if there were, he would have been up there with Palmer and Nicklaus as the best of the best. For Jacklin, though, this stint at the top of the game wasn't destined to last.

Things began to turn for the worse in 1972, back at the Open Championship. Jacklin, still just twenty-eight, came into the seventeenth hole in the final round tied with Lee Trevino. He reached the par-5 in three shots, giving himself a fifteen-foot birdie putt, whereas Trevino had been in trouble since the tee and sailed his fourth shot over the green. It was a massive advantage for Jacklin, and Trevino, glum after his big mistake and in a fit of self-pity, congratulated Jacklin in the fairway on his "win." The American was almost casual over his fifth shot, seeming to have conceded defeat, but in a moment that would gut Jacklin, his chip went in the hole. It wasn't the first time Trevino had holed out—to Jacklin's memory, it had happened over and over during the two days the men were paired, and Trevino never should have been that close in the first place. The fact that it happened again, at such a critical moment, seemed cosmically unfair. Jacklin overreacted, determined to make birdie, and ran his aggressive putt three feet past the hole. He missed his par putt and, unbelievably, went into the eighteenth trailing by one. Rattled, he made bogey and Trevino won.

It's not an exaggeration to say that the 1972 Open broke Tony Jacklin.

"I was done after that," he told James Corrigan of *The Telegraph* years later. "It knocked the stuffing out of me . . . something, I don't know what, died inside me that day."

Nicklaus and Palmer approached him that night at the Greywalls Hotel to reassure him, to tell him not to let one day affect his outlook, but he couldn't help it.

"I felt bloody sick," he told Rick Reilly. "Nothing's fair. Life and golf are for the takers. You've got to take it, grab it, and keep it. Never give anything away."

He had given it away, and as a player, he'd never get it back—at least not on the biggest stage. Two years shy of his thirtieth birthday, he'd lost his edge, and he never seriously contended at a major championship again.

The years went on, and at the 1975 Ryder Cup, the soles of the plastic shoes he was given for the event came off during his singles match with Raymond Floyd. At the 1977 installment, he got in an argument with team captain Brian Huggett that ended with Jacklin being left out of the Sunday singles session. That spawned a deep bitterness at how the event was being run, and it came to a boiling point in 1981 when he and Seve were left off the team in favor of Mark James.

"We were practically frappéed every time we turned up," he said. "You go into it knowing that you're going to get lambasted, basically."

After the snub of 1981, Jacklin was done with the Ryder Cup. He was suitably bitter and wanted nothing to do with the organization, the captains, or the event itself. Moreover, he'd been so open to expressing his opinions, including his refusal of a vice captaincy, that he was pretty sure the feeling was mutual—the institution wanted nothing to do with him, either.

Which is why it came as the greatest professional surprise of his life in the spring of 1983 when Colin Snape at the British PGA and Ken Schofield, executive director of the European Tour, found him on the driving range of Sand Moor Golf Club in Leeds and asked him if he wanted to serve as the next Ryder Cup captain.

"You could have knocked me down with a feather," he said. "I was in total bloody shock."

Aside from personal qualms, Jacklin's chief problem was how he and his fellow players consistently felt like second-class citizens, to the extent that they didn't know who would be paying for the dry cleaning. Early in Ryder Cup history, Walter Hagen made it a priority for the Americans to travel in style, and at this point they were taking the Concorde to events and had the best in clothes, facilities, food, and drink, while the Europeans were stuck with disintegrating plastic shoes and musty locker rooms—at best.

He told Schofield and Snape that he needed time to think about it. And though their approach may have seemed sudden to Jacklin, and in the grand scheme of things it *was* a quick decision, it had been brewing for months. In fact, there was a full-fledged battle happening in the inner ranks of the British PGA and the European Tour, the central argument of which was whether the captain of the Ryder Cup team should be a much older, distinguished player—a position handed out as a sort of lifetime achievement award—or someone younger, more of the players' generation, perhaps in the twilight of his career, who knew them better and might understand more precisely how to compete and win. There were multiple committee meetings, with players like Bernhard Langer and Bernard Gallacher pushing for a younger captain, but by the end of 1982, there was no resolution in sight.

Two factors decided the argument in favor of a younger captain. One is that the 1983 Cup in Florida was fast approaching, and they still hadn't made a choice. Today, it would be unthinkable to name a captain with less than a year to go, but by the time they secured Jacklin, the Ryder Cup was four months away. Second, the organizing bodies had just barely survived the hunt for a new sponsor, and they knew that if the matches didn't become closer, they'd be stuck in the same position two years down the road. Anything that promised a better chance of winning became a priority, and eventually, the Gallacher/Langer faction won out. To men like Snape and Schofield and Lord Derby, the radical choice to offer the captaincy to a disgruntled thirty-eight-year-old didn't seem quite so radical anymore . . . even if they didn't particularly like him.

Jacklin's first instinct was to tell them to shove it, but then he started thinking about all the grievances he'd been nurturing, and the fact that the Ryder Cup was so close at hand. He wondered if this was a real opportunity to change things, and he dreamed up a wish list. He wanted carte blanche to run things how he saw fit, which included flying the Concorde to Florida, getting a proper clothing deal, being able to take their caddies to America free of charge, having a team room with all the food and drink they'd need, and getting three captain's picks. He decided to bring them that proposal, and if they said no, well, no harm done.

If his shock on the driving range had been great, it was even greater when Schofield and Snape said yes—to everything. They'd have to move mountains to make some of it happen, since the coffers weren't exactly overflowing, but they had the Bell's Scotch money, they needed to be competitive, and they needed Jacklin to say yes. So *they* said yes first, and Jacklin was left with no choice but to accept.

Lord Derby had been hanging around Sand Moor, too dignified to ask Jacklin directly but very much anxious for his decision, and the two men chatted afterward. They weren't particularly fond of each other then, and the relationship would only get worse with time. But that day at Sand Moor was probably the high point of their relationship. Both men got what they wanted, and at one point, Jacklin felt bold enough to bring up another problem he'd been thinking about for two years.

"What about Seve?" he asked.

"You've accepted the captain's job," Derby said. "He's your problem."

* * *

The Fourth Meeting: Spring 1983, the Dining Room, Prince of Wales Hotel, Southport, England

Later that summer, the Open Championship would be played near Southport at Royal Birkdale, but Jacklin's immediate priority was to meet with Ballesteros. They worked it out within a week of Jacklin accepting the job, and when they met for breakfast at the Prince of Wales Hotel, Seve's eggs grew cold as he vented every one of his Ryder Cup grievances to Jacklin.

"I said, 'Well, I agree with every bloody thing you said,'" Jacklin remembered. "'They're all a pain in the ass, but I'm in charge, we do what we want, and I can't do it without you. I've accepted the job, but without you, we're not going to be competitive.'"

Jacklin also brought up how becoming a Ryder Cup star would improve his image in the UK, which was of no small importance to Ballesteros at the time. In the end, his anger assuaged, Seve seemed to deflate.

"Okay," he said. "I help you."

"And *my God*," Jacklin remembered, years later. "Once he committed, he was unbelievable."

That was the last of the four critical meetings. The end result was the emergence of a unified Team Europe with the money to compete, Tony Jacklin as captain, and Seve Ballesteros leading the charge for the players. It would have been unimaginable just two years earlier, but on one side of that table at the Prince of Wales Hotel sat a captain with unprecedented freedom who was about to revolutionize the whole event, and on the other side sat a player who was angry and uncertain, but who was bound to become the greatest Ryder Cupper of them all.

When Seve Ballesteros said the words "I help you," they were still months from setting foot in Florida. But in that moment, before anyone on either side even knew it, the fifty-year reign of the Americans had come to an end.

CHAPTER THREE
Winter 2020, Edgerton, Wisconsin

Stricker

"I hate to talk, first of all."

—Steve Stricker

"He's too quiet for anyone to have any good stories ... he's one of those guys who just cruises along and isn't going to draw any attention to himself."

—Jim Furyk, to *Golf Digest*'s Dave Shedloski

Bob and Carolyn Stricker were extremely kind people, and for more than an hour, they sat with me in the living room of their home on Jenson Street, spoke about their lives, and even let me photograph the house. When it was all over, Carolyn refused to let me walk to my next stop, a newspaper office, and insisted on giving me a ride, stopping along the way so I could take a picture of the town welcome sign featuring her son and the other Edgerton, Wisconsin, native of note, novelist Sterling North. In our hour together, they had a lot to say about their family, their town, and what made Steve Stricker who he is today. And so it feels slightly strange that the thing I remember most came early in our interview, when I asked them what Steve was like as a young boy. There was a long pause while they looked at each other, and it was Carolyn who broke the silence.

"I don't know," she began before trailing off. More silence, and then Bob picked up with a story about the time Steve brought home a dog named Pepper—a story that ended up being more about the dog than the boy. Later, when I mentioned that I found him to be particularly observant at the Presidents Cup in Australia, I asked if he had been that way as a boy.

"I don't know," said Bob.

"I don't know either," Carolyn agreed.

I was disappointed with those answers at the time, but later, I found them important and even revealing. It wasn't that they didn't know what he was like—they did, and they told me a good deal in our time together. It was more the situation that put them off, the nature of the question, and their own style of communication. They weren't stoic or harsh, but there was a midwestern simplicity to them that didn't leave much room for introspection. Despite their kindness, I discovered that talking about themselves, or their thoughts, was outside their comfort zone, at least to a stranger with a tape recorder.

Their son Steve was cut from the same cloth. He had the same simple resistance to baring his soul, but more than that, he considered family an inviolable fortress. At the Ryder Cup, one reporter tried to ask him about his daughter, Bobbi, an aspiring golfer, and he shut the conversation down immediately. Nor has he said much publicly about his older brother, Scott, who passed away at age fifty-one shortly after Stricker served as vice captain at the 2014 Ryder Cup. His private life is a refuge, and very few people see past the fortress walls.

One of the first times I ever saw him in person, at the 2013 Accenture Match Play Championship, he was playing Ian Poulter in the fourth round. I was there to see Poulter, the greatest match play golfer of his generation with the sole possible exception of Tiger Woods. Walking down the first fairway, Stricker was just a few feet ahead of me when he paused to introduce himself and shake hands with the official scorer, the standard bearer, and then me. I had never seen this before, and haven't since—typically, a golfer thanks these people after their rounds, usually in a perfunctory manner, by signing a ball or a glove. They never interact *during* a round, and my first cynical instinct was to wonder if Stricker was a phony, if this was his way of furthering his brand as a quintessential "nice guy."

Eight years later, I have to laugh at the idea. If there's one thing Stricker loathes, it's a spotlight. As he told us at the Ryder Cup, he actually dislikes the simple act of talking, and there's very little he fears more than public speaking. At the opening ceremonies of the Whistling Straits Ryder Cup, he became so nervous that he told the entire Wisconsin audience that he rooted for the Bears, not the Packers, which earned him a round of hearty boos—the first and probably only time a home captain will be booed by his own crowd.

"That didn't go so good," he admitted to the media afterward, and even Dustin Johnson zinged him a few days later in a team press conference, saying, "Next time, let's not tell all the Green Bay fans that you're a Bears fan." (Stricker can blame his father for that one—Bob Stricker pointed out to me that they lived closer to Chicago than Green Bay, and his own father had season tickets to see the Bears back when they played at Wrigley Field. When Bob got to see a game of his own in Chicago, it ensured that he'd be a Bears fan for life, and ditto for his son.)

Even on the golf course, the spotlight was sometimes difficult for Stricker. In a long and successful playing career, it has to be said that in the most pressure-filled moments, he didn't always respond well, which is why he's one of the best American golfers never to win a major, and perhaps why in three Ryder Cups his combined record was 3-7-1.

It's also why, when he was chosen as Ryder Cup captain, he was viewed in some corners as an uninspired choice for a struggling American team. If the pick didn't generate a ton of controversy, it's because it wasn't a surprise—it had been telegraphed for a number of years that Stricker would get the captaincy in his home state, and any chance of a different outcome vanished when he captained the American team to an easy Presidents Cup victory in 2017. That accomplishment solidified him in the Ryder Cup pecking order, but earned him little credit otherwise, since American success in that competition is considered a foregone conclusion.

The Ryder Cup is a very different beast, and for some, the concept of picking a player who had never won a major—Stricker was the first to hold that distinction in American Ryder Cup history—made little sense, particularly in such an important year. There was an implication of weakness, bolstered by the fact that in his twelve victories on the PGA Tour, the stress of playing in front of people for seventy-two holes was such that he inevitably broke down in tears. Could a man like that lead a team?

Those who asked the question fell prey to a common error, which is the belief that being a good player makes you a good coach. It's not true in golf any more than it is in any other sport. In fact, it was the qualities that made Stricker a top-tier player despite his unlikely origins— his steadiness, his incredible ability to prepare, and his resolve to move on toward his goals even after multiple disappointments—that would define his legacy as a captain.

* * *

Driving into Edgerton on a grim February afternoon, you see what you might expect to see—fields of hay lined with bound bales, fields of chopped corn, light snow everywhere, tractors, truck stops, a BP, a Piggly Wiggly, red barns, low storage sheds with wide aluminum siding, repair shops, a motel, an old general store. Edgerton is an old tobacco town, and there are remnants of that history in the brick warehouses downtown and the stretch of Queen Anne homes that speak to a bygone affluence. After tobacco left, it was a GM town. When the Janesville Assembly Plant shut down in 2009, it became ... well, it became what so many small towns have become, which is a mix of many things, some of them contradictory. A conservative bastion dotted with Trump signs; a liberal bedroom community for Madison, the nearby capital with the state's flagship university; a place hit by economic difficulties; a place working to revive its downtown.

Bob Stricker spent his life here as an electrician, wired many of the town's buildings, and knew everybody in Edgerton so well that Stricker Electric rarely took outside clients. His own father was a carpenter, his mother came from a farming family, and though he's not entirely sure of their ancestry, there's little doubt that the Stricker name is German. Carolyn, whose background is German and Norwegian, is the daughter of a homemaker and a worker at the old Nunn Bush shoe factory in Edgerton, and she spent her working career as a secretary at a hospital. They are, of course, good Lutherans, and they imparted values of politeness and fastidious organization to their children. Nicki, Steve Stricker's wife, would later claim that you could eat a plate of food out of the back of Bob's truck, and her father, Dennis Tiziani, the longtime coach at the University of Wisconsin, once joked that you could learn everything you needed to know about Steve Stricker's precision by watching the meticulous way he put on a pair of shoes and socks.

Bob's father began building the house on Jenson Street the day the Japanese bombed Pearl Harbor, and as a child, Bob would spend all his free time at Edgerton Towne Country Club just a few feet away up a steep hill (driving his mother, who lived and died by the schedule of farm life, crazy in the process). It was only nine holes then and, despite the name, a public course. Locals called it the "goat ranch," and it was marked by hard, hilly ground with plenty of undulations, narrow fairways between woods, blind tee shots, and small greens. The par-4s were short, the par-3s were long, and it put a premium on a player's wedge game. Bob became a strong golfer, and when his sons were born, they followed in their father's footsteps. They excelled at all sports—Steve was an all-conference basketball player his senior year—but golf was their favorite, and if they weren't nearby at Towne Country Club, they were at the Racetrack Park treating the grassy areas like their personal driving range.

Steve, four years younger than Scott, was constantly tagging along, and Scott liked this about as much as most older brothers enjoy a younger shadow.

"We'd let him in the foursome," Scott told *Sports Illustrated* in 1997, "and he would grunt the ball out there off the tee, and we'd needle him, 'C'mon, Arnie, try a little harder.' There was some friction. I think we made him want to beat us that much more."

Mike Hesselman is the manager of Towne Country Club today, and since the days when Stricker would walk up the hill to play, they've added a back nine; it's straighter, to the relief of many. He and his parents are friends with Stricker, and when we met, he had played with him in Naples just weeks earlier. He confirms what everyone else in the town says: yes, Stricker really *is* that nice.

As a senior in high school, Hesselman finished second at the Wisconsin state championships, losing in a playoff. Stricker was there watching him, and together with his family, they went out to dinner that night. Hesselman was upset, but Stricker spoke with him about his game, relayed some stories about some of his own hardest losses, and generally made him feel better on what was the toughest competitive day of his life.

He's not the only one with a story like that. Stricker still lives in Madison, and it's not uncommon to see him show up at an Edgerton basketball game or a fish fry at the Decoy with his parents. As long as there aren't too many out-of-towners—there usually aren't—he's rarely bothered. As for his home course, Stricker still plays in a fundraising outing every year, and he's fronted money to the club in the past when they've found themselves in a tough spot.

Diane Everson, the publisher of the *Edgerton Reporter*—a weekly newspaper so thoroughly small-town that they hold a claim as the oldest continuously published paper in the state, and so old-school that Everson herself has managed to resist signing up for Twitter—spoke of the "glow" Stricker brought to the town. He gave a "significant" donation to the new hospital, volunteers at Thanksgiving meal outreach, and has been in the newspaper office to ask for coverage on projects at the golf course.

Bob Samuelson worked at the *Edgerton Reporter* for thirty-three years and was probably the first journalist ever to cover Stricker. He has a degenerative nerve disease now, and lives in the Edgerton Care Center surrounded by the sketches he's drawn of his favorite athletes. (The portrait of Stricker holds a place of pride all by itself.) Band-Aids cover his hands, he has trouble lifting his head, and he speaks slowly, but he still becomes emotional when talking about Stricker.

"I've always used one word to describe Steve," he said, "and that's *class*."

Samuelson was around when Stricker was winning high school championships and was considered the best high school golfer Wisconsin had produced since two-time US Open champion Andy North. He covered him occasionally in college, and again when the PGA Tour came nearby, but he mostly lost touch once Stricker moved to Madison. Years later, when Stricker was inducted into the Edgerton sports hall of fame, Samuelson was the master of ceremonies. His disease had begun to take effect, so he was using a walker to get around, and the two things he remembers most about that night were the way Stricker broke down crying when he accepted his plaque, and how the bulk of his attention was on Samuelson himself.

"He kept coming back," Samuelson said. "Saying, 'Bob, are you gonna be okay? Are you gonna be okay?' That sort of thing. And I guess it just fits with everything that people see in him."

He told me about the time Stricker came back to town to play at a men's invitational golf tournament at Towne Country Club, blew everyone away with back-to-back scores of 66, and then refused to ever play again, such was his embarrassment. It's a reflection of later stories from his life, such as the time he refused to allow Kohl's to put his name on the sleeves of their sponsored line of shirts.

Samuelson occasionally went to see him play at the now-defunct Greater Milwaukee Invitational, or the John Deere, and even then, surrounded by reporters from bigger outlets, Stricker would single him out and make time to talk.

By the time Stricker was in his early teens, his parents knew he had a special talent, but nobody was quite sure where it would take him, least of all Stricker himself. He won high school state championships, the state amateur, and three state opens, and he was very much on the radar of Tiziani, the Wisconsin coach. But Tiziani couldn't offer him a full scholarship, and the only other major school recruiting him, Illinois, could, so he chose Ed Beard and the Illini. He knew Tiziani was upset, but the two stayed in touch, and when Stricker had trouble, he'd often call for advice. Tiziani informally became his coach, and occasionally at Big Ten championships, an odd sight would present itself—the Badgers coach instructing the best player from rival Illinois.

* * *

Stricker's first ever plane ride came on a recruiting trip to Illinois, and it was the start of his introduction to a much bigger world. It was an overwhelming new world, one that left him unsure of himself and his skills. He was a two-time All-American at Illinois and a three-time Big Ten champion, but he never won the NCAAs or a major amateur event, and he maintained the mentality that he wasn't good enough, that he was too limited coming from the north, and that he didn't belong in the upper levels of the sport. Such was his insecurity that upon finding out his freshman roommate was from Atlanta, an honest-to-god city, he was sure their relationship would be impossible. (It wasn't—he and Kevin Fairfield became good friends.)

One summer during college, at Cherokee Country Club in Madison, he was working with Tiziani when a lifeguard walked by in her bathing suit.

"Who's that?" Stricker asked.

"My daughter," said Tiziani.

That was the day he met the woman who would become his wife, and in time Stricker's life would be inextricably tied in with the Tiziani family. Dennis would coach and help him manage his career, Nicki (an excellent golfer herself) would serve as his caddie, and Dennis's son Mario would eventually become Stricker's manager and agent.

After college, Stricker started out on the Canadian Tour. He attempted to pass the PGA Tour's Q-School every year, and every year he failed to move past the second stage. Finally, on his fourth try, he earned his Tour card, and despite his lingering sense that he might not belong, he took immediate advantage, making twenty-two of twenty-six cuts and notching four top-ten finishes. He got his first win at the Kemper Open in 1996, and his second at the Motorola Western Open.

When the 1997 season began, he came in with high hopes that not only would he win again, but he might soon score a huge win and take his place among the very best players in the game.

That all changed when he played with Tiger Woods.

The two men were paired together for the first time at the Pebble Beach Pro-Am in February—two months before Tiger won his first major at Augusta—in a group that included Kevin Costner and Bryant Gumbel. Stricker felt he was striking the ball well, but he was dismayed to find that on hole after hole, Tiger was driving it past him—not just barely, either, but by forty or fifty yards. After the round, he stewed on the day, and finally told Nicki in a fit of despair that he simply couldn't compete on that level. Today, he calls it his "first big blow to my confidence."

"My round with Tiger made me introspective," he wrote later for *The Players Tribune*, "and for the first time I began to doubt myself. All the early mornings on the range hitting balls until my hands were torn with calluses; all the hours spent practicing during the frigid Wisconsin winters; all the memories I had of being on the course with my father; in my mind, at that moment, it truly seemed as though all of the time and effort I had put into the game of golf had been rendered utterly meaningless."

There you see it again—the sense that no matter what he's achieved, he doesn't *really* belong, and can't really consider himself an elite golfer. He began to struggle, and that struggle coincided with falling out of love with tour life. His sponsorships and obligations meant he had to travel more than ever before, sometimes out of the country, and in a case of poor timing, his true nature as a small-town homebody began to reassert itself. It grew worse when his first daughter was born, and though his parents traveled with him to help for a year, it wasn't long before it became clear that Nicki would have to give up her job as caddie. After that, Stricker truly felt alone, and his happiness waned.

So did his game. There were highlights here and there, and he even managed to win the biggest tournament of his professional life in 2001 at the WGC-Accenture Match Play Championship—his last two opponents, Toru Taniguchi and Pierre Fulke, weren't especially notable, but it's interesting to look back and see that he defeated Pádraig Harrington in the first round—but in general, the next few years were a story of struggle.

After a particularly tough round in Doral, his playing partner, Jack Nicklaus, took pity on him and gave him a lesson, but even that couldn't help for long. By 2004, he had lost his playing card and had to rely on sponsor exemptions for the next season. There were a thousand technical explanations for what had befallen him, but they all boiled down to the same thing: he was trying to fix what didn't need to be fixed, in an effort to chase away the feeling that he wasn't good enough.

Strangely, that was also the start of his turnaround. His time at home rejuvenated him, and in 2006, when he made fifteen of seventeen cuts, he was voted the Tour's Comeback Player of the Year. Thus began the golden age of Stricker's life as a professional. In the next six years, he won nine times on the PGA Tour, including two FedExCup playoff events, and rose as high as number two in the world. To golf fans, he became a household name, known for his incredible putting, his steadiness, and, less happily, his unfulfilled close calls at major championships.

He also played three Ryder Cups in his heyday, winning in 2008 under Paul Azinger and losing two straight nailbiters in 2010 and 2012. He learned from all of them, just like he learned from his vice captaincies in 2014, 2016, and 2018, and from leading the US to a lopsided victory at the 2017 Presidents Cup.

In fact, he had Tom Watson to thank for his future captaincy. In 2014, Watson and his vice captain, Andy North, wanted someone younger as a vice captain, someone with insight into the current players. Perhaps it was North's Wisconsin connection, or maybe Watson subconsciously saw Stricker as the kind of personality who wouldn't challenge his leadership. They picked him, and he managed to survive what proved to be a debacle for the US team with his reputation intact.

He had two other lucky breaks. The first was that he was the perfect age when the task force was formed after 2014—just slightly past his prime, but young enough to know and relate to all the modern players in a way that made him a useful vice captain for men like Davis Love III and Jim Furyk. The second factor, and likely the decisive one, was that the 2020 Ryder Cup was set to be held at Whistling Straits in Wisconsin. It was an easy leap to make—put the Wisconsin native at the helm. Stricker himself thinks that if that Ryder Cup had been somewhere like California, he wouldn't have been chosen. But he entered the captaincy pipeline, and in 2019 he got the call from PGA of America president Suzy Whaley: his time had come.

* * *

There are very few people close enough to Stricker to say they know him intimately, and Dennis Tiziani is one of them. I met Tiziani in the winter of 2020 at Cherokee Country Club, where he's now the principal owner, and on the Uber ride to the club, my driver began ranting about religion.

"It's all real," he said as we drove out of the city and into the gray February morning. "All gods and goddesses under Jehovah."

It felt like good preparation for meeting Tiziani. He's a big man, with a sharp nose and eyebrows that dance when he speaks, and that day he wore a Carhartt jacket over a large flannel. Unlike Stricker, he has a philosophical bent—at one point, on the topic of managing a player, he quoted Umberto Eco: "If you wait by the river long enough, the bodies of your enemies will float by." Nor was he shackled by midwestern stoicism; here was a man who enjoyed talking, and was very good at it.

"My question," he asked rhetorically early in our meeting, "is where do you take your mind when you want to hide? There are priorities of faith, family, education, and golf. All items that no one can take away. Your trust can be put totally in them. Outside these items, all occasions must be verified."

He was talking about Stricker and his "simplistic" approach to life. He'd known him since he was in high school, when Stricker first showed up at Cherokee looking for instruction and would amuse himself in the downtimes by making caricatures out of matchsticks. Tiziani knew early on that Stricker wasn't a worldly kid by nature. He had to be drawn out, encouraged to let his natural competitive energy come to the forefront. Tiziani understood the paradox, which is that beneath his quiet demeanor, Stricker *was* competitive—"He'll eat your eyes for olives," as Tiziani put it. And yet, he was also someone who had an instinct to hide. Those opposite impulses would forever be at war in his career.

Davis Love III, another one of the few people who was allowed inside Stricker's inner circle, also brought up this paradox when we spoke about the captain.

"Other players know that that Steve Stricker on the Tuesday of a PGA Tour event is not a really good partner to have in a gambling match," Love said. "But on Thursday when the bell rings, the guts and determination come out, and he's going to play great."

As Stricker's instructor, Tiziani often used metaphors Stricker could understand, and what could be better than electricity? "Some people only have the capability of 110 volts," he'd tell him, "but you are wired for 220 volts." He sensed early on that Stricker could see things differently than even he could, and Tiziani was no slouch—he had played on the PGA Tour before becoming Wisconsin's coach. Stricker was a great listener, but he'd apply his own spin on every lesson, introducing elements that Tiziani couldn't foresee; such was his genius.

"He's one of the only players I've ever seen that can hit the ball out of a fairway bunker and not take a grain of sand," said Tiziani. "One year in the John Deere, on eighteen, he hits it in a bunker, and his caddie says, 'Just hit it in the front; we'll get it up and down and make the playoff.' He said, 'Give me a 6-iron.' Took it out of there to the back of the green, made the putt, and won the tournament. The caddie said one thing, but he had a totally different idea."

At one point, showing me a *Life* magazine with Ben Hogan on the cover (and obviously believing I was smarter than I really am), Tiziani waxed poetic on Hogan's "secret" in ways that were instructive about his own personality, even though I had no clue what he was talking about.

"I sat with him, I watched him, so I understood," he said of Hogan as he gestured to various parts of his body. "And everyone points to the secret as being up here, from a bowed position to a set position. And they always put the circle up here. *That's not where it happens!* It happens in the first six to eight inches away, and how you take the club away to go ahead and then turn and set to get to that position. *He didn't even know his secret!* I can tell you 90 percent of people teaching have no idea what I told you."

He was speaking about Hogan, but more than that, he was speaking about Stricker. Everything he taught him—everything that *anyone* taught him—would go through the filter of his unique mind before it was applied on the course. Trust, but verify.

Together, the two were able to have an exceptionally honest relationship. That was true when they worked on Steve's game—"I have the end of the rope," Tiziani told me. "I'm going to dip you into shit, but I'm going to be able to pull you out of it"—and in life.

Tiger Woods became friends with Stricker, and it was Tiziani who told Stricker why. It happened for two reasons, the old coach said. First, because Tiger knew he could beat him—Stricker wasn't threatening, at least at the start. Second, because Tiger looked good by association when he hung around with the nicest guy on Tour. If he was friends with Stricker, he couldn't be all bad.

It reminded me of a story Ted Bishop told after his tenure at PGA of America was up, about how Phil Mickelson and Tiger would tease Stricker that he'd never be a Ryder Cup captain because he couldn't win a major. It seems harsh, but that was the hierarchy, and that was the role Stricker occupied in the orbit of the alpha males.

When Tiger's infidelity became public and all the sordid details came out, Stricker had two responses. The first was to buy Nicki a new and improved wedding ring as a way to reaffirm his faithfulness, and in that gesture you can see both his disgust with Tiger and a sense of guilt by association. His second response was to remain Tiger's friend, to move toward him rather than away, and support him in his time of need.

Tiziani was also the first to say that in a perfect world, Stricker would have more than just four captain's picks, because it would allow him to choose players that could win without being detrimental to the team. (Little did he know that when the pandemic hit, Stricker would embrace the chance to add two more picks, giving him six.)

"Phil Mickelson's a loser in the Ryder Cup," Tiziani said, on the topic of detrimental players. "What the fuck are you doing with him?"

It was with some regret that I said goodbye to Tiziani, perhaps the most colorful character I met in my travels, and I didn't realize at the time that so much of what he said would foreshadow issues that would come up for Stricker at the Ryder Cup.

I went outside to look at Cherokee Country Club in the snow, walked past the sickly cedars, and saw the geese roaming the grounds and the Catholic Church across Sherman Avenue. I made my way to the long trailer where Stricker famously practiced in the dead of winter after driving his daughter to school, hitting balls from the heated bay out into the snow drifts covering the range, at the frozen flags, losing every yellow ball to the winter. It's where he made and remade his game, where the hours would slip by such that when he got home, he'd apologize to Nicki, surprised by the passing time.

And I thought of what his mother said, when I asked her to describe her son in a single sentence.

"He's somebody who cares."

I thought she was referring to the famous niceness, but now I think it meant something more—that he cares deeply about everything in his orbit, including his own success. He always has, no matter what happened to him, no matter how far he fell. What his critics failed to understand when he became captain is that the simple act of caring, in such a deep way that it leads to meticulous preparation, to the dull, committed hours ensuring that no matter what else happens, nobody will ever be able to say that you didn't try *everything* . . . well, when it comes to the Ryder Cup, that counts for a whole hell of a lot.

CHAPTER FOUR

1983, Palm Beach Gardens, Florida

The mysteries of Seve . . . part one
of the Jacklin trilogy . . . the scare at
PGA National

"Seve and I shared a car at one point as we traveled to get our clubs fixed in 1979 . . . I tried to explain that it's a much easier game from the fairway and that he should try and work on slowing his swing down, especially at the all-important time when he was coming down the stretch at a tournament.

He said, 'But you don't understand, Tony.'"
—Tony Jacklin, from *My Ryder Cup Journey*

It's easy to forget today, in an era when the vast majority of Ryder Cup dysfunction has been associated with the American team, that it used to be the Europeans and British who fought and bickered and seemed to shoot themselves in the foot at every possible opportunity. There is a qualitative difference in the two kinds of dysfunction, though; while modern American failure stems from ego and personality clashes, the old British and European teams were a study in pathology, and the pathology was inevitable loss. Everything that went wrong stemmed from the original problem: they couldn't win.

This ironclad reality had all kinds of side effects. In the best case, it was the bravado Tony Jacklin mentioned, the forced swagger as they threw themselves against the juggernaut year after year. In the worst case, it was the posturing and feigned indifference of Mark James and Ken Brown in 1979. All were symptoms of the disease of losing.

Tony Jacklin's chief job as captain, then, was to create a culture in which his players believed—*truly* believed—that they could win. His work began with the 1983 Ryder Cup at PGA National Golf Club in Palm Beach Gardens, Florida. The first matches were set to begin about four months after he accepted the job, and the task in front of him was monumental. Although he had negotiated for three captain's picks, they had settled those terms far too late in the game to implement for 1983, which meant the team would be chosen entirely from the European Tour money list.

Jacklin negotiated with the European Tour and the British PGA for upgrades in certain areas; by allowing fifty fans to travel with the team in exchange for a donation, they were able to afford to fly on the Concorde jet; by cutting a deal with a clothing brand called Austin Reed, they were able to secure high-quality team uniforms; that summer, Jacklin flew to Florida to meet Jack Nicklaus, the US captain, and in his tour he found the team room he so desperately craved.

All of these changes were designed to make his team feel on equal footing with the Americans, and not like a poor relative flown in from the country to be embarrassed by his richer cousins. It was a start, but Jacklin knew it wouldn't cure the underlying problem by itself. To infuse his players with true belief, he needed a lieutenant on their level, someone who could translate his passion for winning into a competitive spirit among the team that would be impossible to resist. And he thought he had found that person in Seve Ballesteros.

* * *

It's interesting to note that in America today, Seve Ballesteros seems to be thought of chiefly as a Ryder Cup legend. It makes sense on one hand—his greatness is a historical fact—but on the other hand, how quickly we forget that unlike fellow Ryder Cup legends like Colin Montgomerie,

Lee Westwood, or Ian Poulter, Ballesteros's excellence extended to the major championships. He was a five-time winner in the world's biggest events, the first European ever to win the Masters, and easily one of the three greatest European golfers in the history of the sport. If Jacklin was the man who planted the first flag for Europe in America, Seve was the next step in the evolution, someone who stood on his shoulders and exceeded him.

More remarkably still, he did it under some of the same hostile conditions Jacklin knew, but perhaps worse. Quoted in Ballesteros's obituary for the *Washington Post*, Peter Kessler said, "He never felt like he got the love he deserved. He played with a chip on his shoulder. He just wanted to be one of the guys with the Americans, but they all thought he was coming in and taking money right out of their pockets."

There was a racial component to Seve's time in America that Jacklin never had to contend with. He wasn't exactly Jackie Robinson, and the majority of the American crowds loved him and his daring style, but there were isolated incidents where he was targeted for his ethnicity. At the 1983 Ryder Cup, an American journalist persisted in calling him "Steve" even after he had been corrected, which was also common in galleries. At one tournament, an announcer stepped out as Seve approached the tee and said, "Let's give the little spic a big hand." And in general, people were very comfortable impersonating his accent, including an R&A official named Graham Brown who led off a dinner speech in 2007 with a Seve impression before getting in trouble for segueing into more overtly racist humor targeting Asian and Black people.

All of this was compounded by relationships with American governing bodies that soured over time. He missed a tee time in 1980 at the US Open and was disqualified, and later in the 1980s, he fell into a long-standing feud with PGA Tour commissioner Deane Beman over membership requirements. In fact, Seve was an expert at making enemies, both on the course and off—he was the kind of man who slept with a .38 revolver under his pillow as an adult. Bernard Gallacher once said of him that he "needed to feel that the world was against him. He wanted to lead, to beat people." John Hopkins, in a feature at *Global Golf Post*, wrote, "You never needed to tell Ballesteros there were dragons around the corner . . . he knew."

And yet, none of it changed him. To study Ballesteros extensively is to see qualities he shares with a man like Michael Jordan, particularly his ability to hold grudges. He published a memoir in 2007, for instance, that's full of complaints about everyone who ever wronged him. That quality gets to the heart of his competitive genius and his all-encompassing drive to win—particularly when paired against just one or two opponents.

The parallels with Jacklin continue in his upbringing. Seve, too, came from relative poverty, and was somewhat of a longshot to become a professional golfer. He grew up in a fishing village called Pedreña on the northwest coast of Spain near the city of Santander. His father was a farmer, and their small house was surrounded by donkeys, rabbits, and chickens. Ballesteros was the youngest of five sons, and he was born with a defect that made his right shoulder hang lower than his left. He took up boxing, and he learned golf by hitting on the beaches of Pedreña and sneaking onto a local course to play after hours.

His uncle Ramon Sota was one of Spain's best golfers when Seve was a child, and Sota finished sixth at the 1965 Masters. Sota held an interesting place in the young boy's life—Seve rarely spoke about his influence as a teacher, but his countryman Manuel Piñero later said that Sota inspired him in a different way.

"Seve wouldn't admit he learnt a lot from Ramon," Piñero said, "but I think Ramon was the first master in that part of the world. Ramon always talked about Arnold Palmer and Nicklaus and that the Americans were unbeatable. It was impossible for him to beat them even though he was a fantastic player. Seve wanted to show his uncle and his people that he could beat the Americans. He wanted to show that he could do what some people thought was impossible."

Like Jacklin, he quit school at age sixteen, and like Jacklin, his success was instantaneous. At age nineteen, he finished second at the Open Championship, and he actually led on the final day before Johnny Miller tracked him down. Very quickly, Ballesteros became known for his creativity and his almost magical short game. For those of us who never saw him play in his prime, it can be difficult to understand the aura that surrounds this part of his game, but for those who were there, the stories take on an almost mystical tone. One of his caddies, Billy Foster, told a story of a tournament in Switzerland when Seve found himself in front of a wall on the eighteenth hole.

"He was perhaps 10 feet from the wall and the wall was 10 feet high," Foster said to the journalist John Hopkins. "There were fir trees above the wall and he saw a chink of light in the trees about 4 feet above the wall. He had half a backswing. Four times I asked Seve to chip it out, wedge it onto the green and make par that way. I envisaged his ball hitting the wall, rebounding into his face and killing him and I'd have no boss and no percentage money. I pleaded with him. My last words to him were: 'I know you're Seve Ballesteros but you're not f—— Paul Daniels. Chip it out will you, please?'"

Seve wouldn't listen. Foster watched the dust come up from his shot, and though he couldn't see the ball, it soon became clear that it had cleared the wall, stayed low enough to slice through the gap in the trees, and landed about a yard from the green. On his next shot, Seve chipped in for birdie.

"I went down on my hands and knees to bow to him," Foster said. "I thought he was God."

These stories—of his magic, of his surreal, inexplicable ability—abound. There are more than a few people who think Seve Ballesteros played a significant part in Europe winning the 2012 Ryder Cup . . . about sixteen months after he died.

* * *

At age twenty-two, he won the Open Championship, and he did so in quintessential Seve style, hitting only four fairways in the last round. On the sixteenth tee, he even hit into a parking lot, his ball stopping next to a white car, and some people think he did it on purpose to get a better angle at the hole. If he did, it worked—he made birdie and beat Jack Nicklaus by three. He was the youngest winner of the Open Championship since the turn of the century.

Of course, Seve embraced the notion that he hit into the parking lot intentionally. Later in his career, stories circulated that when he changed his swing, he took photos and videos of his old swing and burned them in the American desert. None of it was true, but there was something mythical about the man to begin with, and he was never afraid to burnish the legend.

By 1983, he had three majors and had just won his second Masters in April. The world rankings were still three years away, but it's likely he was either the world's best golfer or among the top three. Everyone knew that, but they didn't know that he was about to become a Ryder Cup juggernaut. His only previous experience was his 1-4 showing in 1979, when Larry Nelson and Lanny Wadkins ruined his trip to West Virginia. It wasn't hard to see that he was important to the team, but Jacklin may have been one of the few who recognized what was coming.

"I was a sort of pioneer," Jacklin said, "and Seve was the same. He won multiple times over here and was a leader. And he had that same outlook: 'You're not better than I am just because you put USA after your name.' As far as any of us were concerned, they hadn't corralled ambition."

The other factor that became a massive part of the Ballesteros storyline is that to his opponents, he was a constant pain in the ass. There are countless stories of him coughing during a backswing or shuffling his feet, or engaging in various other forms of gamesmanship, but like everything else with Seve, it's difficult to parse out truth from myth. What's certain is that he lived inside the heads of his opponents, particularly the Americans, and they were constantly reacting to things he did or that they *believed* he did. It sometimes got to the point that the Americans would explicitly be at fault, as in 1991, when Paul Azinger and Chip Beck accidentally used two different balls in an alternate shot match—against the rules, at the time—were called out by Seve, and then became angry at him even as they slowly realized what they'd done. It shows that where he went in the Ryder Cup, conflict followed, and while it wasn't always his fault, he created a force field around himself that affected everyone.

The remarkable truth, though, is that unlike the vast majority of professional golfers or athletes, he was able to adopt a combative pose and still play at his best. There's a reason most golfers don't seek out high-tension situations with a colleague—it doesn't help anyone. When Rory McIlroy and Patrick Reed had their incredible front nine duel at Hazeltine in 2016, and emotions hit a fever pitch on the eighth hole after their exchange of long birdie putts, they felt a need to put their arms around each other and defuse the intensity. Even so, they both struggled for the rest of the round—it's almost impossible to maintain that level of animosity and still play at the highest level. Impossible for everyone but Seve.

It's one thing to practice gamesmanship, but it's quite another to do it and win. Nothing is quite so infuriating to an opponent, and to this day, long after his death, Americans remember how he got under their skin. In the oral history *Us Against Them* by Robin McMillan, Curtis Strange tells the story of an exchange with Ballesteros in the 1987 Ryder Cup at Muirfield that perfectly illustrates how he could worm his way under his opponents' skin:

> On the first hole of one match in 1987, I wanted to fucking kill him . . . Seve had a chip from just off the green. I had a long putt down the hill and putted it past the hole. Olazábal putted, then wanted to putt out, but I said, "Well, wait a minute, wait a minute, you can't do that. You're right on my through line." Seve came charging up. "That bother you?" he said. "That bother you?" I said, "Yes, that does bother me."
>
> And so Seve stomped over to his chip and chipped it right into the back of the hole—then walked off the green pumping his fist at me! And I almost had to applaud him. More power to him. Goddamn, I was so mad I wanted to kill him.

That was Seve—always ready to stir up trouble, but also ready to deliver results. (And always at the center of reactionary responses from his opponents—according to Olazábal's caddie, Strange was trying to intimidate them from the beginning of the match, going so far as to complain about the way the caddie stood while holding the flag.) Even the stories of the times he lost carry a certain sense of the supernatural. Hal Sutton and Larry Mize gave Seve and José María Olazábal their only loss in the pairs session of the 1987 Ryder Cup, and while it remains one of the proudest moments of Sutton's career, when he told the story in the summer of 2021, Seve was still the starring character.

"It was the first time they ever got beat," he said. "I hit it like this on the first hole, Seve made a thirty-footer, I hit it like this on the second hole, Seve made a thirty-footer. Anyway, I was 5-under through five holes, we were 1-up. So we got to sixteen, I was the only guy to hit the green. Seve and Larry both missed it left; Olazábal missed it right. Olazábal chipped it all the way across the green; Seve chili-dipped it, which he never did. And I hit it about six feet behind the hole. And Seve after he chili-dipped it, he was standing over the ball off the green, and I said, 'Larry, what do you think he's going to do?' And Larry said, 'He'll make it.'

"Which of course he did."

* * *

It might be a better story if the Americans were arrogant or at least cocky about their chances in 1983, considering how the last fifty-six years had gone, but in fact, many of them had a suspicion that things were about to get tough.

"We knew, even if the rest of America didn't, that we were going to have to play our absolute best if we were going to keep the Cup," Ben Crenshaw said, and Nicklaus felt the same way.

The Americans were loaded again, led at the top by Tom Watson—who had won three majors in the previous two years and was inarguably the best player in the world—major champions like Raymond Floyd and Fuzzy Zoeller, and Lanny Wadkins, the best Ryder Cup player in US history. Wadkins was the kind of player who would introduce himself to an opponent by saying, "Hi, lunch," as if that opponent were a meal he was about to eat.

"Wadkins was the cockiest son of a bitch you ever met in ten lifetimes," Jacklin said. "He was an arrogant bastard. But in the nicest way."

Among all American players, Wadkins is one of just three with twenty Ryder Cup wins—his overall record is 20-11-3—but the other two, Arnold Palmer and Billy Casper, played in the easier pre-European era. He had a well-earned reputation for toughness. It's no coincidence that he and Larry Nelson were the ones to spoil Ballesteros's first Ryder Cup in 1979 by going 3-0 against him in the pairs sessions. However, due to the arcane rules for qualification at the time, and the lack of captain's picks, Larry Nelson was left off the 1983 team. So was Hal Sutton, who had just won the PGA Championship in August but had been on the PGA Tour for only three years and thus wasn't eligible. In their place were players like Jay Haas, Craig Stadler, Calvin Peete, and Bob Gilder—all talented, but not exactly as feared as the men they were replacing.

This dynamic was also at play for the Europeans, where Jacklin would have to wait until 1985 for his captain's picks to kick in. Ballesteros was in, but he was the only player who had won a major at that time. Future champions like Bernhard Langer, Nick Faldo, Ian Woosnam, and Sandy Lyle were on the roster, along with a seasoned veteran in Bernard Gallacher and an emerging Ryder Cup stalwart in Sam Torrance. But the Europeans, too, had their own low-profile types: Paul Way, Gordon Brand, and Brian Waites.

On the first morning, in alternate shot, Faldo and Langer took down Wadkins and Stadler, and José María Cañizares paired with Torrance to notch a win, but the session ended in a 2-2 tie when Seve and Paul Way lost to Tom Kite and Calvin Peete 2&1. Way was the youngest player on the team, and though he never fulfilled the promise of his early career, he was known at the time as a confident, combative player—a "cocky little bugger," per Jacklin—even at the age of twenty.

Jacklin could have been in an awkward position with Seve, his team leader. He had begged him to play, told him he couldn't do it without him, and in doing so sacrificed some of his power and authority... at least potentially. But there was something paradoxical about Seve, because while he seems like the kind of person who might demand special powers in such a situation, he was almost completely deferential to Jacklin. This was in stark contrast to someone like Jack Nicklaus, who had so many ideas and held such a lofty position in the game that he was known as a thorn in the side to his captains. At the 1981 Ryder Cup, European captain John Jacobs was speaking with Dave Marr, the US captain, and mentioning how much difficulty he had with Mark James and Ken Brown in 1979. Marr expressed his sympathy and said that he only had one difficult player.

"I know who that is," Jacobs said. "The one who knows everything about everything."

That was Nicklaus. But Seve, with his similarly strong personality, never went down that path. When Jacklin showed him the lineup card for his approval or sought out his advice on some partnership, Seve would say, "No, you do it, you're a great captain. I don't need to see it."

All of which speaks to his comprehensive ability to see what it took to win on a very sophisticated level. It's as if he knew intuitively that undermining Jacklin, or even holding a special place among his peers, wasn't the way to foster unity and team spirit, and that gave him a surprising and paradoxical humility. It also helps explain how, despite being hated by the Americans, he was a beloved figure among his countrymen and his teammates, to the point that when you ask the Europeans about him today, many of them still break down in tears.

It's also why Jacklin paired him with Way. If Seve had his druthers, he would have played with his countryman Cañizares, and he was slightly upset at the Friday-morning loss—his Ryder Cup record was now 1-5-0. He told Jacklin that he felt he was being asked to be a parent rather than a partner to the young Englishman, at which point Jacklin pointed to Seve's head and said, "You *are* his father, Seve. You are, in here. That's exactly why you're well paired together. Is that a problem?"

A light went on in Seve's head, and he told Jacklin that no, it was no problem. Together, he and Way went undefeated in their next three matches. (This spirit of subsuming himself to the team was a key element of Europe's Ryder Cup future, even for the very best players. The same could not always be said for the Americans.)

After a strong afternoon session, in which Ian Woosnam played a terrific back nine with Sam Torrance to defeat Tom Watson and Bob Gilder 5&4, despite literally shaking from nerves, the Europeans led by a point. It was only the second time in history they'd ever held a lead after the first day.

Then they started getting unlucky. On Saturday morning, Lanny Wadkins and Stadler went 3-down to Brian Waites and Ken Brown, but roared back and won on the eighteenth hole when Stadler chipped in from twenty-five feet. Faldo and Langer won again, which was interesting because Langer asked Jacklin to rest him, and Jacklin, showing his usual strong instinct for reading people, told him, "Absolutely not." But in the anchor match, Watson and Gilder got their revenge against Woosnam and Torrance in a blowout. It was tied at 6-6, and after a split in the afternoon session, with Faldo and Langer winning their third match and Ballesteros and Way upsetting Watson and Gilder, they headed into Sunday singles tied at 8 points apiece.

Throughout this Ryder Cup, Jacklin had been willing to try new ideas that seemed radical at the time, and not just in preparing his team before the event, but on the course too. For one thing, he told Gordon Brand Jr. that he wouldn't be playing until Sunday singles. This idea has largely been discredited and abandoned by now, particularly after Mark James's captaincy in Brookline in 1999 when the three players he sat for the first four sessions all lost in the horrific Sunday singles meltdown, and in fact Brand would lose in 1983 as well, but it showed that Jacklin was exploring the limits of his captaincy.

Nicklaus, in contrast, was committed to getting his players equal playing time. The Americans knew they were in for a tough fight, but that didn't mean they were willing to alter their traditional view of the

Ryder Cup, or to engage in what we would now consider the modern tactics of preparation and strategy. He may have known what was coming from his adversaries, but to actually *do* something about it was a very different thing in 1983. How do you avoid complacency after decades of obliterating your opponent, even if you sense the winds of history changing? How do you justify meeting Jacklin on his own ground? It was an easier switch to flip for the Europeans, because they *had* to do something different, but not so easy for the Americans. In 1983 and for many years after, they were almost imprisoned by their past success, and incredibly reluctant to change.

That dynamic reared its head when the two captains presented their Sunday singles lineups. Traditionally, captains had placed their best players at the back of the lineup, and knowing that Nicklaus would likely adhere to tradition gave Jacklin a big opportunity. He decided to front-load his lineup, putting Seve, Faldo, and Langer as his top three. The idea was to steal a few early wins, establish momentum, and let the players at the bottom lineup take confidence from the early results. This type of strategy is commonplace now, but it was so unexpected at the time that when Nicklaus saw Jacklin's lineup, he actually exclaimed, "You can't do that!" He was still mired in the old way of doing things, and it allowed Jacklin to stun him with a guerrilla tactic that he couldn't possibly anticipate.

It worked brilliantly for Jacklin, at least for a while—his three best players drew Zoeller, Haas, and Morgan, and when all three raced out to big leads, it seemed as though Europe would put 3 instant points on the board and take an enormous first step toward stunning the Americans. In the lead match, Ballesteros took a 3-up advantage with seven to play on Zoeller, who was in pain from a back injury, but Zoeller somehow won four holes in a row, forcing Ballesteros to win the sixteenth just to bring it back to all square. That was where it stood on eighteen when both men hit into the rough. Zoeller pitched back onto the fairway, but Seve's lie was so bad that he could only hack it 20 yards into a fairway bunker 250 yards from the hole.

With the lip of the bunker directly in front of him, he took out his 3-wood, which looked at the time like an act of insanity. What happened next is considered by some to be the greatest shot in Ryder Cup history—Seve managed to pick the ball clean and hit it all the way to the green. The shot has grown in myth because it wasn't on television, which means we have to rely on eyewitness accounts.

"I was lucky enough to be 20 yards behind Ballesteros when he hit that 3-wood from a bunker," John Hopkins wrote later. "And as soon as I realized how daring a shot he was attempting, shivers ran up and down my spine. The ball came out of the bunker barely disturbing a grain of sand, bent 30 yards in the air and ended by the side of the green. That was unquestionably the most thrilling shot I have ever seen and I never expect to see another like it."

Zoeller responded with a great shot of his own, and they halved the hole and the match, but somehow, despite blowing what looked like a massive lead against an injured opponent, Ballesteros managed to gild his reputation.

It was a critical half from Zoeller, though, because Faldo and Langer both won. Jacklin's strategy came with its downsides, and in matches four through six, Brand, Lyle, and Waites all lost, giving the Americans an edge. Paul Way beat Curtis Strange to cap a tremendous Ryder Cup—Strange began to panic that he was going to be on the first American team to lose at home—Torrance and Kite halved, Stadler took down Woosnam, and Ken Brown, who had been such a nightmare in 1979, delivered a huge point against Floyd.

That left two matches on the course with the score tied at 13-13—Watson holding a slim lead over Bernard Gallacher, and José María Cañizares in a tense duel with America's star, Wadkins. Just like Seve, Cañizares held a 3-up lead with seven holes to play, but Wadkins chipped away until he was 1-down coming down the eighteenth hole. If Europe could win, they'd have 14 points and be just a half point from securing a stunning victory.

After a strong drive and layup on the par-5 eighteenth, Cañizares had about 105 yards left, but he left his approach short of the green, in the tall grass. Then Lanny Wadkins stepped up for his third shot. If you watch video of it today, you can see a flash of lightning in the sky after he swings. The ball stopped eighteen inches from the hole. He halved the match, and moments later Watson closed out Gallacher on the seventeenth hole.

The Americans had won, and Nicklaus, relieved beyond belief not to have been the first American captain to lose at home, went out to where Wadkins had hit his sand wedge and kissed the divot. He also invented a new nickname for Wadkins that night: "Wheelbarrow." As in, "This guy's balls are so big that he has to carry them around in a wheelbarrow." A year later, they presented Wadkins with a golden wheelbarrow to commemorate his shot.

* * *

"My most vivid memory of the 1983 Ryder Cup was patting Seve on the back and saying 'hard luck' and then seeing when he turned round that his eyes were full of tears."
—Warren Darrell, Paul Way's caddie

It's almost impossible to describe the level of disappointment the Europeans felt at that moment, having come so close to accomplishing the unthinkable. The competition felt different to them than ever before, more positive and more intense, because Jacklin had done his job well. In the end, though, it was hard to ignore that the result was the same: America kept the cup for the thirteenth time in a row. You can imagine the dark sense of inevitability settling over them as they marched into their team room.

Seve Ballesteros sensed it too, and he knew he had to act.

"We were all in the team room feeling down and dejected," Nick Faldo remembered, as related in David Feherty's *Totally Subjective History of the Ryder Cup*. "Half of us felt we should have won and the other half were not sure ... At that point, in marches Seve. He had his fists clenched, and his teeth were bared, just like he is when he's excited, and he kept marching around the room saying to everyone, 'This is a great victory, a great victory.' Then he said, 'We must celebrate,' and he turned the whole mood of the team around. That was the spark, Seve in 1983. By 1985, we knew we could do it."

"The Sunday night at Palm Beach, he was extraordinary," Torrance added. "He made us all, even Langer, shout out, 'We will beat them.' He had tears streaming down his face. It was ridiculous the amount of emotion that was shown. He said, 'Don't cry when we lose. Cry when we win. We are going to beat them.'"

Tony Jacklin, for his part, had a moment when he thought to himself, "What did I do wrong? What could I have done better?" And though he was always his own worst critic, he couldn't think of much. A few tweaks here and there, sure, but overall he knew he had made the right decisions.

The Americans sensed it too. Nicklaus spoke for everyone when he said that they wouldn't be the favorites at the Belfry in 1985, and that the close score in 1983 was no fluke. The Americans had lost before, rarely, but never in the history of the Ryder Cup did they consider themselves underdogs. The tides were changing.

The perception of the Ryder Cup was starting to change too. That year, in 1983, there was no television coverage on Saturday—ABC didn't want to deviate from college football, so they only showed a scoreboard at halftime—and just two hours on Sunday. Still, this was the first time the Ryder Cup had ever been on American TV. When Ballesteros hit his miracle shot on eighteen, there were not yet any cameras there to record it because it came too early in the match. On that dramatic Sunday, there were about one thousand spectators on the entire course. At Whistling Straits thirty-eight years later, almost fifty thousand fans attended each day, and more would have come if the course had the capacity.

The result in 1983 was the beginning of the end of the Ryder Cup as a forgettable exhibition. The wave of American dominance had just crested with the victory at PGA National. That wave was going to crash, and it was going to crash hard. Perhaps the best way to describe what changed in 1983 is that up until that moment, the story of the Ryder Cup had been one kind of story, and that story was about America. Starting that weekend, it became another kind of story, and this one was about Europe.

CHAPTER FIVE

Spring 2020, Kohler, Wisconsin

*Whistling Straits, the links course that
wasn't . . . Herb and Pete . . .
Stricker's dilemma*

*"Incredibly creative, controversial, wasn't afraid to take
chances, did things that didn't really make sense, certainly
didn't make sense to me . . . I don't know where he came
from. He has no precursor—everybody always says, Alister
MacKenzie is who I follow or whatever. But not with Pete.
Pete just showed up, and he had no precursors, and nobody
could even copy him. Nobody even tries. He was a complete
original, and that's genius."*
— Brandel Chamblee, on Pete Dye

*"Mr. Kohler, he always comes up with some wild ideas. I
never listen to him. But the deal is, his courses are successful."*
— Pete Dye, to Gary D'Amato

If you live in an American home with running water, there's a decent
chance that you see the word *Kohler*—probably without noticing it, at
this point—multiple times every day. The Kohler Company, based near
Sheboygan in a town named after itself, Kohler, Wisconsin, does many
things, but they're most famous nationwide for plumbing fixtures. On
showerheads and sink faucets, the Kohler name is emblazoned everywhere in the nation's kitchens and bathrooms.

The company began, as so many massive American companies began, on the strength of a tireless entrepreneur in the late 1800s. John Michael Kohler was born in Austria, his father emigrated to America before his son's tenth birthday, they became successful dairy farmers in Minnesota, and the younger Kohler married well and became the mayor of Sheboygan. After taking over his father-in-law's steel and iron factory, he had the idea in 1883 to attach ornamental feet to a pig trough and sell it as a bathtub, and to make a very long story short—and skip more than one hundred years of innovations, profit, political influence, strikes (including the longest labor dispute in US history), and various other triumphs and controversies—the Kohler family today is worth billions of dollars.

Herbert Kohler Jr., whom everyone in the company orbit calls Mr. Kohler, took over the company in 1972 at age thirty-three, and until he handed the reins to his son David in 2016, he oversaw the continued growth and expansion of the Kohler juggernaut. He was eighty-two when the Ryder Cup came to Wisconsin, and when he appeared on television for the opening ceremonies, with his white beard and his walking stick, he looked every bit the formidable patriarch.

He knew very little about golf as a young man, and though he'd play once a year in a local event using the hickory-shaft clubs that belonged to his father and were otherwise kept in the basement, the closest the family came to golf was when they'd ride their horses across a course in Kohler on Sundays. Then, in the early 1980s, they renovated an old building that had served since 1918 as a living quarters for Kohler factory workers. This was the American Club. A Tudor Revival building featuring coarse red brick, steep gables, and dormers, it had been a modest dormitory with a picturesque exterior, but with millions committed to the redesign, including two extensions, Herb Kohler transformed it into the only five-diamond resort hotel in the Midwest. (When it was time to pick out accommodations for the Ryder Cup teams, it was the obvious—and only—choice.)

As the Kohler Company's tourism arm, Destination Kohler, began to grow, and people traveled to the American Club, more and more began to fill out suggestion cards with a common request: they wanted to play golf. Kohler's head of business development was a strong golfer, and after tossing around the idea for a week, they decided to build a resort course near the American Club. After all, they had the land.

The search for architects began in 1982. They found a team of two men from nearby Chicago that had designed courses for the PGA Tour. It seemed at first like the perfect fit, and Herb Kohler hired them. Before long, a problem emerged.

"We discovered a rather interesting but strange philosophy," Kohler told me. "They believed that the tee of a par-3, or the landing area of a par-4 or par-5, should always look down on the hole."

Kohler adheres to the company mantra of "living on the leading edge of design," and in a way that he admitted was naïve at the start, he had ambitions to attract major championships to Wisconsin. The only way to build a championship course where the green was forever visible on approach shots was to make it very long, but these courses would be in the Sheboygan River Valley, with major changes in elevation. It might work as a resort course with golf carts, but it would be a big problem for tournament golf.

"Three days after we hired them, we fired them," he said, laughing at the memory. "They were in there shaking their heads; they didn't understand. 'Why in the world?'"

The search began again.

"We went through some of the big names on the list," Kohler recalled, "and one of these was this odd character. He had just finished Sawgrass for the PGA Tour, and the players were upset, to put it mildly. Who in the hell would build a target golf course that more often than not would embarrass them—as their home course!"

He took one of his characteristic pauses, and the amusement was evident in his eyes.

"I found it rather intriguing."

That same designer had also just finished a course called the Honors in Chattanooga, Tennessee, on land much like the rolling terrain of the river valley. It was a beautiful course, and it was well suited for amateurs.

Kohler thought he could combine that concept with the tournament caliber of Sawgrass to create a track that would be playable for all skill levels but also attract the biggest tournaments in the world.

Thus began the courting of the legendary designer Pete Dye.

When Dye first came to Wisconsin, he saw the sign as he entered the town of Kohler—population 1,934—and was taken aback at the concept of designing a course for so few people. But when he drove by Kohler headquarters, he said, "Well, I guess you can pay your bills," and they set to work. Like Kohler, Dye was a man of artistic temperament but also of tremendous will.

"They're both irascible characters," David Kohler said. "They're both stubborn. On many levels, these characters could never work together. But because they're both really good at what they do, and they're both very creative as artists, there's such a deep respect and a fun kind of admiration because they would both enjoy giving the other one a barb."

That mutual admiration took time, though, and their relationship almost blew up permanently over a dispute involving a stand of trees during the construction of their first project, the River Course at Black-wolf Run.

"Fundamentally, I'm a tree hugger," Herb Kohler said. "But Pete never let anything get in his way. Now, he'll plant a hell of a lot of trees, but that is not his first concern."

The last hole to be built at the River Course was number seventeen, and Kohler wanted it to back up to the rapids for aesthetic reasons. Dye insisted that it was too far from the next tee, and had a different layout in mind. The problem was, Dye's intended hole ran right through a grove of elm trees—one of the few clusters that had survived the elm beetle.

"Beautiful things," Kohler said. "Eighty, ninety feet tall. And I just wouldn't agree to cut those trees down. So we were in a stalemate."

One day, Dye called him up and requested a meeting at noon to iron out the last details. Kohler couldn't make it, so he called Dye and said he'd be there later in the afternoon. His day stayed busy, and when he finally drove his old, beat-up Jaguar to the course—he'd had snow tires put on so he could get through the mud—it was 6:30, and he didn't see a living soul. What he did see was a giant pile of smoking timber. Dye had cut down the entire grove of elm trees and burned them. His D8 bulldozers were still hot to the touch, but Dye had skipped town.

Kohler called him in a rage, demanding he return—"We're going to have a conversation about trees and how we get along in this life"—and was on the verge of firing him. Dye came back to face the music, and somehow the relationship, both professional and personal, survived. But Kohler learned something important about Dye, which is that like many artistic zealots, he would take massive risks for his vision, even if it meant pissing off someone with great power like Herb Kohler, who wasn't used to having the people he paid defy him.

Even afterward, Kohler told me, Dye was an expert at the soft lie, agreeing to certain concessions that he had no intention of following in order to push a project forward. The two men would become close friends, to the extent that their families would vacation together, but Kohler learned that as the price of Dye's great talent, he'd have to navigate that slippery aspect of his personality.

In 1988, they opened the River Course at Blackwolf Run. It proved so popular that they built another nine, and then another nine after to complete their second course, and when that filled up with reservations, they began to look for the next plot of land. They settled on a pancake-flat former military airstrip (and, according to local legend, a former meeting ground for drug mules moving product up and down the east coast of Wisconsin) on Lake Michigan.

It wasn't easy for Kohler to acquire the five hundred acres of land. To do so, he had to negotiate with the Wisconsin Electric Power Company, which had purchased the land with the idea of installing a power facility at a later date. They told him it would be impossible to sell—their policy was to buy land well in advance, often leasing it to farmers for up to fifty years until the time came to build a utility. At one point, the CEO told Kohler that he didn't hate the idea of a world-class golf course near one of his facilities, and the image of a golf course around a nuclear power plant gave Kohler shivers. But he agreed with the broader point in order to move the negotiations forward. Eventually, they made Kohler an offer—if he bought a nearby tract of land from a local farmer and traded it to the company along with some cash, they'd give him the land he wanted for his golf course.

Holy shit, thought Kohler, *that's something we've got to do*. It took him seven months to negotiate with the farmer, and the longer it went, the more the farmer figured out Kohler's true purpose, and the more expensive the proposition became.

"It wasn't cheap," he said. "Oh, dear."

But he sealed the deal in 1995, made the trade, and then discovered that eight acres on the southern end of the property he had acquired was technically considered a wetland because of the plant growth. A long battle ensued with the Department of Natural Resources, but with an assist from the Army Corps of Engineers, they reached a deal whereby they'd engage in "mitigation"—increasing wetlands elsewhere (on a three-to-one ratio) in order to develop the part that was on the site of their golf course.

Finally, with those obstacles out of the way, they were free to build a course. And that's when things became even more challenging, because Kohler's mandate to Dye was, on its face, outrageous—he wanted him to make this flat piece of land look like Ballybunion, a rolling links course on the west coast of Ireland.

* * *

Dye was unique in how he designed his courses. Rarely did he plot anything on paper or use the software that is now ubiquitous in course construction. Throughout his life, he never even owned a cell phone or computer. Instead, he would walk the course with his dog—every dog he had was named Sixty, a reference to the price he paid for the original dog—working with his shapers as he moved, like an artist on his canvas. Some holes, like number seventeen at Whistling Straits, he first drew on a cocktail napkin.

Aesthetically, Dye loved deception—to create the impression of incredible danger where none exists, as on the eighth hole at Whistling Straits, where from the fairway there's an impression that the back of the green drops immediately off a cliff, when in fact there's plenty of land.

He often went the opposite way, too, creating illusions of safety when the reality was danger. He lived to make golfers uncomfortable, as any recreational golfer teeing off at the tenth hole at Whistling Straits can attest. To reach the fairway, you must carry a wide chasm, but the landing zone slopes diagonally downward even as it presents an uphill façade, which introduces an element that is equal parts awkward and menacing, and which is entirely intentional. Just for kicks, he stuck a bunker right in the middle of the hill, which means that even if you manage to hit a good shot, you may end up trapped.

The professionals are now so long off the tee that the bunker doesn't come into play for them, but I can personally attest that for recreational golfers, simply having the length to carry the waste area provides no relief; standing over that tee shot was the most unsettled I've ever felt on a golf course. And this is Dye in a nutshell—he's a master at the psychological elements of course design, and has the sadistic streak to see it through.

Like any artist, his work was never done—he'd return often to make changes, like nearly bisecting the long sixth green to add a bunker where the center used to be, in order to create an extra penalty for players who opted to play safe and wound up short of a back pin placement.

The problem he faced with Whistling Straits was obvious: This was not Irish linksland, with its sandy, treeless landscape bridging the mainland and the beach. It was a flat piece of property by a lake, and to make it look anything like Ballybunion would mean to manufacture it from thin air. To see it through meant working on a scale that only a billionaire who refused to hear the word *no* could achieve. They moved acres of dirt to create elevation changes and brought in more than seven thousand truckloads of sand so Dye could place hundreds of bunkers at strategic and aesthetic spots around the course. (The natural soil, despite being on the water, is rocky clay rather than sand, meaning they had no help in creating bunkers from the terrain.) The great irony, of course, is that the features of a links course exist because of nature—bunkers are where sheep huddled together against the wind, fairways and greens are where animals grazed—and here they were altering the landscape to create an artificial resemblance to nature as it looked thousands of miles away.

"His intention is for someone to stand on the tee box, and here's a bunker, there's a bunker over here, none of them are in play, nobody's ever going to hit into them, but they're put there intentionally for the panorama," said Mike O'Reilly, the golf operations manager at Kohler. "All over the golf course, you'll see the same types of things, and it's like, 'Wow, look at this hole!' But the greens are quite large, and the course is very playable if you choose the right tees."

Whistling Straits is often credited as the first golf course in America to feature fescue fairways—a staple of British and Irish links courses—beating out the Bandon Dunes original course by about a year when it opened in 1998. Since then, it has been copied by other high-profile courses going for a linksy look, including major championship sites like Erin Hills and Chambers Bay. Fescue is a temperamental grass, and Chambers Bay paid for its risk dearly when the greens were in poor condition for the 2015 US Open—in 2018, they switched back to poa annua—and fairway issues at Erin Hills got so bad that they returned to bentgrass. For fescue to prosper, it requires climates with low humidity and sandy soil, and it doesn't respond well to golf carts, which is one of the reasons why the Straits course is walk-only.

When I visited Whistling Straits in the fall of 2019, Chris Zugel—then the superintendent, since promoted to director of golf course maintenance for all five Kohler courses—took me around the course. There are trees here, mostly pines, ash, oak, and birch, and on the right day you can see bald eagles flying from their nests in the top branches, but as far as the course is concerned, they never come into play. The Straits course is naked to the elements, especially the wind when it comes roaring down the coast, and only the man-made elevation changes provide pockets of respite. The landscape is dominated by Dye's bunkers, the long reddish grass in the rough called bluestem, and juniper bushes that mostly grow in clumps along the mounds and berms, which are rarely in play for professionals (but often enough, as I discovered, for amateurs). Elsewhere, in the areas originally designated as wetlands, you can find Queen Anne's lace, the reedy phragmites grass, milkweed, and cattails.

In layout, this is a classic down-and-back course, with the front nine making a circuit to the south of the clubhouse, and the back nine doing the same to the north. Almost everywhere, there's a view of the cliff that drops down to the shores of Lake Michigan and the gray, frequently choppy water beneath.

The visual effect of the project is stunning, and speaks to the beauty of the land and to Pete Dye's brilliance. There is something undoubtedly a little strange about transforming the geography to such a degree, perhaps something artificial and a bit unsettling if you think about it too long. When you see this kind of thing in the American desert, particularly in Arizona, the juxtaposition of a dry, arid landscape with the plush green fairways of a tournament golf course, kept alive with obscene amounts of water, feels inherently wrong. Yet at Whistling Straits, fabricated though it may be, the overall atmosphere is engaging, comfortable, and somehow familiar. Despite the millions spent to alter the visual spectrum, there is a marked unpretentiousness about the place, and to use the painting metaphor again, it's like living inside a pastoral watercolor by your favorite artist.

Even the buildings, though they don't resemble the local style in the slightest, seem to fit well and create an aura of rustic comfort. There are only three—the clubhouse, the Irish Barn, and the Champions Locker Room. All are made of a gray-hued rubble stone, with slate for the roofs, and the emphasis is on a kind of Scottish-hunting-lodge type ambience—stone fireplaces, dark wooden décor, huge timber supports—rather than size. Running in front of all three, overlooking the ninth and eighteenth greens, and with a view of Lake Michigan in the distance, is a stone patio and a grape arbor. At the Ryder Cup, the clubhouse became the team headquarters for the US while the Europeans gathered in the Champions Locker Room. The Irish Barn, made to look like an old cathedral, with crosses cut into the stone high along the façade, played host to the "one year to go" captains' press conference in the fall of 2019.

In spirit, this is an autumnal venue, or even a winter one, the kind of place that feels like home for people who call fall their favorite season. It looks fine in the summer, but like so much of northern Wisconsin, it takes on a different kind of romance when skies are gray and a chill is in the air. It earned its right to host major championships in June and August, but a late September Ryder Cup was a more natural fit.

* * *

Herb Kohler rarely uses the word *vision* in terms of how he developed golf courses, but there was never any doubt in his mind that he wanted to host major championships at his courses. The notoriety appealed to him as a businessman, and he preferred the rarity of majors to an annual event that would lead to more wear and tear on the courses. Kohler's vast influence and wealth, and the quality and visual beauty of the courses, made forming connections with the governing bodies relatively easy.

"If you can create a little competition," he told me, "all the better."

Blackwolf Run hosted the US Women's Open in 1998 and again in 2012, but it was Whistling Straits that was designed expressly to lure in men's majors. In terms of the competition between the PGA of America and the USGA, Kohler said that it was a "little unfair" because Alice Dye, Pete Dye's wife and partner, was on the board of the PGA. Kohler began working with the PGA of America, specifically then-president M. G. Orender, and reached an agreement that sent the PGA Championship to Whistling Straits for 2004, 2010, and 2015. Baked into that deal was an understanding that this would be a trial run, and that if all went well with attendance and corporate sponsorships and other logistics, there was a possibility that the course could host the Ryder Cup.

After the 2004 event, won by Vijay Singh, they'd seen enough, and in January 2005 it was announced that Whistling Straits would host the forty-third Ryder Cup in 2020.

Even then, difficulties persisted. At one point about ten years later, some of the big corporate sponsors of the event began to get cold feet. Whistling Straits wasn't near a major metropolitan area, and they worried that they couldn't make as much money in Kohler, Wisconsin, as they could on the East or West Coast, or even in a place like Medinah or Hazeltine very near to a big city. The PGA of America absorbed their concerns, and came to Kohler ready to jump ship; they didn't think the numbers were there.

"In the end, we had to guarantee $20 million," said Kohler, "and that wasn't counting any media dollars. It makes you shake a little bit."

There was no need to shake—a month after the Ryder Cup concluded, Kohler learned that the total revenue for the Ryder Cup exceeded any other golf tournament in history. On Thursday, Friday, and Saturday, the merchandise sales broke every previous record.

* * *

There was a lot of talk in the years leading up to the Cup that Whistling Straits would benefit Europe. It *looked* like a links course, after all, but the important fact these optimists were ignoring was that it didn't *play* like one. It's one thing to duplicate the visual style of the British seaside, and even to incorporate fescue fairways, but this was still America, and Whistling Straits was still played through the air.

That phrase, "played through the air," is used often, and what it means is that although Whistling Straits's fescue fairways are built on a base of sand just like a links course, the turf is still softer, which means that the ball won't "run" to the same degree that it would on a seaside track in England or Scotland. Plus, where those courses typically have open layouts with wide landing areas that feed toward the greens, Dye's design of Whistling Straits includes many holes where the fairway before the hole narrows significantly, or the approach contains a significant elevation change. That means even if the fairways were conducive to a bump-and-run links shot—they aren't, because the ground isn't firm enough—Dye's design would make it impossible.

If you want to hit your ball onto a green, you have to *land* it on the green, and you can only do that by carrying it through the air. Lucky for the players, the greens are bentgrass, a species that efficiently stores water and creates a softer landing area. Unlike a links course, where fescue or poa annua greens are often too hard to hold even a short iron shot, thereby forcing the bump-and-run tactic, the receptive greens at Whistling Straits will reliably reward a precise approach.

It's why players like Jason Day, Bubba Watson, Vijay Singh, Dustin Johnson, and Martin Kaymer had great success at its PGA Championships—like so many long American courses, it rewarded length and precision iron play, and you certainly weren't going to see anyone play a bump-and-run. And as Day proved in 2015 when he set a new major record with a winning score of –20—since tied by Dustin Johnson at the Masters—the Straits Course can be very easy for the pros under the right conditions.

"There's been some talk about, 'Does this course favor Europe because it's a links-style course?'" said O'Reilly, the golf operations manager who had previously been head pro at the Straits for ten years. "Absolutely not. You play the ball in the air. You're going to hit it in the air and land it on the green. You're not running things up. That's not how it was built to be played."

Still, unlike Hazeltine, which hosted the 2016 Ryder Cup, the American captain would not be able to expand the fairways by cutting down the rough ... or at least not much. The natural contours of the course could not be altered, and some perceived this as a European advantage.

"I'm interested to see down the road what Steve has in store, but it doesn't look like you can do a lot with this golf course," Pádraig Harrington said at the one-year-to-go presser. "As much as it was obviously designed and built there, it looks like it's just in a natural setting all its life."

"I still think the picking of courses is one of our biggest problems," Stricker told me in 2019. He pointed out that the Europeans pick courses that are typically part of the European Tour circuit, so they're familiar with them ahead of time, whereas that's rarely the case in the United States.

I brought up the idea that Whistling Straits wasn't ideal from a layout perspective.

"No," he said, "it's not."

What Stricker explained is that the PGA Tour has evolved to where most of its courses feature wide fairways, low rough, and bunkers that are no longer in play for all but the shortest hitters. That marks a change from when he first came on Tour, when you had to play *away* from bunkers rather than just soaring past them, and there was a premium on hitting the ball straight off the tee because the rough was higher. That means the players who have the most success on Tour today are long, aggressive, and fearless, and they are rewarded by the typical Tour course. In Europe, though, the courses are narrower, with more punitive rough, and that, in turn, produces a different kind of winner—someone more precise, with greater control, and perhaps not as long.

In practice, the distinction between American and European golfers today is not that neat. For one thing, most European golfers who make a Ryder Cup team today spend plenty of time—usually most of the time—on the PGA Tour, and many of them live in Florida. On average, they are just as long or almost as long as their American counterparts. The regional differences in styles of play and relative strength have been all but erased by the global nature of the game, and it's a constant worry of Team Europe veterans that the Americanization of European golf will eventually destroy their team solidarity and erase their unique identity.

With all that said, the 2016 and 2018 Ryder Cups were excellent examples of course layout providing a huge boost to the home team. At Hazeltine, Davis Love III turned the course into one giant fairway, freeing his bombers to fire at will, and America won in a romp. In Paris, Thomas Bjørn opted for high rough and narrow fairways, such that accuracy off the tee became more important than distance, and America was thoroughly unprepared. (It didn't help that Bjørn had the greens running at incredibly slow speeds.) All weekend long, they played into his hands by missing fairways, and yet again the home team won in a blowout.

The tricky thing for Stricker was how to take advantage of his right to control the course at a venue that was, at heart, seemingly uncontrollable. Working with Zugel and O'Reilly—both of whom admitted, without hesitation, that helping Team USA win was part of their job—he could tinker with certain elements, such as the speed of the greens. Beyond that, the one move he could make was to cut as much rough as possible before the land became steep and rose to the berms and ridges and juniper bushes. They did what they could under the guidance of Kerry Haigh, the PGA of America's chief championships officer, but going in, they knew it wouldn't be anything like the home course advantage that had been created over the last two Ryder Cups.

All the while, Zugel and O'Reilly had to balance that preparation, plus the construction of bleachers and hospitality tents and various other structures, with keeping the course playable for the public. Theirs was a stressful job, with long hours and multiple bosses. They didn't have an official title like "vice captain," but in terms of their value to Stricker, perhaps nobody but the players themselves were quite as important.

CHAPTER SIX

1985, Sutton Coldfield, England

*The Belfry . . . part two of the Jacklin
trilogy . . . the twilight of
the American gods*

*"I'm often asked what gave me the most pleasure, the two
major victories or my Ryder Cup captaincies? Thank God I
don't have to choose. That's all I can say."*

—Tony Jacklin

At the Belfry in 1985, the Europeans were infused with belief after the close call at PGA National, their team was even better than in 1983, and they were once again being captained by Tony Jacklin, armed now with three captain's picks. For the first time ever in the Ryder Cup, they would be the favorites.

But there was a dark underbelly to this belief, and it came down to a simple but terrifying question: What if they lost?

There have not been many "must-win" years in Ryder Cup history. The designation is more art than science, but there's no sense before the European era that there was ever anything that came close, for the simple fact that the United States was the overwhelming favorite, and there was barely ever a "could-win" situation for the British. After that, America had enough historical weight to carry them through the tough decades that came, and it was only in 2016, at Hazeltine, that they experienced the first Cup they absolutely had to win in almost one hundred years of competition.

For Europe, 1985 was their first must-win year. Tony Jacklin, their George Washington, had proven himself in Florida, and the team could easily chalk it up as a moral victory. By 1985, playing at home, there was no more time for moral victories.

The Ryder Cup was at a major fork in the road. Yes, the Europeans were energized, but the facts on the ground were still dire: America had won or retained thirteen straight times, a period spanning twenty-eight years. Put a different way, they had lost exactly once in fifty years. And from the money side, this was the end of the two-event sponsorship from Bell's Scotch Whisky.

So what would happen, just at the moment of their apparent rise, if the Europeans lost? Would they be able to find a new sponsor? Would Tony Jacklin return for 1987? If he didn't, would Seve bother playing? What if their next captain was a dud right at the moment when they were reeling? Would the Ryder Cup even come back? And if it did, would it just fizzle out and die a few years later, as had been its apparent destiny just five years earlier?

Ron Wills, a British writer for the *Mirror*, put it best on the eve of the 1985 Cup: "If Europe's golfers don't beat the Yanks at The Belfry this weekend," he wrote, "they may never beat them."

In many great trilogies, the second act often gets overlooked. The first act is the thrilling introduction, and the third act is the dramatic conclusion. The Jacklin captaincy trilogy from 1983 to 1987 is no different. The first episode was the shot across the bow, falling just short, and the third was the death blow to the juggernaut. But it would be a mistake to ignore 1985. This was the Cup that made the rest of it possible, the fulcrum on which the whole lever of the modern event hinged.

The Europeans had everything to prove—to the golf world, to the Americans, to the sponsors, and to themselves. They had to show that

1983 was no fluke, and at stake was the entire institution of the Ryder Cup. How's that for pressure?

*   *   *

The return of Tony Jacklin as captain in 1985 is one of the all-time no-brainers; nobody else could be trusted to lead the team at such a critical juncture. Today, no matter how well a captain performs for either team, he is limited by custom to just one time at the helm—there are simply too many candidates to accommodate anyone more than once. (Colin Montgomerie tried for a second spin in 2014, but was shot down in favor of Paul McGin-ley, and only Davis Love III has served twice in recent history, the second time under extreme circumstances in the wake of the task force.)

That's a luxury the Ryder Cup can afford as an extremely profitable venture, but in 1985, profit was only a glimmer of a dream, and Europe needed the captain who would give them the best chance to win. In fact, Jacklin wound up captaining four times, and he could have gone more if he'd wanted. But he grew tired after the third go-round, and it was only the intervention of Sam Torrance and Seve Ballesteros, among others, that saw him come back in 1989 for what would be a 14-14 tie and Europe retaining the trophy.

In 1985, Jacklin still had a few more tricks up his sleeve. The first were his captain's picks, which wasn't something he invented, but which he expanded from two to three, and which gave him a profound edge over the Americans. Ryder Cup qualifying today is byzantine and difficult to understand on both sides, but in the 1980s, it was an outright mess, particularly for the Americans. In 1983, Larry Nelson won the US Open but still somehow failed to make the team. Tom Watson won the Open Championship and barely made the team that year, while Hal Sutton won the PGA Championship—the flagship event of the organization that runs the actual Ryder Cup—and wasn't eligible because he hadn't yet spent three years on the PGA Tour.

There were no captain's picks to fix this situation, and it would cost them dearly in 1985, when Tom Watson missed automatic qualification by one literal stroke at the PGA Championship when he bogeyed the final hole on Sunday. Lee Trevino, the US captain, was being interviewed about the Ryder Cup on ABC that day, and while listing his players, he included Watson. Jack Whitaker, the interviewer, told him Watson didn't make it, and all Trevino could say was, "Oh." There wasn't a thing he could do about it.

Today, we have statistics to show us that captain's picks tend to perform better than players who make the team in the last few automatic qualifying positions, but at the time, it was mostly instinct that told Jacklin he'd need them. And in fact, his three picks in 1985—Nick Faldo, Ken Brown, and José Rivero—would perform poorly as a trio. But the Americans' lack of picks cost them dearly, and they wouldn't learn the lesson and implement captain's picks until 1989; even then, it took until Paul Azinger's captaincy in 2008 before they allowed any captain more than two. What Jacklin had done, beyond 1985, was give Europe a serious advantage for the years to come.

Jacklin's next trick was the course itself. The Belfry was not a beloved venue, and in fact was very new. Nor was it a links course, which befuddled many observers—why would you hold the European Ryder Cup at a parkland-style course rather than one of Britain's famous seaside tracks? The answer, of course, is financial—the Brabazon Course at the Belfry was built in 1977 by the British PGA at cut-rate prices (the whole thing cost only £350,000). The organization moved their headquarters to the Belfry, and there were major economic incentives to hosting the Ryder Cup . . . which is why they did it again in 1989, 1993, and 2002, with a brief interlude in Spain in 1997.

The same criticism has been leveled at other European venues like Gleneagles and Le Golf National, and there's some irony in the fact that Whistling Straits in Wisconsin looks the most like a links course of any venue the Cup has been staged at since the 1970s. Nevertheless, the Belfry had a handful of risky holes, including the drivable par-4 tenth and the par-5 eighteenth where water is in play all the way to the green, and it has served as a strong Ryder Cup venue.

Along with complaints about the course, many thought that playing away from the linksland gave the Americans an unnecessary advantage. What they didn't realize was that Jacklin was about to implement his next great innovation as a captain: course control. He worked with the greenskeepers to make sure there was no rough around the hole—the Americans were too good at pitching from two-inch grass, and he wanted to take that shot away and put a premium on chipping, which his golfers excelled at—and he wanted to slow the greens down to erase the advantage of the Americans, who putted on fast greens on the PGA Tour and were simply less attuned to the slower, damper greens that the Europeans grew up playing.

This kind of tweaking is commonplace now—it happens at every Ryder Cup—but it was a major change of tactics at the time. And just as with captain's picks, it would take the Americans a long time to catch on. In fact, according to Paul Azinger, when he contacted the PGA of America about making changes to Valhalla in 2008, chief championships officer Kerry Haigh told him he was the first American captain to ever make the request. That's a twenty-three-year lag, a span in which Europe lost a home Ryder Cup just once and the Americans lost at home three out of five times.

All that said, the Belfry was still an "American course" by British standards, and Lee Trevino was ecstatic in the lead-up, saying, "My guys love this course!" Jacklin was not going to win a Ryder Cup simply by mowing some grass.

But he thought he might win by continuing to foster a strong team connection. Once again, he ensured that his players had the best rooms, the best food, the best drink, and a centralized team room where it would be natural to gravitate and socialize. He took pains—with the help of his wife, Vivien—to make sure that everyone from the caddies to the players' wives were a part of the family environment.

The biggest advantage for Jacklin, though, were the fans. There hadn't been very many raucous Ryder Cup crowds in the history of the event at that point, and certainly none in the United States, but in 1985 the

British fans at the Belfry understood the situation—the Europeans had a real chance to win. They rose to the occasion in a big way, putting out the kind of collective energy, complete with singing and heckling, that differentiates them from American fans. This kind of mass demonstration carries with it real intimidation, and in other settings (like a soccer match) can teeter precariously on the brink of violence. It was all fairly unprecedented for a Ryder Cup, even in Europe. In *Us Against Them*, the American Bruce Lietzke said that the 1981 Cup, just four years earlier, was positively polite.

"We were still in the days when this was going to be an American victory and the Ryder Cup was truly just a quaint little social gathering of Americans and Europeans," he said. "It was just a very quiet event."

Ryder Cups of the past were a rare occasion for fans in the United Kingdom to come out and see the best American players, many of whom otherwise never came overseas except for the Open Championships. Under those conditions, it was golf's version of the US basketball Dream Team going to Barcelona for the 1992 Olympics—they were such megastars that every crowd became a home crowd, and heckling or booing them was out of the question.

By 1985, those days were over. The near-miss at PGA National had signaled to Europe's fans that a new reality had set in, and they knew their players were equals. It changed everything, empowering them to be as boisterous as they might be at a soccer match, and it stunned the Americans.

"They were rooting like hell for their own team and didn't give a rat's ass about you," said Curtis Strange. "So that was an eye-opener too."

"When I would miss a putt, people would cheer," Peter Jacobsen said. "And I thought, 'You know, you're not supposed to do that.' But Lanny Wadkins said to me, 'Get used to it. These people *want* us to lose.'"

Much of the criticism can seem tame by comparison today, particularly the concept of cheering at a missed putt, which is now practically a requirement in Ryder Cup matches, but like so many things about the 1985 Cup, a lot of this was very new, and the newness was shocking.

You can contrast the American reaction to a later figure like Jim Furyk, the American captain in 2018, who was booed heartily by thousands of fans on Friday morning when he walked down the long steps by the first tee in Paris. It was so loud, and lasted for so long, that members of the European team actually apologized to Furyk.

"I told them, 'Don't you *ever* apologize for that,'" Furyk said later. "That was the best fucking part of my week. I loved it. I didn't even take it negative. We were like Darth Vader coming down there . . . I waved. I thought it was awesome."

Furyk was prepared for it—he had seen it plenty in his career. Thirty-three years earlier, the Americans were nowhere near ready, and it affected players like Strange deeply. Trevino, the captain, claimed that even the players' wives were "hissed at" on Saturday, and nobody was quite as angry after that Ryder Cup as Hal Sutton.

"British golf fans have always had a reputation for fairness and appreciation of the game," he said. "But none of our guys saw any of that this week. Their behavior was disgraceful . . . I was verbally abused, and if this is British sportsmanship, then it is a sad day for golf.

"I don't need the money," he added. "I play golf because I enjoy it. If the crowds ever get like this in America, I wouldn't hit another ball."

(Incidentally, American fans *would* get like that in America, and Sutton would play in three more Ryder Cups and captain another.)

Jacklin's response to all that?

"I bet Hal Sutton can't wait to get back to America and head straight for McDonald's," he said.

* * *

"It's one of the greatest honors of my life. But Lord, I wouldn't want to be captain of the team that loses."

—Lee Trevino

As the fans rose to the occasion, so did the Europeans. In 1983, Seve Ballesteros was the only major winner on the roster, but at the Belfry,

Bernhard Langer and Sandy Lyle had joined the ranks with major wins in 1985. Paul Way, who had studied under Seve, won the British PGA, and players like Ian Woosnam and Nick Faldo and Sam Torrance were stockpiling wins on the European Tour.

Still, this team was not on the level of the Americans. They almost *never* were, as Tony Jacklin has conceded, which makes the format of the Ryder Cup, where the benching of four players each session leads to significant strategic maneuvers, so critical to the competitiveness of the event.

Even without Tom Watson, the Americans came in strong. Tom Kite, Curtis Strange, and Lanny Wadkins were all in the midst of very good Ryder Cup careers, and though Trevino had four rookies, two of them, Andy North and Sutton, had already won majors, while Craig Stadler, Hubert Green, Raymond Floyd, and Fuzzy Zoeller were all major champions too. Wadkins might have been the only juggernaut, but the depth was formidable.

Trevino, one of the most fascinating figures in American golf as a player, took the helm as captain, another interesting coincidence when you consider his history with Jacklin at the 1972 Open Championship.

The most that can be said about Trevino as a captain is that he was something of a nonentity.

"We didn't have an intense preparation," Jacobsen said, "I think because in Lee Trevino's years of being on the Ryder Cup team, they were so dominant. Lee had just gotten married, and I think his mind was more on his marriage and having a good time. Lee said, 'You guys can play. You guys know how to handle this. Go get 'em.'"

Trevino, a six-time major champion, had managed to win a major as recently as the year before at the PGA Championship, despite a bad back, and he finished in a tie for second in 1985. Today, if that happened, you'd expect a thousand articles about whether Trevino should make his own team, but it's a sign of the times that there was almost no discussion of him playing at the Belfry.

Trevino had two main personality quirks. The first was that he was always talking. He kept up a constant dialogue on the course, to the irritation of some of his fellow players. At an event in the United States, partnered with Trevino, Jacklin once got so fed up that he told him that he'd rather just play golf and not talk.

"You don't have to talk," Trevino answered. "You just have to listen."

The other quality is his even keel. Aside from a long feud with Augusta National, the so-called Merry Mex was known for a steady, happy temperament on the course. That was on full display in his 1972 duel with Jacklin, when he took an almost ho-hum approach to chipping in a slew of critical shots and breaking Jacklin's heart.

It's a fascinating captain versus captain dynamic. On the one hand, you have someone who goes with the flow of life, doesn't get too high or too low, and has an almost Zen-like mentality. On the other, you have someone who has constantly operated with the need to prove himself, mostly to Americans, and as a result has the impulse to try to control all elements with rigorous preparation in order to safeguard himself from the vagaries of chance.

Ask yourself this: Which of those two mentalities would be better as a player, in the crushing pressure of a major championship?

And then ask a very different question: Which one would be better as a Ryder Cup captain?

*   *   *

Jacklin was a big believer in pairing two copacetic personalities together, and in 1985 his stars were the Spanish pair of Seve Ballesteros and Manuel Piñero. Together, they won three of four matches, and this Ryder Cup represented a coming-out party for Spain generally. When you compile the records of every country that has participated in the Ryder Cup, Spain is at the top, above even America. The term *Spanish Armada* has been used to describe the best pairings over the years, and they've been absolutely critical to Europe's success. In 1985, the collective record of the four Spanish players was 10-3-1, and they've been on a tear ever since.

Peter Jacobsen, playing in a match against Piñero and Seve, was shocked by the intensity they brought to the event.

"They're both very good friends of mine, and I guess I was expecting a little bit more camaraderie," he said in *Us Against Them*. "There really wasn't much. It was pretty much a dog-eat-dog match from their standpoint. I didn't realize how intense they were or how intent the Europeans were on winning until that match. I thought, wow, these guys are really here to play. I'm not a bulldog competitor like a Lanny Wadkins or Raymond Floyd. I want to win, but I don't want to lose a friendship over a match."

It's almost quaint to hear someone talk this way about the Ryder Cup, but it's another example of how seriously the Europeans were taking things, and how far the Americans lagged behind.

Paul Way and Ian Woosnam scored two victories of their own, but the pairing of Langer and Faldo that had worked so well in 1983 had lost its magic, largely because Faldo was going through a divorce. He played so poorly on Friday morning that he told Jacklin to bench him. It presented the captain with a tough choice—in 1983, he had heard the same request from Langer and told him no. With Faldo, his instincts led him in the opposite direction, and showing his usual ability to read people, he sat him until Sunday singles. Langer wound up playing with three different partners in the next three sessions and winning 2 points.

America took a quick 3-1 lead after the first session, and the Europeans fought back to a 1-point deficit in the afternoon. The turning point came on Saturday morning, in the final match of the four-ball session. Craig Stadler and Curtis Strange were taking on Bernhard Langer and Sandy Lyle, and it transpired that the Americans were 2-up with two holes to play. On the eighteenth hole, Stadler had an eighteen-inch putt to win the match. If he made it, the United States would maintain its 1-point lead, and if he missed, it would be knotted at 6 points apiece heading into the afternoon.

One of the recurring truths about human nature is that people, when they tell a story, always seek to find meaning in specific moments, and they want those moments to explain everything that followed. Sometimes, it's possible to force a narrative structure on something that was messier and more complicated in real life, to make order out of chaos in ways that fall short of truth. And maybe all of Team Europe is guilty of that when it comes to what happened on the eighteenth green to Craig Stadler. Or maybe they're not.

All we know for sure is that what happened in that moment, what happened over the next two days, and what they say about it now: that the entire Ryder Cup changed in an instant, and not just for 1985, but for the entire history of the event.

Stadler missed the putt.

"I was standing right there on top of him, helping him read it, although there wasn't anything to read," Strange said. "At that moment, you don't say anything. You certainly don't say, 'That's all right.' He might slap you upside the head, because it's not all right."

Alistair Tait, writing in his biography of Seve Ballesteros, narrated the action in the team room, where Seve and the others were watching (Seve and Piñero had just lost their only pairs match of the week): "There was bedlam in the European team room. Seve leapt out of his chair when the ball missed the hole. The chair went tumbling and Seve came down with a bang and landed on his back. His teammates were hammering on the wall to the American team dressing room. The dream was alive. The Europeans had halted the American juggernaut . . . it was game on."

Tony Jacklin was on the course, and watching Stadler filled him with pity. But when he saw Seve moments later, he sensed nothing of the kind. If anything, the Spaniard smelled blood.

"From a personal level, I never wanted to beat anybody by him screwing up," Jacklin said. "I wanted to have my best game, and I wanted to kick their ass, and I remember seeing Stadler miss this putt, and my immediate reaction was shock. And Seve said, 'This is it!' He picked up on it immediately."

From there, it was a nonstop European torrent. They won 3-1 in the afternoon to take a 9-7 lead into singles, and when the last match was in the books, Seve was so excited to see the score that he growled and slapped the table in the team room. Jacklin, remembering how he had stacked the singles lineup with early strength in 1983, decided that Trevino would remember it too, and this time he put his strength in the middle. It was a significant gamble, because Trevino, as predicted, led with his best players, but Jacklin felt that the middle of his lineup would come through.

He had another piece of fortune—that night, Manuel Piñero was so primed from his victories that he was marching around the locker room, saying, "I want Wadkins. I want Wadkins." Jacklin considered it, and it sounded like a good idea.

"Little Manuel Piñero was a great guy, good friend of mine, and he was typical of what America didn't understand about match play," he said later. "He wasn't a great stroke player, but match play was his forte. He was like a little terrier dog; he'd grab onto the ankle, and he wouldn't let go."

Jacklin knew it was likely that Wadkins would go out first, so he put Piñero's name in the number one spot. When the lineups were released an hour later, sure enough, the matchup was set.

"When Manuel got to know he was playing Wadkins, he jumped," Jacklin remembered. "*Jumped.* Little guy. Jumped four feet in the air."

The next morning, against America's greatest Ryder Cup golfer and one of the most intimidating figures in the history of the competition, Piñero took a 2-up lead with back-to-back wins on the tenth and eleventh holes, and he wouldn't give an inch. In the end, he beat Wadkins 3&1.

"It was the opportunity he wanted," Jacklin said, "and he kicked his ass and beat him. The reaction from the rest of the field when they saw Manuel had taken care of Wadkins . . . Can you imagine what that does? God, if he can do that . . ."

Lanny Wadkins played Ryder Cups all the way until 1993. When the chips were down in 1983, he stepped up and hit one of the greatest shots in Ryder Cup history. He's a living legend. But nobody plays long in this event without some bad memories—not even Lanny Wadkins. This was the biggest, most important loss of his Ryder Cup career, and it's not even close.

Piñero's win meant that America would have no early momentum, and from there, Jacklin's plan worked to perfection. In the middle of the order, from spots three through seven, Europe won 4.5 out of 5 points. It was Sam Torrance, on the eighteenth hole, who had the chance to secure the win. His opponent, Andy North, hit the ball into the water, and Torrance hit the drive of his life. As he walked up the fairway, the moment overwhelmed him so much that he began to cry. Torrance was a player who never won a major championship, and he was experiencing the most important moment of his entire career. He didn't stop crying until he had buried the birdie putt that secured Europe's first Ryder Cup win in twenty-eight years. The shadow of his arms shot out over the green when the ball was still three feet from the pole, and he stood in that pose, weeping, while Jacklin and the others rushed to embrace him.

Renton Laidlaw, the BBC Radio commentator who passed late in 2021, was calling the action with his partner John Fenton, who had been with the BBC for a long time and seen plenty of Ryder Cups. Laidlaw knew the moment would be special to him, and after setting him up—"We haven't won this since 1957"—he threw it to Fenton. Fenton, whose job it was to narrate those special moments, and who was very good at it, was so overcome that he couldn't say a word.

* * *

Curtis Strange, still on the fifteenth hole in a match he'd eventually win against Ken Brown, heard the celebrations up ahead, the roaring and the chanting and the singing, and he summed up the feeling for all the Americans: "God, it's a terrible thing, isn't it?"

The Europeans drank champagne on the clubhouse roof and later threw Tony Jacklin into a pool, ruining his good suit. Lee Trevino was uncharacteristically bitter. He singled out Wadkins's loss to the press, was "ungracious" at the team dinner, and never congratulated Jacklin. According to Andy North, after his loss to Torrance, Trevino wouldn't even talk to him.

Perhaps this bitterness is understandable. The Germans have a great term, one of their classic long compound words: *Gotterdammerung*. It was part of an opera cycle written by Richard Wagner in the late 1800s, and the rough translation is "twilight of the gods." Viewed historically, 1985 is the American Gotterdammerung—the moment when an unbeatable team lost the unbeatable aura that had surrounded it for decades, and suddenly looked, in so many ways, vulnerable. This is history viewed in hindsight, of course—nobody knew at the time that Europe had just begun a run that would see them win twelve of the next seventeen Ryder Cups. How could they, with everything that came before?

Whether they knew it or not, the American Ryder Cup experiment was about to take a sharp dive into an abyss of losing and dysfunction, and Lee Trevino was a harbinger of things to come.

Not only would Team USA fail to understand how to get out of the abyss, but for decades they wouldn't make an intelligent effort because they didn't want to admit they had fallen in the first place. Every US captain and every player and every pundit who ever said, "They just happened to play better," was somebody stuck in the blind cycle of losing that began in 1985. Tony Jacklin and Seve Ballesteros hit them with a punch so devastating, and so comprehensive, that they wouldn't recover for years.

CHAPTER SEVEN

Spring and Summer 2020, Jacksonville, Florida, and Kohler, Wisconsin

The end of the world

"It was a professional crisis no one could have adequately prepared for, and it all unfolded here—in a dim, cozy conference room on the second floor of the TPC Sawgrass clubhouse. Huddled inside the Board Room, surrounded by oil paintings of the former commissioners, the Tour's executive leadership team met for more than 12 hours on March 12, 2020, trying to come to grips with an existential threat to their business."

—Ryan Lavner, GolfChannel.com

In time, the PGA Tour would distinguish itself as one of the best, most efficient sports leagues in terms of handling the COVID-19 pandemic and staging safe events while minimizing the expensive days and weeks of total shutdown. It did not start out so smoothly.

As recently as a week earlier, at Bay Hill, when Tyrrell Hatton won his first PGA Tour event, nobody was really talking about the novel coronavirus. Yes, we *knew* about it, at least vaguely, but it seemed like nothing more than the latest almost-pandemic that would, for most people, be no more than a blip on the radar. Nothing about COVID-19 seemed particularly different from SARS, or bird flu, or swine flu, or Ebola, or any of the other public health scares that left most of us untouched.

One week later at the Players Championship—the PGA Tour's flagship event—everything had changed. On Tuesday, the Ivy League canceled its postseason basketball tournaments, and if that was the first sports domino to fall, Wednesday, March 11, was D-Day: the Golden State Warriors announced they'd play their home game that night without fans, the NCAA announced all of March Madness would be played without fans, and almost every major conference followed suit. Utah Jazz center Rudy Gobert became the first American athlete to test positive for the virus—after jokingly touching a microphone and several teammates' belongings, no less—and that night, the NBA announced the suspension of its season. The next day, the ATP announced a six-week suspension, Duke University bailed out of the ACC basketball tournament, and all the conferences that had gone fanless a day earlier now followed suit in canceling. Major League Baseball canceled spring training, the NCAA canceled all spring and winter sports, and the NHL put a pause on its season.

Throughout this chaos, the PGA Tour at first resisted the rush to cancelation. It was understandable—this was the most important event of the year, a favorable media rights deal had just been inked, the timing could not have been worse, and after all, golf was played outdoors with minimal human contact. Wasn't that enough? All the while, for what it was worth, they had the support of the White House and health officials on all levels.

It was business as usual for Thursday's first round, even as the Tour began to weather criticism from various corners, including a few players. By noon, as the pressure mounted, they opted to hold the rest of the event with no fans. But the optics grew worse as the day went on, with players beginning to worry publicly, including Rory McIlroy, who said, "Today's overreaction could look like tomorrow's underreaction."

That night at 6:45, the Tour restated its goal of continuing the tournament, but when Disney canceled operations at 8:30 p.m., the writing was on the wall. Soon after, the Players Championship was canceled, and the Tour wouldn't return for three long months.

By that point, the people making the decisions had endured two sleepless nights. On the Golf Channel Friday morning, when commissioner Jay Monahan was asked by Mike Tirico to describe the last forty-eight hours, he could only say, "They've been hard. They've been really hard."

* * *

Jason Mengel, the Ryder Cup tournament director, has a strange role within the PGA of America, and the better he was at his job, the stranger it all became.

His journey started at Western Michigan University, when he had no idea what he wanted to do with his life and chose advertising and promotion more or less because he thought it gave him the best chance to work in sports. His senior year, he had a marketing internship at the Buick Open, loved it, and returned to work there for five years when he graduated. He didn't see much room to advance, so he jumped in 2006 to the PGA of America to become the operations manager for the 2008 PGA Championship in Oakland Hills outside Detroit. The day after the event, he and his wife found out they were pregnant just as they were preparing to move to Atlanta to prepare for the 2011 PGA Championship.

That's the rub with Mengel's line of work—because he's adept at organizing and running tournaments, he has to move to a new tournament location almost immediately after the previous event has finished. In that case, the family news prompted him to seek a different path, and he returned to the Buick Open. It didn't last long—General Motors, who ran the tournament, went bankrupt the next year, but Mengel's skills were still in high demand, and he was right back with the PGA of America in Atlanta.

From there, he was promoted to tournament director and took the growing Mengel clan to St. Louis for the 2013 Senior PGA Championship, then to Whistling Straits for the 2015 PGA Championship, then to Charlotte for 2017, and finally back to Wisconsin for the Ryder Cup. Mengel has three kids now, and all of them were born in different states.

"It's just like anything," he said. "It is what you make of it. We've tried to look at the positives in it, and our kids are getting exactly the type of, um, eye-opening worldly experience that we hoped they would out of this."

Mengel and I spoke in late February 2020 for forty minutes in the trailer on the grounds of Whistling Straits, which had been his office for two years. There were eleven PGA of America employees on site at the time, and that number would grow slowly and then exponentially with the addition of operation assistants, a host committee, hundreds of staff from PGA of America headquarters, and more than four thousand volunteers. What we didn't know is that in less than a month, the coronavirus would shatter a good portion of the work he had done since the fall of 2017—it was so far removed from our minds that we didn't speak about it once.

Mengel's job is the ultimate in multitasking, and it is perpetually stressful, considering he has to oversee every aspect of an event that welcomed around 250,000 people, had an economic benefit to Wisconsin of around $135 million, and is the biggest moneymaker by far for the PGA of America. In the midst of that run-of-the-mill, ordinary professional stress, he noticed in the spring of 2019 that he was feeling weakness on the right side of his body. It got bad enough that he went to the family doctor, and in late May an MRI showed a meningioma—essentially a tumor in the lining of the brain. When the results came in, his doctor told him he needed to be at the emergency room at St. Luke's Hospital in Milwaukee by the end of the day.

Over the next month, Mengel had four brain surgeries and spent almost the entire month in the ICU. His symptoms improved, but he had to have a final surgery in November, and by February, when we spoke, he was only just concluding his radiation therapy. He had lost most of his hair, had the scars to show for it, and will need MRIs regularly for the rest of his life, but the good news was that the tumor wasn't cancerous.

That summer, he was right back to work. Mengel has a hand in everything at the Ryder Cup, from hospitality to marketing, PR, ticket sales, volunteers, spectator services, and coordinating with local governments, and his presence is critical. On the day we spoke, he had scheduled meetings about everything from programming the opening ceremonies to transportation and vendors.

It's all "proactive preparation," but perhaps the most important part of his job, at least from a profit perspective, is securing corporate sponsors and coordinating the construction, from scratch, of the hospitality venues that will host them. That's where a good chunk of the money comes in, and at that point, he'd done his job well enough that he'd sold most of what he needed to sell with plenty of time to spare.

So much for that.

*　*　*

More than a year later, two months before the Ryder Cup, Mengel told me he was glad we never talked about the coronavirus that day in February.

"My answers probably wouldn't have been great in hindsight," he said.

Like everyone else, the PGA of America's Ryder Cup team was caught by surprise at the spread of COVID-19. Unlike the PGA Tour, they didn't have to react immediately to an ongoing event, and even when other leagues began to pause, they were optimistic that nothing would change with the Ryder Cup.

There were a few very good reasons for pushing ahead. On a competitive level, they thought it could end up being a flagship event during a time when other sports and events were being canceled left and right, and that took on a new urgency once the Tokyo Olympics were postponed. There was the chance that the Ryder Cup could have a stage of its own, and at the very least fill the "patriotic" void left by the Olympics.

Financially, it almost felt imperative for them to press forward. At the Whistling Straits Ryder Cup, the contracts were written in such a way that all corporate and hospitality clients, vendors, and volunteers were free to step away should the event be postponed, which would mean an incredible amount of legwork to get them to stay, and to fill the gaps left by those who bailed out. Even the ticket holders could ask for refunds, and those tickets would have to be resold.

From a broader perspective, a delay in the Ryder Cup would have knock-on effects across the world of professional golf. The PGA Tour's Presidents Cup would inevitably have to be delayed by a year, the LPGA's Solheim Cup would either have to be delayed by a year or accept sharing the same year with the Ryder Cup, and most pressingly of all, the European Tour would have to wait three more years to stage its home Ryder Cup in Italy. Among all of golf's major governing bodies, the European Tour has always stood on the shakiest financial ground, and it depends heavily on the Ryder Cup for survival—in years when it isn't played, they lose money, and in years when it's staged in Europe, there's a windfall. To move the Ryder Cup back wouldn't be a death blow, but it would be painful.

Meanwhile, the Masters and the PGA Championship announced that they would be postponed, the Open Championship announced its outright cancelation in early April, and almost at the same time, the US Open announced a delay. That meant that even if the Ryder Cup were held on its normal date, the qualifying structure would be completely disrupted, and they might have to compete with major championships in the fall.

In short, a nightmare.

* * *

In March, *The Telegraph* in London reported that the Ryder Cup was expected to be postponed. The source of this information was never revealed, but it was wholly inaccurate—the PGA of America put out a statement saying it was false, and Pádraig Harrington, on a radio show, expressed shock, saying, "Now that I'm on the inside, you go, 'Wow, it really is made-up stuff.'"

"There's no way that any media outlet could have known at that point," Mengel said, "because we had literally ten different scenarios on the table."

In fact, that report galvanized the PGA of America, and Seth Waugh, the CEO, later said they were pushing hard to make that report look like a "Dewey Defeats Truman" headline—false in retrospect. They ran through several ideas, such as only allowing ten thousand fans on the course per day, but in discussions with local health authorities, it was not at all clear that the risks were acceptable. The other option was to stage the event with no fans, as the PGA Tour did when it resumed play in June. But it's one thing for a Tour event to be played on empty courses, and quite another for a Ryder Cup. Rory McIlroy, in late April, said publicly that a Ryder Cup without fans was "not a Ryder Cup," and that he'd rather delay by a year. (This was somewhat ironic, because not only did a Ryder Cup with no fans give Europe its best chance to win, but McIlroy himself had been verbally abused, sometimes in heinous ways, the last time the Ryder Cup was in America.) Waugh knew Rory was right, and ultimately the concept was a nonstarter.

The *Telegraph* story put Mengel and his team through a wringer of stress. As the pandemic raged on, it became clear that no vaccine would be developed in time. They met multiple times a week, and finally started meeting daily to update the situation, while Mengel would liaise with everyone from his corporate partners to the Kohler Company.

"Every other day went by without numbers getting better," Mengel remembered. "It became more and more of a concern. Certainly by the time we got to late spring, it was front and center, and you couldn't miss it."

As spring became summer and the nightmare stretched into late June, the time to start building the structures needed to stage the Ryder Cup was fast approaching, which meant that a decision had to be made. By that point, it became obvious what they had to do, and on July 7, Waugh, Jay Monahan, and Guy Kinnings, deputy chief of the European Tour, held a press conference over Zoom to announce a one-year postponement.

Baked into that announcement was the potential of something even worse—if they couldn't play in September 2021, Waugh said, the event would have to be canceled outright.

For the next six months, Mengel was forced to scramble to keep as many corporate clients, ticket holders, volunteers, and vendors as he could, while renewing land leases in places where Kohler didn't own the land. He managed to retain 80 percent of his corporate partners and an even higher percentage of ticket holders and volunteers, and by December, he began trying to fill the void. Mengel took pains to put the whole thing in context—he didn't lose any family members, he had a good job, and so forth—but there's no doubt that his already stressful job had become something closer to frantic.

When we spoke in early July 2021, he told me that morale among his team had begun to pick up from its lull the previous spring and summer. New trailers were arriving to accommodate the increased staff, loads of wood and steel began to show up on site, and the first bleachers were being built on the course. Mengel was working twelve-hour days and preparing for the workload to go even higher. That was fine with him, because now the adrenaline was setting in, and the finish line was in sight. He'd also managed to secure new corporate clients to get his total close to where it had been after the first postponement, and that was both a triumph and a relief.

Mike O'Reilly, the golf operations manager, echoed what Mengel said about the feeling around Whistling Straits.

"It was a little bit of a bad vibe and aura because of what happened to the Ryder Cup," he said. "We literally had been planning this since 2005, so you have fifteen years of buildup, and then we're told the party's not coming to town. We lost that excitement a little bit, but now it's back."

* * *

O'Reilly was under the gun almost as much as Mengel. Along with his Ryder Cup responsibilities—he was on the executive committee, and also oversaw the scoring and contestant services committees, the former of which involves a slew of independent elements like transportation, evacuation, marshals, refreshments, practice facilities, and more—he had to watch the tee sheets at all of Kohler's golf courses empty as travelers canceled their plans and the country went into lockdown. On top of that, the courses were entirely booked for September 2021, the date of the new Ryder Cup, which gave him more logistical headaches to sort through.

He was back in the zone by July 2021. Golf was booming in part because of the pandemic, and he was in the process of keeping the resort going full speed ahead while construction was ongoing—the Straits course would remain open to golfers until September 11, just two weeks before the Cup.

I had asked Mengel several times what made people like him and O'Reilly good at their jobs, what qualities got him there in the first place and allowed him to troubleshoot these enormous crises, all while dealing with a serious health scare of his own. Finally, through various caveats and disclaimers, and crediting his "support staff" at length, he gave me an answer.

"Being levelheaded is a key to this," he said. "When you get to this time, working ninety, one hundred hours a week, dealing with crazy things each and every hour, it takes a special temperament to do that. Not everybody has that, but I think it's the same trait we all share on the ground here . . . the ability, whatever the situation might be, to keep calm."

O'Reilly echoed those sentiments.

"I could skate along, just enjoy the whole thing and not, you know, give my all to really help support and promote and just be involved in everything," O'Reilly said. "But I don't want to look back and be like, You know what, they hosted the Ryder Cup at a course that I love, and it's my family there, and I didn't give it my all."

Still, what had brought spirits low previously was uncertainty, and uncertainty remained—the delta variant had begun to spread, infection numbers were rising in America, and there was still every chance that a nasty late surprise could end the Ryder Cup. Mengel and his team were not in the clear and wouldn't be until it was over—that was their unlucky fate, working an event like this in strange times.

By the time we met for the second time, Mengel had no more than thirty minutes. After that, he was off—there were meetings with scaffolding company Arena; Levy Restaurants, the main concessionaire; and Barton G, who would be handling interior design. Within a month, there would be a thousand people on site, and he'd be overseeing them all. There was no time to worry about journalists, pandemics, or brain tumors—the Cup was happening, and there was a schedule to maintain.

CHAPTER EIGHT

1987, Dublin, Ohio

*Jack's nightmare . . . the Death Star goes
down . . . part three of the
Jacklin trilogy*

*"There was just no camaraderie, no energy, synergy, what-
ever, in our team. But that's a very important part of the
European team. Losing is bad enough, but losing and then
having to watch a celebration is even worse."*

—Larry Nelson

If 1985 was Europe's must-win Cup, the stakes in 1987 were equally
simple to understand: for the first time ever, in exactly fifty years of competition, Jacklin and his players had a real chance to beat America in
their own backyard.

Jack Nicklaus, taking the captaincy for the second time as the Ryder
Cup came to his home course, Muirfield Village in Ohio, had two big
problems. The first was the US selection process. Even after watching
the Europeans innovate with three captain's picks in 1985, the US system was in a dire state. Not only did they still lack captain's picks, which
wouldn't come into the process until 1989, but ironically, the increasingly
massive purses on the PGA Tour were working against them. In 1960,

total purses were just north of $1 million on Tour, but by 1983 that had increased to $17 million, and by 1987 it had almost doubled to $32 million.

That meant the best players could play fewer tournaments and still make huge amounts of money. In time, the Ryder Cup points process would account for that, and captain's picks would add flexibility. But in 1987, the system was far behind the reality, and as a result, players who played more frequently—the ones who were not rich—could stockpile points. For the second straight Cup, Tom Watson, who finished second at that year's US Open, was out, while Nicklaus's lineup was loaded with rookies and other inexperienced players, from Dan Pohl to a young Payne Stewart to Andy Bean to Mark Calcavecchia. It was also potentially unlucky that Scott Simpson and Larry Mize, two other rookies, had each won their one and only major in 1987, qualifying for the team.

His other problem was the fans. Muirfield Village had sold out every day, and the crowds promised to be jam-packed, but while the Europeans had fully realized the scope of the Ryder Cup in 1985, here too America was lagging a couple years behind.

"It was an irony in a way," Jacklin said, "but the vast majority of the gallery were Memorial attendees [the annual PGA Tour event held at the course], so a lot of people in the gallery were clapping just as hard for our putts as they were for American putts."

The partisan atmosphere for the home team was completely missing, partly because TV coverage had been nonexistent before 1983. When the aggressively neutral atmosphere became apparent during Friday's matches, a desperate Nicklaus discussed the situation with John Hines, the club manager, and together with the PGA of America they decided to buy thousands of tiny American flags and hand them out to the fans on Saturday in the hope of drumming up some patriotic spirit.

It changed nothing—the fans were still polite to both teams, and the only difference was that now they had little flags to wave around. In response, the small band of Europeans chanted, "You've got the flags, we've got the players!" Even Hal Sutton's attempts to rile up the crowd, as a measure of revenge for the bitterness he felt in 1985, didn't work. (This would be the very last time America had this issue—starting in 1991, even as tactics and strategy continued to lag behind the Europeans, the fans caught on to the intensity, and since then, the Ryder Cup has boasted a loud, raucous, and frequently unfriendly atmosphere no matter where it's played.)

Tony Jacklin had two problems of his own. The first was that the PGA of America, in tandem with ABC, very much wanted to extend the Ryder Cup to four days and introduce a second singles round. The decision was financial—even though ABC would basically roll over in two years and let NBC nab the TV rights from under their nose, they were starting to get a preliminary sense that the Ryder Cup could be getting bigger, particularly with the revenge motive for the Americans. The idea also served a second purpose, which was to give the United States a competitive advantage—they usually had the deeper team, and were particularly strong in singles.

Jacklin recognized the danger in all this, and acted fast with the only weapon at his disposal—he threatened to resign if the changes went through. He knew the PGA of America could not have cared less about his resignation, but his success in 1985 gave him a tremendous amount of leverage with the European Tour. They backed him, and eventually Nicklaus told his team to forget it. This would prove to be a massive decision not only in 1987—when it was likely decisive in terms of the final result—but for all the Ryder Cups to come, when the Americans often held their own or crushed the Europeans in singles but were routinely outplayed in pairs matches.

Jacklin's other issue was revenue sharing. The British PGA desperately wanted to keep 50 percent of the cut from the Ryder Cup, which was suddenly starting to seem like a very big fish that would yield very big profits, while Jacklin and the players thought it was ridiculous that just because they owned the Ryder Cup once, they should continue to reap all the awards when it was the players of the European Tour who were doing all the work. As someone who had made his living not as a club pro but as a touring professional, Jacklin felt especially passionate about defending the players. The conflict got so bad that the PGA even threatened to send British club professionals to defend the Cup in Ohio—a wild, irrational gambit that would have likely killed the Ryder Cup for good. Jacklin won this argument too, earning a compromise 60/40 split in favor of the European Tour, but also earning the lasting enmity of Lord Derby. (The mutual bitterness from that particular fight lingered so long that Jacklin suspects Lord Derby stood in the way of him receiving a knighthood.)

Still, the problems faced by each captain, and the way those problems were resolved, were a perfect representation of how the Ryder Cup ran for both sides. The Europeans were able to solve their disputes and even prosper from the resolution, while the Americans were completely stuck in an untenable stalemate.

* * *

Larry Nelson came into 1987 with a 9-0-0 record in the Ryder Cup. He was the first player, and for many years the *only* player, to go 5-0 in the current format in 1979, and he had followed that up with a 4-0 effort in 1981. Not that it was any surprise—Nelson took up golf at age twenty-one, amazingly late in the game, after serving in the US infantry in Vietnam. To say that his game improved dramatically in a very short time is to understate it, and by the time his career was done, he'd own ten PGA Tour victories and three major championships. Someone with this kind of natural skill and life experience wasn't bound to be very intimidated even by a pressure cooker like the Ryder Cup, and in his first two campaigns, he was flawless. In 1987, he came in hot, having won the PGA Championship in a playoff against Lanny Wadkins, his partner from 1979.

It's remarkable, then, that in 1987, which was to be his final Ryder Cup, he finished 0-3-1. He remembered it later as a "terrible week" where the Americans were almost universally confused about Nicklaus's pairings. They played in practice rounds with familiar partners, but when the tournament came, they were all split up. Nelson himself expected to play with Wadkins, and for good reason, but on the first day, in the morning session, he found himself matched up with Payne Stewart. They played poorly, and were beaten 1-up by a new Spanish team that would go on to be the greatest duo in Ryder Cup history: Seve Ballesteros and the rookie José María Olazábal. Over the years, this latest version of the Spanish Armada would play together fifteen times, winning a staggering 12 points from those matches. (Ballesteros had an American caddie named Nick de Paul, who, eager to prove that he was loyal to Europe, poured shots for his fellow European caddies and told them to "whip these motherfuckers' asses.")

That match serves as a perfect microcosm not just for the 1987 Cup, but for everything that was coming down the pipeline—American mismanagement, European chemistry, and a major strategic imbalance between the two teams that was more than enough to overturn America's natural talent advantage.

While Ballesteros and Olazábal top the all-time pairs points list, the duo sitting in a tie for second place also made their debut in 1987. Nick Faldo was rising in the world rankings in 1987, and had just won his first major that summer at the Open Championship. Ian Woosnam, just a year younger, won four times in Europe in what constituted his breakout season. The two men were not particularly friendly, and Woosnam had paired with Paul Way brilliantly in 1985, while Faldo and Langer had been stars together in 1983. On paper, none of this made a great deal of sense. But Jacklin, showing yet again his unerring instinct for pairing personalities together, decided to run out Woosnam and Faldo Friday morning. They beat Wadkins and Larry Mize 2-up, won again in the afternoon over Hal Sutton and Dan Pohl, halved against Sutton and Mize Saturday morning, and then went out Saturday afternoon and played a four-ball session against Curtis Strange and Tom Kite that Jacklin marveled at, saying, "I never thought I'd live to see golf played like that." They birdied the first five holes, went 10-under through fourteen holes, and won a 5&4 victory.

Starting Friday afternoon, Jacklin's other big pairing idea, Bernhard Langer and Sandy Lyle, won their first of three straight matches. Everything he touched turned to gold, while Nicklaus's meandering style yielded nothing but confusion and failure.

Things got so bad for the Americans that in the Friday-afternoon four-ball session, they lost all four matches. It was the first time they'd ever been swept in a session at home, and it sent the Europeans into Saturday with a 6-2 lead. They managed to build on the lead Saturday, culminating with a brilliant Langer approach on the eighteenth hole in near darkness to secure the final point, and had a 10.5-5.5 edge as the teams got ready for the nasty, unpredictable beast that is Sunday singles.

* * *

"Often, as a sportsman, the more you want something, the more difficult it is to stay in the present."

—Jacklin

Today in the Ryder Cup, a 10.5-5.5 lead would be considered almost insurmountable. There have been two instances where teams trailed 10-6 and managed to win the Ryder Cup on Sunday, and one of those, in Medinah in 2012, saw the visiting Europeans mount the comeback. That day represents the most remarkable, against-the-odds moment in the history of the Cup, and as Pádraig Harrington said, "That's why they call it a miracle." That day, the Europeans were so good that they would have overturned a 10.5-5.5 deficit too, at least enough for a 14-14 tie to retain the Cup. In 1987, the Americans had to do even better—they needed 14.5 because of Europe's previous victory, which meant they'd have to win an outrageous 9 points out of 12 in singles.

They almost did it. From the moment the day began, it was a nightmarish scene for the Europeans, who saw American colors everywhere on the scoreboard. Most of Jacklin's stalwarts, from Woosnam to Faldo to Lyle to Olazábal, lost. Nicklaus ran his five rookies out from the second through sixth spots, and they managed to win 3.5 points, with only Howard Clark of Europe coming through against Dan Pohl. Bernhard Langer could only get a half point against Larry Nelson (controversially, they went good-good on short putts on the eighteenth hole to split the match, when it might have behooved Nelson to take a chance on something odd happening), and Lanny Wadkins was back to his old self, pounding Ken Brown 3&2.

With the score at 12-11, the Europeans seemed to catch an enormous break when Ben Crenshaw, upset at himself for three-putting the sixth hole, swung his putter at a buckeye on the ground and shattered the shaft. Two holes later, Nicklaus came to ask how he was doing, and he had to admit to the captain what had happened, and that he'd have to putt with a 1-iron for the rest of the round. Nicklaus was appropriately annoyed, but in what began to look like a miracle, Crenshaw stayed close to his opponent Eamonn Darcy, roaring back from 3-down at the turn.

According to Darcy's caddie, Darcy became immediately frightened when he learned about Crenshaw's mistake, because he realized how bad it would look if he lost to a player without a putter. When Crenshaw took the lead on the sixteenth hole, it had the feel of a monumental upset, but then he flew the green, lost the hole, and did something on eighteen that became a running theme for the Americans: he drove into the water.

As it happened, the United States only won the eighteenth hole once in eight tries on Sunday, and though they would win 7.5 points in the session, it could have been more. Darcy ended up with a treacherous six-foot downhill putt to win his match against Crenshaw, and though his Ryder Cup career had been frankly miserable to that point—he entered the match 0-8-2, and Jacklin had only played him once before Sunday—he became the first of many unheralded Irish players to strike a big blow in a critical moment on Sunday—a group that would later include Christy O'Connor Jr., Philip Walton, and Paul McGinley.

He made the putt to stave off disaster for the Europeans, and his team needed just one more point with three matches left on the course.

Wadkins beat Brown in a must-win match for the Americans, but then the comeback came to an abrupt halt. Seve Ballesteros, just months from retaking the number one ranking in the world, finished off Curtis Strange 2&1 to put Europe over the mark.

Though it had been sloppy and terrifying on the last day, Jacklin's brilliance in establishing an overwhelming lead over the first two days had been enough—*just* enough—to give Europe its first ever victory on American soil.

If 1983 had been the warning shot, and 1985 had proved that the Europeans were a winning team, at least at home, 1987 was the victory that transformed the Ryder Cup forever. The thing that had never been done in sixty years, and that had seemed impossible, was now a reality—Europe won in America.

Jacklin would go on to captain once more, the 14-14 draw in 1989 that allowed Europe to retain the Cup—after US captain Raymond Floyd announced his team as the "twelve best golfers in the world," no less—but this was fundamentally the end of his trilogy. A remarkable turnaround had been achieved in the space of less than five years, and when José María Olazábal danced a celebratory jig on the eighteenth green at Muirfield, it symbolized the definitive power shift that had just occurred.

For Nicklaus, the loss was brutal, though his stature within the game perhaps made him the best man to shoulder the burden. When you say the name "Jack Nicklaus" today, nobody thinks at first glance about the 1987 Ryder Cup, or that he became the first US captain to lose at home. He is one of a small handful of people whose careers were so legendary that he could escape that ignominy.

Nevertheless, though he put a good face on it, he was upset. In 1983, he had been moved to tears by the tension on Sunday that barely kept him from becoming the first American captain to lose at home, and now, four years later, his great fear had been realized. He told the press that the Americans had grown soft under pressure because they played for so much money, while the Europeans, with less competition, had more chances to compete for titles under pressure. He said explicitly,

"Our guys just weren't quite as tough as their guys," and in a move that's almost shocking in its display of bitterness, he gathered the entire team together in his home after the matches to lecture them, to the extent that they were late for the closing ceremony. What possible good could have come from this is hard to discern—years later, Nicklaus felt bad about it—but it speaks to the intense pain of the loss.

Neither Nicklaus nor Jacklin nor anyone else realized at the time how bad things would become for the Americans. In fact, the true scope of it took time to develop. After the 1989 draw, the US team won the Cup back in the War By the Shore at Kiawah Island, and they won again at the Belfry in 1993. But that would be the last time they'd win in Europe for twenty-nine years and counting, and in the meantime, the Europeans would begin to win frequently in America. Tony Jacklin started something profound that captured the spirit and passion that had been missing for his side in the Ryder Cup, and he established a template that could be passed down through the years.

The Americans should have been scrambling as early as 1987 to figure out what was going wrong and how they could fix it, but instead they chose—collectively and almost unconsciously—to believe that what had happened was a fluke. Yes, Europe was better, they conceded that undeniable fact, but as the years passed, they adhered to the mindset that a Ryder Cup among equal talents is essentially random, that sometimes they would play better, and sometimes the Europeans would, but all thoughts of strategy or team building were blown out of proportion. Call it arrogance, complacency, or lack of imagination, but they stuck to this belief even as the results showed a pattern that was anything but random. Europe won, and won some more, and won some more, defeating superior American teams, sometimes by margins that couldn't be called anything but embarrassing.

It was Jacklin who started the European renaissance and carried it to its dramatic triumph in 1987. The organizational powers handed him the keys to Team Europe out of desperation, and he showed everyone who was watching exactly how to conduct a winning Ryder Cup campaign.

But the Americans had been too successful for too long on the strength of talent alone to study the lesson. In that sense, they were victims of their own success, and it would be years before they could humble themselves enough to learn. In the interval—a long, painful interval—Europe was free to conduct the Ryder Cup on its own terms.

CHAPTER NINE

2020–2021, America

*The wild postpandemic ... an
American team forms*

Before the pandemic struck, in 2019, Tiger Woods, Brooks Koepka, Shane Lowry, and Gary Woodland won the year's four majors; Kevin Kisner won the WGC Match Play; Patrick Reed and Justin Thomas won playoff events; and Rory McIlroy won the Players Championship, the Canadian Open, the Tour Championship, and a WGC event, along with the PGA Tour's golfer of the year award.

Each of these results had huge Ryder Cup implications at the time and came with serious emotional resonance. Tiger's victory at the Masters needs no embellishment—it was the most famous major victory ever—and it was almost as poignant when the Irishman Shane Lowry won the Open Championship the first time it was contested in Northern Ireland since 1951, with the "Troubles" defining that nation's geopolitical landscape in the decades between. Rory's victories seemed to presage a return to his superlative form, Koepka's four majors established him as the greatest talent of his generation, Woodland achieved a long-sought breakthrough, and Kisner solidified his status as one of America's greatest match play golfers.

By the time the Ryder Cup came around in 2021, none of it mattered. Besides the fact that the globe was wracked by a pandemic, each of those stars had endured a reversal of fortune. Gary Woodland simply dropped off the map after his US Open win, plummeting from twelfth in the world all the way to one hundredth by the end of 2021. McIlroy's momentum faded, and he managed to win just a single PGA Tour event in the next two years. Kevin Kisner was the most hurt by the pandemic, destined to come up just short of the Ryder Cup again; Lowry would fade enough that he had to rely on a captain's pick from his countryman Pádraig Harrington; Thomas would be stripped of his Ralph Lauren sponsorship after an on-course slur; Koepka would become infamous for a feud that would, in some people's minds, paint him as an unrepentant bully; Reed would be smeared as a cheater (again), endure a disastrous Presidents Cup, and nearly die of COVID-19 in a Houston hospital; and Tiger Woods would break both of his legs in a gruesome car crash while traveling twice the speed limit on a February morning in California.

In the two years after the start of the pandemic, golf followed life—as the American Ryder Cup team took shape, everything we thought we knew was turned on its head.

* * *

When golf resumed after the break at the Charles Schwab Challenge in Texas, there was one name on everyone's minds: Bryson DeChambeau.

It's unclear whether DeChambeau was a polarizing figure from birth—we'd have to ask his parents, and they might not appreciate the question—but he's certainly divided fans since emerging into the public eye as a relentlessly innovative golfer. From equipment to strategy to his own body, DeChambeau has never been afraid to tinker in ways that go against the sport's inherited wisdom, to the point that when he has an idea like putting side-saddle croquet-style, he'll have a special putter made to give it a shot. (It did not work.) When the pandemic hit, he committed himself to a new and radical project: gaining strength and mass by virtue of a comprehensive weight regimen and diet. He returned as a bulked-up megalith, and his new style of play touched a nerve like nothing else. To witness the result in person was both strange and awe-inspiring, and the reactions, to put it mildly, were mixed.

Some were excited by the radical, power-based approach, but others fell somewhere on the spectrum between irritated and threatened. For the naysayers, the most frustrating part is that it actually worked. When the PGA Tour returned after the COVID-19 shutdown, DeChambeau, twenty-six at the time, had gained twenty pounds of muscle and forty pounds overall, registered ball speeds approaching 200 mph, and proceeded to register four straight top-ten finishes and a victory at the Rocket Mortgage Classic. With the added power—his 350.6-yard average that week set a PGA Tour record for an event winner—he took the distance revolution to dizzying heights. His success annihilated one of golf's presumed truisms: a player who adds that much weight and muscle will be restricted in his movement and sacrifice touch.

And so another truism emerged. A chorus of analysts and fans alike believe that DeChambeau couldn't maintain this mode of play, or his lifestyle, without getting hurt. More muscle equals more susceptibility to injury, the thinking went, and his new body made him a ticking time bomb. After all, look what happened to Tiger.

It was a comforting thought for those who felt distinctly uncomfortable watching Bryson transform their favorite sport, but the fact was that working with Greg Roskopf, a trainer who had spent years with NFL players and other top-level athletes, DeChambeau had gained weight in strength while taking care to maintain a muscular balance. At least in the near future, no injury was forthcoming.

The project culminated in September at Winged Foot Golf Club, an A. W. Tillinghast course outside New York City, where DeChambeau won his first major championship at the delayed US Open. There, in difficult conditions, he bided his time over the first three days and came into Sunday's final round trailing Matthew Wolff by two shots.

For Wolff, just twenty-one years old, it was a huge chance to match his friend Collin Morikawa as yet another impossibly young major winner. His career was on a shocking upward trajectory—just months after winning the 2019 NCAA individual championship, he won the 3M Open, becoming the ninth-youngest winner in PGA Tour history. His profile was so big at the Wyndham Championship, I made it a special priority to speak with him. Standing outside the autograph area, I met one of his managers, and told him that I was going to try to talk to Wolff.

"Just make it fast," he said.

"I only have one question," I told him, and he seemed mollified. "The problem is, it takes twenty minutes to ask."

He didn't so much as crack a grin, and when I spoke to Wolff moments later, the reception was just as frosty. There are certain interviews that are doomed from the start because the player is annoyed, and this was one.

"I haven't thought about the Ryder Cup at all," he said. Two more questions followed by two more terse one-word answers—no and no—and I gave up.

The next year, at the Players Championship just before the pandemic shut things down, I spoke to Collin Morikawa and Viktor Hovland about the trio of young stars, and they both referred to Wolff as "immature" by comparison. But at the US Open, he had the opportunity to do something spectacular.

Unfortunately, Wolff was on the verge of a mental health crisis that would spoil his next year, and in tough final-round conditions at Winged Foot, he faded with a 75. It was still good enough for second place, and he was one of just two players at even par or better for the tournament. But the other player, Bryson DeChambeau, shot 67 on a day when the next best score in the entire field was 70. He finished at −6, and the victory at his national open served as the exclamation point on everything he'd tried to achieve in the past year.

* * *

"So many times I relied on science, and it worked every single time."

—DeChambeau, following his US Open victory

DeChambeau's win at Winged Foot was perhaps the most consequential result for golf since Tiger Woods won the Masters in 1997—he had the courage not just to seek out innovative ideas, but also to pursue them with monomaniacal energy. His commitment was so rigorous, so fanatical, that it had the effect of making everyone else look like a dilettante.

The ultimate legacy of his astonishing win at Winged Foot—a course that was supposed to be the antithesis to and kryptonite for the DeChambeau style—is that he could no longer be dismissed as a pretentious pseudoscientist. That comfort was gone, and it was time to reckon with a reality that forced from the mouths of the doubters the three most painful words imaginable.

He was right.

"I don't really know what to say, because that's just the complete opposite of what you think a US Open champion does," Rory McIlroy said. "Whether that's good or bad for the game, I don't know, but it's just—it's not the way I saw this golf course being played or this tournament being played. It's kind of hard to really wrap my head around it."

"Everyone talked about hitting fairways out here," Xander Schauffele said on Sunday, when asked about DeChambeau. "It's not about hitting fairways. It's about hitting on the correct side of the hole . . . You'd rather be the guy in the rough with a lob wedge than with an 8-iron or 7-iron."

There's a story, almost certainly apocryphal, about Christopher Columbus attending a dinner party at a nobleman's castle after his voyages. At one point, a guest spoke up to say that discovering a new trade route to the Indies wasn't such a great accomplishment; really, anyone could do it. Rather than respond, Columbus asked for an egg. When it arrived, he challenged everyone at the table to stand the egg straight on its end. They all tried, and they all failed; the egg toppled every time. When they were done, Columbus took the egg, cracked the end, and stood it straight up with no problem. "And now that I've shown you how it's done," he said, "any fool could manage."

Bryson DeChambeau had cracked the egg, and he should have been embarking on the best year of his life. It didn't work out that way, but that had nothing to do with his game, which secured him an automatic berth onto the Ryder Cup team.

* * *

The US Open was actually the second major held after the restart; the first, which was staged on its original date, was Augusta's PGA Championship at Harding Park in San Francisco. It was the first major in more than a year, and was played without fans. A packed leaderboard on Sunday included players like Dustin Johnson, Paul Casey, Brooks Koepka, DeChambeau, Tony Finau, and Justin Rose. In their midst, starting the day two shots off the lead, was twenty-three-year-old Collin Morikawa—a player who had already earned the respect of the golf world with two PGA Tour wins, and who had nearly added a third before blowing a short putt against Daniel Berger.

A year before I met Morikawa at the 2020 Players Championship, he was a student at the University of California, Berkeley. He relayed that fact to a group of gathered media on Wednesday morning at Sawgrass because he woke up that day, looked on Snapchat, and saw a picture of himself from exactly a year ago practicing his short game at Cal. One year hence, he was preparing for his first Players Championship, and the image he presented was one of incredible polish, particularly in contrast with the other rookies.

"I'd say I'm fairly mature," he said, referring to Viktor Hovland and Matthew Wolff, his playing partners for Thursday's first round. "Viktor's mature, but you know me and Matt are on opposite ends of certain maturity levels on certain things, but that's just who I've always been . . . I love knowing everything, knowing all the information."

In a TaylorMade hat and Adidas shirt, he sipped coffee with brown sugar and cream from a Starbucks cup and fielded each question with the thoughtfulness of someone who had graduated at the top of his class from media boot camp. Like many players of his generation, his voice was faintly redolent of Tiger Woods—not to the same degree as Patrick Reed, who often sounds like he's doing a good impression of the greatest golfer to ever live, but enough so that it made you think he had been influenced in his younger days.

Morikawa had the shadow of a mustache above his lip, a bright flash of a smile, and a good-looking face that was slightly pock-marked. He was genuinely insightful and witty, as when he noted that a "generation" in professional golf, by the current media definition, tends to encompass a span of about one year, and that we'd abandon him for a younger model the first chance we got.

Mostly, though, I couldn't help noticing how good he was as he fielded questions, how comprehensive his composure, how thorough his thought process. At one point, while expressing his gratitude for the experience of his caddie, J. J. Jakovac, he joked about how he had surprised Jakovac by asking if he was organized—something that matters a great deal to Morikawa. Then he spoke of what appealed to him about Jakovac, who had been Ryan Moore's caddie for years.

"When I look back at the people he's caddied for, it's not like he's bouncing around," Morikawa said. Then, as if some internal censor began to blare, he caught himself midsentence. He realized that it might sound insensitive to caddies who *do* bounce around, that it was a judgment on their character, and he sought to immediately correct himself. "But I know caddie's a tough job," he said, "and day by day, it can go by in a second."

It all happened quickly, without any change in his facial expression, but it made clear how quickly his brain worked, and how conscious he was, moment to moment, of his own image and how it was being perceived.

This capacity for quick self-correction and clarification reveals itself often in his speech. When I asked about his upbringing—his parents owned a commercial laundry service that delivered napkins, tablecloths, and more to restaurants around Los Angeles—he told me about how his parents "tried" to take up the game of golf around the time he was born, and then he seemed to think this might sound condescending.

"I say 'try.' They *did* take up the game," he said.

Max Homa, another Cal Berkeley product, considers Morikawa a friend. When I asked him to describe Morikawa, Homa was effusive, while simultaneously highlighting the steadiness inherent to his character.

"He's a robot!" Homa said. "I don't know that there's one thing that you could even knock about the guy. He is nice, he's brilliant, he's thoughtful, he keeps to himself when he needs to. He's the guy you want to be around when he wants to be, he's pretty much a perfect golfer, he hits the ball as straight as you could hit it, as solid as you could hit it, he putts it well, he chips it well, he's who everyone would want their kid to grow up to be like."

The word *robot* stuck out to me, and I asked him whether that meant he is boring in his professionalism and constancy.

"No, no," Homa corrected me. "He's like the perfect robot. He's like if I built a robot . . . it's not like if a scientist built a robot, it would be like if a dude built a robot."

* * *

Homa's "perfect robot" description is an intriguing one, because Morikawa is a machine on the golf course, so incredibly error-free that at Sawgrass, he was the active PGA Tour leader in most consecutive cuts made. Most of his success stems from his iron game, which is Tiger-like in its efficiency—he finished second only to Justin Thomas in the "strokes gained: approach" category for the 2019–2020 season, and a year later he was first, the only player on the Tour to gain more than a stroke per round against the field.

On Sunday at the 2020 PGA Championship, he moved into a tie for the lead for the first time with a birdie at the tenth hole, tying Casey and Scheffler at –10. As the rest of the leaders seemed to be stuck in place, Morikawa holed a short pitch to take the lead on fourteen. Then, on sixteen, the short par-4, he pulled off one of the greatest pressure shots in PGA Championship history (Bob Denney, the longtime PGA of America historian, put it in the top three). With his driver, Morikawa hit a ball that carried 274 yards, moving left to right with his trademark fade, to a green that very few golfers had reached that day. The ball landed softly in the fringe and rolled to within six feet.

"It's brilliant, Nick!" Frank Nobilo gushed on CBS. "Absolutely brilliant! *That* is what we've been waiting for. Twenty-three years of age . . . the shot of his life!"

He buried the eagle putt, and two holes later, he was a major champion.

He went through the usual postmajor slump, but I was on hand the next February at the Concession Golf Club to watch him outduel Billy Horschel at the WGC-Workday Championship, hitting flawless approach after flawless approach to win by three strokes over Horschel and Koepka, and the following July he won the Open Championship at Royal St. George's by coming from a stroke behind against Louis Oosthuizen. At twenty-four, he now had an astounding two majors under his belt, and while his contemporaries grinded away, seeking to make their marks, Morikawa had become one of the top three players in the world.

* * *

In all six majors staged after the pandemic, the same name kept appearing on the leaderboard: Scottie Scheffler. He never finished worse than T-19 in any, and he lodged four top-tens. But it was at the WGC Match Play in Austin, where he won a tough group that included Xander Schauffele and Jason Day, and went on to beat Ian Poulter and Jon Rahm in the knockout rounds before falling to Billy Horschel in the final, that he truly caught Steve Stricker's attention. I texted Stricker that Sunday, asking for a comment on the Americans in the final four, and he wrote back, "Very excited to see Scheffler take down two of their top players."

I met Scheffler at the Players Championship, where he sat in the media scrum looking lanky even in a chair. The other reporters had left, and I was alone with him while he spoke about how his time spent on the road, in lonely hotels, had helped him learn about himself.

"What did you learn?" I asked.

"You learn what works for you, you spend time alone in thought, and you kinda learn about what you believe," he said.

"And what do you believe?"

But once again, he evaded with a laugh. Despite this stonewalling, I found him interesting and likeable in our short talk, an impression that would deepen with time and that would also resonate with Stricker when it came time to make his captain's picks.

Scheffler and his family moved to Dallas from Bergen County, New Jersey, when Scheffler was just five. His mother worked as a COO at a law firm while his father stayed at home to raise Scottie and his three sisters. Although New Jersey didn't allow anyone younger than twelve on public courses, in Dallas the young transplant was free to work on his game, and his family joined Royal Oaks Country Club when he was around eight. There, he met his current coach, Randy Smith, the pro who at the time coached Justin Leonard. Scheffler grew up watching players like Colt Knost and Harrison Frazar come through Royal Oaks.

Scheffler never had a specific moment where he committed to golf, mostly because he always wanted to be a professional. At six foot three, he played basketball throughout high school—he called himself a "utility guy" who was good at crashing the offensive glass—but in his heart of hearts, golf was plan A, and there was no backup.

That day at the Players Championship, another reporter approached to ask for advice on covering his first tournament in-person. "You look nervous," Scheffler said, and he joked that the question made him feel too much pressure. But he finally settled on something that felt appropriate: "Just be yourself. I don't know what else to say."

That's advice Scheffler himself heeds naturally—his calm, easy manner doesn't seem to change for anything, and his game was special enough that his caddie, Scotty McGuinness, who has worked with the likes of Jason Gore, Matt Jones, and John Daly, left the PGA Tour to spend a year with him on the Korn Ferry Tour in 2019. The decision paid off—Scheffler won Player of the Year, easily qualified for the PGA Tour, and began to contend with the world's best players at the biggest events, all through the summer and up to the Ryder Cup.

* * *

The 2020 FedExCup playoffs were dominated that summer by Dustin Johnson, who would have won all three events if Jon Rahm hadn't buried a sixty-six-foot putt in the playoff at the BMW Championship to snatch that victory away. Otherwise, DJ was in pure thoroughbred mode, winning the Tour Championship and its $15 million prize easily, and he kept it going through the Masters—held in November that year—when he obliterated the field and became the first golfer ever to post -20 at Augusta National. It was a monumental victory for the thirty-six-year-old Johnson, who before that weekend belonged to a group of superb players like Justin Rose, Adam Scott, and Sergio García who had never managed to win more than one major championship despite careers that merited two or more. Johnson's own history at majors had included a string of bitter disappointments, including the infamous late penalty at Whistling Straits and a three-putt on eighteen to hand the 2015 US Open at Chambers Bay to Jordan Spieth. Now, he had a Masters to add to his US Open title, and two things were true: his legacy was as complete as it needed to be, and it felt like there would be more to come.

* * *

At the Sentry Tournament of Champions in January 2021, Justin Thomas missed a short par-putt on the fourth hole, and as he tapped in and scooped his ball, the microphones picked out a single word:

"*Fag.*"

That started the cycle of anger and apologies, which came to a head when the clothing company Ralph Lauren dropped their sponsorship. A month later, his grandfather Paul, a longtime PGA teaching professional, passed away at age eighty-nine, and because of COVID-19, they weren't able to hold a normal funeral service. On February 23, the news got worse when his friend Tiger Woods crashed his car in Los Angeles. Thomas was playing the WGC-Concession and was scheduled to appear in his pretournament press conference just moments after the news came out. Over the Zoom video call, he was clearly despondent, and it looked like he'd been crying.

"I'm sick to my stomach," he said.

When asked if it had been hard to be on the golf course the last few weeks, he nodded.

"It's been a tough year," he said. "I mean, self-inflicted, but yeah, it's been tough."

This was inarguably the lowest, most dismal moment of his career, which made it all the more incredible in March when he came from three shots behind to win the Players Championship for what was his biggest win since the 2017 PGA Championship. That would be his only win of the season, but it would ultimately be enough with a strong summer to qualify for the Ryder Cup team automatically.

* * *

Two months before his accident, Woods had undergone his fifth back surgery, and he told Jim Nantz during coverage of the Genesis Invitational that he hoped to be back for the Masters, and joked that he had lengthened his putter so he didn't have to bend over as far.

Woods fractured bones in his right leg when he crashed the Genesis GV80 SUV courtesy vehicle on the way to shoot a promo with NFL quarterbacks Justin Herbert and Drew Brees, but it wasn't until April that LA County Sheriff Alex Villanueva announced the results of his investigation. Woods had been traveling almost ninety miles per hour in a forty-five-mile-per-hour zone, there seems to have been no other car on the road, and while he continued to insist that there was "no evidence of any impairment," thus justifying the absence of any kind of blood test, the twenty-two-page report revealed that an empty and unlabeled pill bottle had been found in Woods's backpack at the scene. Other details emerged; Woods was "disoriented"—he thought he was in Florida—and somewhat combative, two symptoms consistent with traumatic brain injury. It was also revealed that while traveling around the bend on Hawthorne Boulevard, he seems to have never hit the brakes, and may not have even taken his foot off the gas. No conclusions were ever firmly established, and when asked about it directly late in 2021 at the Hero World Challenge, he offered no further details and directed journalists to the police report.

It was impossible not to think back to 2017, when Woods had been found in Florida asleep behind the wheel of his car, and tests revealed that he was under the influence of Vicodin, Ambien, and other medications. Experts were divided on whether Woods received special treatment from Villanueva in the wake of this crash, but the outcome—severe injuries and the possible end of his playing career—was plenty harsh. It hadn't seemed to be a sure thing that he'd make the Ryder Cup team, even after his Masters victory, but now even the idea of him being on site as a vice captain—a role he had filled with great enthusiasm and skill in Hazeltine—seemed out of the question.

* * *

Since Jordan Spieth's spectacular 2015 season, and his Open Championship victory two years later, his comeback had long been prophesied but never actualized. At the start of 2021, after so many false hopes, he had fallen as low as ninety-second in the world. His issues were manifold but were perhaps most clearly explained in an interview on the *No Laying Up* podcast in 2019.

"For me it was physical," he said. "It started with kind of the putter blade, how I was viewing things, and my alignment got off because my eyes were not seeing where the putter blade was actually pointed, and therefore I couldn't trust it. And then it bled into to kind of my full swing, and I just got off in setup that then I'd try to fix the wrong things, and I'd get down this spiral."

There has always been a deep neurotic element to Spieth's brain, and to hear him retell his struggles is to listen to an anxiety dream. There are three "swing feels" he pursued from bygone periods of transcendence, but none of them were quite accessible, and in the course of trying to fix himself, he routinely grooved new habits that turned out to be harmful, which ultimately put him in a place markedly worse than "back to square one." It cost him sleep, and it's easy to imagine a sense of panic, or something close to it, encroaching on his thought process as he followed one false path after another.

He thought he had things figured out at the time of that interview, but his slow, inexorable fall down the world rankings continued all the way into early 2021. On the few occasions when he got close to contention with a good Thursday or Friday round, he seemed unable to handle the stage, and would quickly tumble down the leaderboard. He knew, and often said, that if the Ryder Cup had been held in 2020 as planned, he never would have made it, and indeed he missed his first team event in years when he wasn't included for the 2019 Presidents Cup. In the meantime, he leaned on his wife for support, but warned her that because he wanted to be at the top of the game again so badly, and because they didn't have a family yet, he was committed to putting in longer hours than ever before.

Then, without any warning, he shot a 61 in the third round of the Waste Management Open in Phoenix. He had some technical explanations for it—"It's reversing how I was steepening the club to shallowing the club transitionally," he said—but the explanation came down to reversing bad habits he had acquired over time and returning to a purer state of swing.

He finished T-4 in that tournament, T-3 at Pebble Beach a week later, T-4 at Bay Hill, and T-9 at the Match Play (losing 1-up to Matt Kuchar in the round of sixteen). Then, on Easter Sunday at the Valero Texas Open a week before the Masters, he finally broke through with his first win in almost four years. Charley Hoffman shot a final round 66 and challenged him every step of the way, but Spieth had all the answers, shooting a 66 of his own to stay ahead by two strokes.

"It's been a road that had a lot of tough days," he said. "I've had people in my corner that have always believed in me even when I've kind of believed less in myself."

* * *

At the WGC-Workday Championship at the Concession Golf Club in Florida, I had asked a number of players what they thought about the original gesture—Nicklaus conceding the putt to Jacklin at the 1969 Ryder Cup—that had inspired the construction of the course. I was surprised to find that many of them, including Justin Thomas and Tyrrell Hatton, had no idea what I was talking about, but the most impressive answer came from Jon Rahm.

"I'm an avid history fan, especially history of the game," he said, "so I know all about Tony and Jack. I'll go as far as saying there's not many players other than Jack Nicklaus that can get away with that in a Ryder Cup. If that happened nowadays, you might get chewed out by some people on your side.

"I think Jack had the future vision," he continued, "giving Great Britain, an island, a tie instead of a loss, which I think benefited the event itself, the future generations of the event, because if the US kept winning every year, it's not fun, right? . . . It's a stamp in history, one more of the reasons he is who he is."

This was one of my first encounters with the intellect of Jon Rahm, and his keen sense of the sport he plays. The Spanish star and current world number one was born in Basque Country in the west Pyrenees, the apparent descendent of a Swiss cabinetmaker who came to the Bilbao area in the early 1800s. In the United States, the Basque region is most commonly known for a long political conflict between the Basque separatist group known as the ETA and the Spanish government. It has been known as "Europe's longest war," and the Basque people were particularly at odds with Francisco Franco, the dictator who ran Spain for decades in the mid-twentieth century and banned Basque language and culture (a culture that is itself subject to many claims and counterclaims regarding its ethnic origin, but whose cultural and genetic distinctiveness likely owes itself to the relative isolation of the Basque Country's mountainous geography).

"We have our own language, our own traditions, and even certain tax laws are a little bit different. So even though Spain is very diverse, there is a difference between Basque and Spanish people," Rahm said. "But it's tough because I'm not . . . anti-Spanish, obviously. I'm Basque as much as I'm Spanish. I represent Spain all over the world, and it's unfortunate the fact that I have to keep saying that every time something like this comes up. But Basque people are very hardheaded, very loyal, and very passionate, and that's kind of something that really just describes me really, really well. And I'm proud to be where I'm from."

Rahm grew up adoring the Ryder Cup, and Seve Ballesteros especially. He laments the fact that Seve's famous shot in 1983 isn't on You-Tube, and he was practically distraught when I told him it hadn't even been on live TV. He has a distinct memory from college of watching the 2012 comeback at Medinah in the team facilities at Arizona State, and he claims to have snapshots of memory as early as the 1997 Cup in Valerrama, when he was three years old. He played in his first Ryder Cup in Paris, and though he lost his two pairs matches, he struck a massive blow for Team Europe on Sunday when he defeated Tiger Woods 2&1, dealing Woods just the second Ryder Cup singles loss of his career.

Rahm's main battle as a young golfer is not his game—he rose to the number one world ranking for the first time in July 2020, at just twenty-five years old—but his anger. He was known in his early days on Tour for extreme outbursts that included throwing clubs, punching signs, and unleashing f-bombs. Over time, he improved, and his best test came in the summer of 2021 at the Memorial Tournament, when he established a six-shot lead heading into Sunday. Because he had come into contact with someone who tested positive for COVID-19, Rahm was subject to the Tour's contact tracing, and on Saturday his sixth test came back positive. The result was that he had to drop out, forfeit a likely victory, and kiss millions of dollars goodbye. Not only that, but it cost him his dream of playing in the Olympics.

It would have been a classic stage for a Rahm blow-up, but age—he has a wife and son now—and his anger-management work paid dividends. He never lashed out, never blamed anyone, never even showed an ounce of bitterness.

Three weeks later, he came to the US Open at Torrey Pines and ticked off the last remaining box on his career checklist by shooting 67 on a difficult final day to overtake McIlroy, DeChambeau, Louis Oosthuizen, and others on his way to winning his first major championship. Just twenty-six, he was on top of the golf world in every way imaginable. He had emerged as Europe's great young hope, and its best counter to the emerging class of brilliant young Americans.

* * *

The Olympic Games were fraught from the beginning, largely because of Japan's shocking mishandling of the COVID-19 virus, but after a year of delay, they were held, and golf made its second straight appearance after being resurrected in 2016. At the Kasumigaseki Country Club in Kawagoe, Xander Schauffele defeated sixty golfers from thirty-five nations to win the gold medal. (Rory McIlroy, Paul Casey, and Collin Morikawa were among the golfers who lost out on a bronze medal in a seven-man playoff.)

Schauffele had been an exceptionally talented golfer on the circuit for five years, with eight top-ten finishes in his last fifteen majors, and while he captured a Tour Championship in 2017 and a WGC event a year later, the knock on him was that he hadn't won quite as much as he should have. The gold medal, prestigious in almost every other sport but still of uncertain merit in the golf world—an average PGA Tour event had a stronger field—was a big step in the right direction.

Schauffele, the son of a Chinese-Japanese mother and a German-French father, was raised in a strict household by parents who didn't understand each other's language when they met, or when they married three months later. Ping-Yi, his mother, wanted to escape the discrimination she faced growing up in Japan with Chinese heritage, and Stefan Schauffele had been a strong athlete whose own Olympic decathlon dreams were smashed at age twenty when a car accident caused by a drunk driver forced him to spend two years recuperating, much of them in hospitals (Schauffele lost vision in his left eye). The Olympic gold medal, some said, meant more to him than it did to Xander, and Xander accused him of "hogging" it after they returned from Tokyo.

Stefan was a man of tremendous willpower, and Xander followed in his footsteps, quitting soccer at age twelve when his coach wouldn't let him play offense. According to Stefan, in a story by Tod Leonard of the *San Diego Union-Tribune*, he told his son the day after he quit that they would start trying to make the PGA Tour.

The project began, and it came with occasionally combustible results, including a fight in which the two of them managed to destroy an entire bathroom. Stefan refused to pay for Xander to play in AJGA events, calling it a "money grab," and in general the trajectory of their relationship resembles many other toxic parent-child sports dynamics that end in disaster. He instilled in him an underdog attitude that the son, also combative by nature despite a laid-back personality off the course, was quick to embrace, but Stefan's short-lived stint as Xander's caddie ended after he called him an "idiot" during a Monday practice round.

Somehow, this complicated relationship worked, or at least it has until now. Stefan is still with Xander at every stop, a constant looming presence with long, unkempt hair, wearing strange outfits that might include capri pants and a straw hat, a cigar in the mouth, and an expression that seems to rotate between a wry grin and a grimace. He likes to remind people that he has been nicknamed "the ogre," and I got a taste of his style at the BMW Championship. I wanted to ask Xander a quick question, but Stefan was aggravated, and made his displeasure known to nearby Tour officials.

Stefan has been Xander's only swing coach—he's not the type to allow someone else to have that kind of control, though he did make a concession in bringing on a new putting coach—and in order to occupy that role, he learned the finer points of teaching from other pros.

It's difficult to know what to think of the relationship now. Sometimes it seems funny, sometimes charming, and sometimes less so, but it's clear there's real love there, and it survived a test that has destroyed many other father-son relationships. And in what might be the biggest year of his life—along with the gold medal, Schauffele was married in the summer—his father was there for every bit of it. He was the biggest figure in his son's life, and occasionally the biggest figure on the course.

* * *

If the lead-up to Whistling Straits was largely a story of youth, there was one notable exception—the strangest major result of all came in May, when fifty-year-old Phil Mickelson somehow outlasted Brooks Koepka to win at Kiawah Island, putting the capstone on a brilliant career. The win truly came out of nowhere. It had been almost a year since his last top-twenty finish, and afterward he would return to the relative mediocrity that had been the status quo. But it posed an issue for Stricker—for years, Mickelson had been a leading personality on the US Ryder Cup team. Even if his form dipped, would it be possible to keep him off the team in a year when he'd just won a major championship?

* * *

As results came in and the golf world soldiered on through the virus, Steve Stricker and Pádraig Harrington kept preparing. Harrington named Robert Karlsson, Luke Donald, Martin Kaymer, Graeme McDowell, and Henrik Stenson as his vice captains, a group notably low on experience. He also opted to take only three captain's picks, not four like Thomas Bjørn had done, while Stricker took six.

Among the early concerns I heard about Harrington's captaincy was that he would overcomplicate things and overcommunicate them. Stricker, temperamentally, would never have that problem. Along with all the logistical issues he dealt with—uniforms, food, and décor, to name a few—he and his team devised a questionnaire to send out to roughly twenty-five players, adding others as necessary. The purpose was twofold—to ask them point-blank who they did and did not want to play with, and to learn more about their personalities so they could potentially match players and pods together in ways that would benefit team chemistry, rather than hurt it. (One early surprise came when Scottie Scheffler said he was eager to play with Bryson DeChambeau.)

His first vice captain was Jim Furyk, the captain in Paris, and in May he added Davis Love III, a two-time captain with a slew of experience, and Zach Johnson, who many saw as the next in line after Stricker. In September, closer to the Ryder Cup, he would add Fred Couples.

I had met Couples at Prestonwood Country Club in Cary, North Carolina, for a senior event in October 2019, and his ability to speak on golf at length made a sharp contrast with Darren Clarke, who reacted to a simple introduction like I'd just threatened him with a baseball bat.

Couples conducted his interviews on the driving range, tan in the sunlight, wearing a zip-up windbreaker, khaki shorts, and white Ecco shoes. There is not much to say about his presence that hasn't been said before, from his good looks to his natural sangfroid. There is a kind of charisma that is less effortful, that just exists as an aura, that pulls you in without trying. It's a quiet kind, and that's what Couples has, and it's why he's such a popular figure with younger golfers.

"We haven't won on foreign soil in twenty-seven years?" he asked. "Is that correct? I mean, does that make sense to you? It doesn't make any sense to me. And you think, why would you even bring that up? But when you're there, everyone brings it up. So if you're a twenty-four-year-old and you don't really know, then you go, Oh, my god, Phil, we haven't won this since '93? And then everything becomes a big deal."

He would know—in his rookie year, in 1989, he lost a crucial match to Christy O'Connor Jr. Long before he became a Masters champion, Couples had a reputation for playing poorly under pressure, and when he bombed one past O'Connor on the eighteenth hole with the match all square, Tony Jacklin told O'Connor that if he could put one on the green, Couples would choke. It happened—O'Connor hit his famous 2-iron, and Couples missed the green with a 9-iron, losing the hole and the match.

I asked if he thought the usual analysis was overblown, and that the weight on American shoulders, which seems to lead to failure after failure, was more in the imaginations of the media and fans than a real phenomenon. That's when his face changed—he looked at me with an expression that went somewhere beyond serious, that demanded to be heard.

"When I played in it, I kept saying, 'How bad can it be?' I mean, we land on the Concord, and there were five thousand people that we had to walk through in a line. Are you kidding me? I was so nervous even in practice rounds. The weight is there."

CHAPTER TEN

2004–2006, Bloomfield Hills, Michigan, and Straffan, Ireland

The disaster years . . . Hal and Phil . . . rock bottom

"It all starts with the captain . . . I understand and I hear, 'Well, guys just need to play better, or they just need to putt better.' Absolutely you do. But you play how you prepare . . . [In 2004] we were told two days before that we were playing together . . . that's an example of starting with the captain. He put us in a position to fail, and we failed monumentally."
—Phil Mickelson, on playing with Tiger Woods at the Ryder Cup at Hal Sutton's behest

In 1989, Tony Jacklin stepped down after four captaincies. His wife, Vivien, had passed from a sudden brain hemorrhage in May 1988, and though he was already growing tired of the captaincy and had entered a period of depression and personal strife—he became tabloid news in England when he had an affair with a sixteen-year-old girl—he agreed to accept the captaincy in 1989 in part so his new wife, Astrid, could experience what had been such a major part of his life for so long. Playing at the Belfry again, the trajectory was similar to 1987—Europe ran up a lead in the pairs sessions on the strength of 3.5 points from Ballesteros and Olazábal, led 9-7 in singles, and then watched as America roared back in singles. This was the debut of American rookie Paul Azinger, who beat Ballesteros in the number one singles spot in the first of what would be many contentious clashes. The US team won the last four matches, but it was only good enough for a 14-14 tie, which meant that Europe retained the cup as the previous winners. Jacklin's captaincy ended with a loss, two wins, and that final "victorious draw."

Jacklin was replaced for 1991 by Bernard Gallacher, who had shadowed him for many Ryder Cups in a position that wasn't quite a vice captain but was a sort of sounding board. When the Europeans came to Kiawah Island, the Americans were ready. The first war in Iraq was in full swing, and patriotic spirit was high. Dave Stockton, the American captain, had his players dress in khaki fatigues, and unlike 1987, the US fans had finally caught on to what had become a serious battle. ABC Sports had shown little interest in maintaining TV coverage of the event, and NBC, still smarting from losing Major League Baseball, swooped in by 1989 to sign a two–Ryder Cup deal for 1991 and 1993.

Unfortunately for them, their chief sponsors, GM and IBM, pulled out when the economy hit the skids in 1991, and they had to scramble with four months left to get *any* sponsors for the event. The ones they cobbled together, which didn't include a single equipment company, were not nearly enough to make up for losing the big fish. They had already lost plenty in sales and revenue when a deep fog hit on Saturday at Kiawah, delaying the start. It forced them to air the competition past 6:00 p.m., cutting into affiliates' local news time and leading to even greater losses. At that point, the instinct of some of the top brass, including new president Dick Ebersol, was to look for a way out of the deal. As the losses compounded, Jon Miller, who was then vice president of programming and is now president of programming at NBC Sports, began to have concerns about his job security. The Ryder Cup was his baby, and, through Saturday morning, it was an unmitigated financial failure.

Then Sunday's dramatic finish happened. In the critical last match, Bernhard Langer and Hale Irwin came to the last hole all square, with Langer needing to win the hole to get Europe to another 14-14 tie and a retained Cup. Langer started well, hitting his tee shot in the fairway, and Irwin courted disaster when he yanked his ball far to the left. What happened next remains one of the greatest Ryder Cup mysteries ever—one way or another, Irwin's ball ended up in the fairway. With modern cameras, it would have been clear what happened, but in 1991 it was all ambiguous. Various stories have circulated about the ball hitting a woman's leg and bouncing back, but Jon Miller claims with absolute certainty that an American fan picked the ball up and threw it back in the fairway. Irwin was still well behind Langer, and the best he could do was bogey. That set up Langer with a par putt to retain the Ryder Cup. He missed.

Jack Welch, chairman of NBC's parent company GE, called Dick Ebersol that night to tell him that it was the greatest sporting event he'd ever watched. Suddenly, the conversation at NBC was no longer about how to get rid of the Ryder Cup, but how to secure the rights for years to come. In three days, the perception of the event was completely transformed in the United States, and NBC still holds the rights today.

Two years later, once again at the Belfry in 1993, the US team consolidated that win, keeping the Cup on European soil with another massive run on Sunday that overwhelmed the Europeans and turned a Saturday-night deficit into a 15-13 win.

In 1995, 1997, and again in 1999, the final score in each match was 14.5-13.5. Europe won the first two, including a second win on American soil at Oak Hill. That year, it was the Europeans reversing a 9-7 pairs deficit on the road to win by a point, punctuated by another obscure Irishman, Philip Walton, earning the winning point, and Per-Ulrik Johansson defeating a US rookie named Phil Mickelson. At Valderrama in 1997, captained by Seve Ballesteros, Europe held a massive 10.5-5.5 lead on Saturday night, but nearly blew it when the US team won 8 points in singles to come within a hair's breadth of an incredible comeback. And in 1999 in Brookline, Massachusetts, in a desperate attempt to hide his weak players, European captain Mark James kept three of them on the bench all four pairs rounds, reaped the benefits by establishing a 10-6 lead, and then watched it all crumble around him on Sunday in what remains America's greatest Ryder Cup triumph ever—the incredible comeback, Justin Leonard's miracle putt against Olazábal, and the narrow victory against all odds.

"He made some fundamental errors that nobody will ever make again," Harrington said of James, "but somebody had to make them."

At that point, the Ryder Cup seemed to have taken on a definite pattern—close matches in which the leader heading into Sunday was likely subject to a furious charge by the opponent. In hindsight, the years from 1983 to 1999 can be considered the golden age of the Ryder Cup, when all but one match was decided by 2 points or less. Europe held a 5-4 record in that stretch, the drama was constant, and there was every reason to believe it would be like this for years to come.

*   *   *

Just weeks before the start of the 2001 Ryder Cup, back at the Belfry, the 9/11 attacks occurred, and the Cup was pushed back a year. The decision was made to keep the teams the same, regardless of what happened over the next year, and both the United States and Europe had players who fell out of form. It was appropriate that after two days of pairs matches, the score was knotted at 8-8. Sam Torrance, the European captain, had made several good decisions to that point, including moving the par-4 tenth tee back to prevent the United States from using its superior length to drive the green. Curtis Strange, the American captain, made a small mistake by shifting his Friday pairings, resulting in two losses for Tiger Woods, but overall, it was a good, tense Friday and Saturday, with everything to play for in singles.

In what would become an important pattern, though, Sam Torrance seemed to learn from what he had seen at Brookline in 1999, stacking his best players at the front of the lineup in an attempt to gain momentum that would echo across the course and spur his team to victory. He expected Strange to do likewise, but remarkably, Strange put three of his best players—Davis Love III, Phil Mickelson, and Tiger Woods—in the last three spots.

Torrance's plan worked to perfection: Europe won 4.5 points in the first six matches, and the Americans were deep in the hole. By the time Paul McGinley made the Cup-clinching putt to halve his match against Jim Furyk (yet again, an obscure Irishman with the match winner), Love, Woods, and Mickelson's matches were rendered irrelevant. It was a massive error by Strange, and one that American captains would make again.

As for McGinley, he had been one of the players whose form had gone to pot over the delayed year. His confidence was nonexistent, and his main thought was, "Fuck me, how am I going to play my first Ryder Cup when I'm way out of form?"

The way he remembers it now, Torrance "played him like a fiddle."

"He knew me better than I knew myself," McGinley said. "He knew how to push my buttons without me even knowing it."

The week before the Ryder Cup, most of the players were in a world championship event, but McGinley hadn't qualified. He got a call from Torrance, who told him that he was going to pick him up Thursday morning to go to the Belfry. He was joined by Lee Westwood and Phillip Price, two other players down on their luck. They had a practice round together, the staff treated them like royalty, and they had the course to themselves. On the way back, in the 7-series BMW Torrance had rented for the day, they drank a bottle of pink champagne, and Torrance told him the plan for the entire week—who he'd play with, when, and where he'd be in the singles.

"He treated me as the most important guy," McGinley said. "He didn't treat me like a rookie. 'What do you think of this, what do you think of that, do you like that idea?'"

After that day, McGinley felt involved, and it buoyed his confidence. He lost his first match on Friday, but on the final match of Saturday afternoon, he hit the 4-iron of his life on the eighteenth hole to steal a half point from the Americans, and when his teammates mobbed him, he felt better than he had ever felt in his professional life. When he came into the clubhouse after his interviews, the team gave him a huge cheer.

"And of course I'm fucking ten foot tall," he said. "I've fucking made it, I've performed on the biggest stage, the biggest pressure."

Torrance hugged him and told him he was going to play him twelfth, because he had played so well under pressure that the match might come down to him. But when pairings came out a half hour later, he was listed ninth. His joy evaporated—suddenly, it felt like he was being hidden. When Torrance returned, he sat across from McGinley, grabbed his head, and pulled him close.

"I know what you're going to say," he told him. "But I had a think about it. Do you know in the history of the Ryder Cup, it's never ever come down to the twelfth match? Ever. So I've put you where this is going to be won."

McGinley felt ten feet tall again. What's interesting about what Torrance said is that as recently as 1991, it *had* come down to the final match, and it's not clear whether he knew that, whether he actually wanted McGinley in the pressure spot, or whether he was telling him what he needed to hear in the moment. What mattered was that McGinley felt infused with confidence. The next day, on the eighteenth hole, with the outcome still very much in doubt because all the matches behind him were close, he pulled his 3-iron approach left of the green. He was "nervous as a kitten," but when he walked across the bridge toward the green, Torrance was waiting for him.

"I was thinking, Fuck me, don't fuck it up now," he said. "And as I'm walking up, here's Sam, on the wall of the bridge, sitting there with a big smile on his face. Just leaning, like, 'Isn't this the greatest thing ever?' No worry on his face."

Torrance stood, put his arm around McGinley's shoulder, leaned in, and whispered, "This is why you're number nine."

McGinley's nerves disappeared, and he felt a rush of complete loyalty to Torrance. Furyk's ball was in the bunker, positioned for an easy up-and-down, and McGinley knew he'd have to match him from a much tougher position. He managed to leave himself ten feet, Furyk knocked his bunker shot to gimme distance, and McGinley had a putt to win the Ryder Cup. It was good from the moment he struck it—he leaped straight up in the air after it fell, and a moment later he was mobbed by his teammates.

Europe managed 2 half points in the last two matches, and the final score was 15.5-12.5. It may have been a coincidence that McGinley had clinched the winning half point, but it was no coincidence that he was in a position to execute under intense pressure while just a week earlier, he had been crestfallen about the state of his game. Sam Torrance had learned a little about setting his lineup from Brookline, but he had learned so much more about managing people from his years as a player, starting with Tony Jacklin. When his time at the helm came, he was ready to put those lessons into place, and this was perhaps when onlookers first began to realize that the Europeans had established a template that made it possible to achieve continuity through the years.

As it happened, that obscure Irish golfer, Paul McGinley, would learn a lot from Torrance, and was infused with ambition to be a captain himself one day. It worked out for him, and all the lessons he learned over the years from men like Torrance would inform his own spectacular captaincy. And so the chain continued, from one man and one year to the next, success building on success.

Beyond Strange's mystifying decisions on Sunday, it wasn't a shameful loss for the United States, but the next two Ryder Cups were about to mark the low point in the American match play experiment.

In 2004, Hal Sutton took the reins for the United States with a team that looked stronger, by far, than the Europeans. He had five major winners, and they had none; he had double the number of players in the world top twenty; and he had a course suited to his team. He made the late, controversial decision to pair Tiger Woods and Phil Mickelson, a bad idea from the start—it took two of the greatest talents, and rather than spreading them between groups, isolated them, placing an enormous target on their backs such that any loss would become a massive triumph for the enemy.

To look at the facts is to sort through a mess. Sutton, who had become one of the spiritual leaders of his team as a player at Brookline (somewhat against the odds, because he was known as a loner on Tour), committed the cardinal sin of keeping his players in the dark until two days before the event. That had been standard practice for many years, but the Europeans had long since started planning in advance, as in the case with Torrance and McGinley two years earlier. Professional golfers are creatures of habit, and nothing is worse for them than uncertainty. It has since become doctrine to give them as much information as possible as early as possible, but Sutton almost seems to have willfully withheld that information, or at least made up his mind far too late. When he did, he paired two stars who didn't especially like each other at that time, who played different balls, and who hadn't had great success in the Ryder Cup in the first place.

Contrast that with Bernhard Langer, Europe's captain, who planned meticulously and kept the players informed at each step. He took care of every detail imaginable, right down to making sure his team wore "positive, aggressive" colors for every session, and that Miguel Ángel Jiménez had a full supply of cigars, olive oil, and red wine. Throughout the process, he was open to suggestions and always had time for his players. In a move that impressed his players even decades later, he designated the other end seat at the table to Colin Montgomerie, going so far as to ask another player to move at the first meeting. It was a show of respect for Montgomerie's stature, but also a way to flatter his ego and ensure that he was on Langer's side all week.

"I played in ten Ryder Cups myself," Langer told me, "and these are the twelve best players on the continent, who have their questions and ideas, and I never wanted anybody to wonder about anything. I wanted them to know what I'm doing, why I'm doing it, and I made sure I told them."

From the start, the Europeans were clearly the more relaxed team, mixing with the home crowd and signing autographs at Langer's behest, and things got so goofy in the lead-up that Darren Clarke's caddie, Billy Foster, stole Thomas Bjørn's cart in a practice, raced it down the fairway while Bjørn and Lee Westwood chased him, fell out while taking a hard turn, and watched as the cart sped on toward a crowd of spectators . . . all of whom managed to move out of the way, barely.

The results were too predictable: the "dream team" of Woods and Mickelson were defeated twice on Friday, first by Colin Montgomerie and Pádraig Harrington, and next by Darren Clarke and Lee Westwood. By Saturday, Sutton was forced to beat a full retreat, breaking up the pairing and praying for a late comeback. But overcoming Tiger and Phil meant a lot to the Europeans, who were fighting with the usual chip on their shoulders, and the score after Saturday was an insurmountable 11-5.

For both Mickelson and Sutton, the bitter memory lingered. Mickelson courted controversy twelve years after the fact by lambasting Sutton before the 2016 Ryder Cup, and in the summer of 2021, speaking at the Country Club of North Carolina seventeen years after his captaincy, Sutton told his side of the story while referencing "The Match," a 2018 exhibition when Tiger and Phil played together again.

"I thought long and hard about putting Tiger and Phil together," he said. "I looked at the world rankings, Tiger was 1, Phil was 3 at the time. I put it in my pocket, and I stopped by Tiger and said, Tiger, let me ask you a question. I'm going to pair you with Phil. 'Would you be okay with that?' He said, 'Oh, yeah, I'd love to do that.' So I said, Give me a few of your balls. So I had these three Nike balls. I walked down to Phil, and he said, 'You don't know who I'm paired with yet?' . . . I threw the balls down. He said, 'You're pairing me with Tiger?' I said, 'You're out there Friday.' He said, 'Thank you very much, that's exactly what I wanted.' I said, 'Okay I just gave you the world's biggest stage. Don't let 'em down.' So I took a big hit for that, and several years later, they paid them $10 million to play together."

The line drew plenty of laughs, but it was clear in these remarks and others that he still felt hurt by the events of that weekend.

On Saturday night, Sutton was lambasted, and Europe's Bernhard Langer was practically bloodthirsty. He had seen enough Sunday collapses and reversals in his time that his priority was to ensure there would be no complacency on the European side. "I want the fucking record!" he said to his team that night.

Unlike previous Ryder Cups, the leading team expanded its lead on Sunday, with seven Europeans winning outright. One exception was Paul Casey. On Saturday afternoon, he was sitting in a cart with Darren Clarke when Langer approached them to talk about Sunday singles.

"I know who they're going to put out first," he said. "They're going to put out Tiger. You two are playing great golf. I want one of you two to lead us out."

The veteran Clarke looked at Casey.

"You're playing great, Case," he said. "Good luck against Tiger."

Langer was right—Tiger got the number one singles spot. So did Casey. Casey lost.

The final score, though, was a humiliation: 18.5-9.5. Yet again, the Americans found what happens when a good, prepared European captain goes up against a captain flying by the seat of his pants who seemed to make his team's dysfunctional elements worse.

There were plenty of lessons to be learned; they learned none.

* * *

The 2006 Ryder Cup in County Kildare, Ireland, was more of the same. At the K Club, Ian Woosnam was the latest European captain to step up to the top seat after years spent observing successful leaders as a player. He was every bit as good, and Tom Lehman's Americans never had a chance. Yet again, a European pair beat Tiger Woods twice. Yet again, Europe romped out to a 10-6 lead. Yet again, they continued to dominate through singles, and yet again, they won 18.5-9.5.

That made three straight victories, and the last two had been embarrassing drubbings. America had sunk to its lowest point, and it became clear that even with a home Ryder Cup on the horizon in 2008, the United States would need to break the pattern of ineffectual captains who refused to learn history's lessons and threw their players out to drown in unwinnable situations.

They would need a visionary to meet what had become a European juggernaut, and for the first time, a visionary was on the way.

CHAPTER ELEVEN
August 2021, Memphis, Tennessee

Brooks and Bryson . . . the long comeback of Harris English

"I played with him at Colonial the first week back out, but I sort of said, 'Okay, wait until he gets to a proper golf course, he'll have to rein it back in.' This is as proper as they come, and look what's happened."
—Rory McIlroy, on Bryson DeChambeau's US Open win

Memphis in August—seven weeks to go until the Ryder Cup. Once again, it was an effort to think of anything but the heat. The scenes at TPC Southwind accosted you slowly, as if in a dream—Rory giving chipping lessons to Brooks Koepka, Ian Poulter wearing polka dots, Xander Schauffele revealing that Steve Stricker sent a text asking for everyone's vaccination status, and Spieth confirming it. On the course, the marshals held signs that said "hush" rather than "quiet," and the somnolent sounds of cicadas and the low whine of the blimp lulled several fans to sleep.

On Saturday at the WGC–FedEx St. Jude Invitational—one of the last big chances to collect Ryder Cup points for both the Americans and Europeans—the mercury hovered generously around ninety, but the humidity was thick enough for a good sweat. I walked with Bryson DeChambeau's group for a few moments. It had been a rough summer for him; his caddie quit on the eve of a title defense, he got pilloried on social media for failing to yell "fore!" after launching a ball into the gallery, and he even managed to insult his own equipment company, Cobra, by saying his driver "sucked," which led to a public rebuke.

Earlier that week, he had been ripped by Geoff Calkins of the *Memphian Press* as "the worst kind of dummy, the kind that likes to pretend he is smart," after telling reporters he didn't take the vaccine because he would "rather give it to people who need it." The implication was that there was a vaccine shortage, which wasn't true, and he went on to say that he was waiting for it to become "really mainstream."

"It's irresponsible, is what it is," Calkins wrote. "It's dangerous and it's selfish."

In response, either to this story or the general reaction, DeChambeau decided he would no longer speak to the media. The *print media*, that is—he didn't dare brush off TV or even radio, but the print boycott started the next day and continued all the way to the Ryder Cup, when Steve Stricker all but forced him to speak to the writers so his absence wouldn't become a storyline.

On Saturday, he woke the crowd from their slumber when he hit a flop shot from behind a wooden fence over a small TV stand and onto the green. For a moment, it was delirium. One loud roar incited others, and around the green they cheered as he ducked under the fence and marched to the green. Several people began yelling the word *science!* Laughter met the cheers, and if you didn't know any better, you might think for a second that DeChambeau was loved.

That wasn't remotely true in the summer of 2021, and you could read it on his face. He never lost the perpetual look of frustration, or grimness, possibly going as far in the wrong moments as pained and forlorn. He does not look happy, and a certain segment of fans—the ones who might have been called frat bros fifteen years ago—seem to identify in him something different, something a little bit uncool, and even when they cheer for him, there's a sharp edge of irony. He attracts people, and he attracts fascination, but not necessarily goodwill. (Incidentally, there were sixteen officers from the Germantown Police Department on site that week, assigned in groups of two to eight players designated by the Tour. These players were obviously the ones most likely to attract big crowds, and for most, like Phil Mickelson, the presence of police seemed superfluous, since the fans who follow him do so out of varying degrees of fandom. With DeChambeau, their presence felt necessary.)

Five holes and four birdies later, DeChambeau was tied for the lead with Harris English and Abraham Ancer at 15-under. Not once did it look like he took much pleasure in the performance, and it was tempting to wonder if the cloud of controversy had worn him down. He marched up the hill after his par on nine, hopped in the cart ready to drive him past the clubhouse to the tenth tee, and soldiered on among the ambivalent, passionate crowds, still with every chance to win again.

In the end, though, he would be undone by the sheer weight of everything that came crashing down on him that summer.

There is a short but robust history of infighting among American golfers at the Ryder Cup. From Mickelson's successful rebellion at Gleneagles to Reed's failed rebellion in Paris to the scuffle between Brooks Koepka and Dustin Johnson that same year, bureaucratic dysfunction seemed to give way to actual family-style dysfunction in the 2010s.

Heading into 2021, it was clear that this year's version would be the feud between Bryson DeChambeau and Brooks Koepka, which started at a low simmer and grew into a monster. By Memphis, DeChambeau was being ritually bullied, with Koepka's encouragement, by fans at every course across the country. Nor was it a story Steve Stricker could ignore—unlike Patrick Reed, it was clear throughout 2021 that both players would qualify automatically for the team, even with the number of captain's picks raised to six. Conflict is not Stricker's strong suit, but it became evident very quickly that there was no way around it—the road to winning the Ryder Cup ran through the Brooks-Bryson feud, and though it was above the captain's pay grade to *solve* it, he would have to manage it. If he failed, it could undermine the team and his entire captaincy.

* * *

If it's possible to put a starting date on the animosity, we have to go back to January 2019, when Koepka complained about slow play, saying, "I don't understand how it takes a minute and twenty seconds to hit a golf ball." He had just played at the Dubai Desert Classic with DeChambeau, and videos emerged of DeChambeau calculating everything from wind to "air density" while preparing for an approach. Bryson's response was tepid, and at this point, it was only mildly personal. Koepka wasn't the only one frustrated with DeChambeau's slow play—later that year, video came out of Justin Thomas and Tommy Fleetwood looking visibly annoyed playing alongside him while he took an absurdly long time over a putt (which he missed), and the English golfer Eddie Pepperell called DeChambeau a "single-minded twit."

"People don't realize the harm they're doing to the individual," DeChambeau said of the criticism, but he hadn't yet felt the real heat.

Later that August, at The Northern Trust, DeChambeau requested a conversation with Koepka, they spoke in a parking lot, and the issue seemed buried. Speaking on a podcast together two days later, DeChambeau laughingly admitted that if it came to a fight, Koepka would "kick my ass."

"He's got that right," Koepka affirmed.

On a Twitch video game stream in January, though, bad feelings resurfaced when DeChambeau poked fun at Koepka's lack of abs from his spread in the ESPN body issue. Koepka fired back on Twitter, writing, "I am 2 short of a 6 pack!" while attaching a picture of his four major championship trophies.

Peace resumed until July, when DeChambeau—his body transformation now complete—confronted a cameraman for getting in his way, and Koepka responded on Twitter with a GIF of the TV character Kenny Powers in a fit of steroid-induced rage. The implication was clear—Bryson was juicing—and a few weeks later, after DeChambeau attempted unsuccessfully to get relief from fire ants, Koepka was caught on video making fun of the situation.

When DeChambeau won the US Open that fall, Koepka told reporters he "didn't watch a shot of it," and during a Q&A on Instagram, when asked why he wasn't talking about Bryson, he said, "If you've got nothing nice to say, don't say it at all."

In May 2021, while being interviewed by Todd Lewis of the Golf Channel, Koepka saw DeChambeau walking in the background and gave an exaggerated eye roll. The video of the outtake was leaked, it once again went viral, and the social media flames were fanned. When it was announced that DeChambeau would partner with Aaron Rodgers in an exhibition, Koepka tweeted "Sorry bro" at Rodgers. DeChambeau responded to say that he was "living rent free in your head," and then Koepka sent out video of a fan calling DeChambeau "Brooksy" during a practice round.

That's the moment when the spat, which up to that point had been almost comical, erupted into something unhealthy. At the Memorial in June, inspired by the video Koepka shared, a small handful of fans began taunting DeChambeau by calling him "Brooksy," which led to three fans being removed—possibly at DeChambeau's request.

"It was flattering," he said afterward. "I think it's absolutely flattering what they're doing."

Later that night, Koepka posted a video on Twitter thanking his fans for shouting his name that day.

"I know I'm not playing, but thank you guys for showing support," he said. "And if your time was, I don't know, say, cut short at the golf course today, DM Michelob Ultra, we're going to be giving out 50 cases of beer to the first 50 people in case their time was cut short, or if they had any trouble at the tournament."

There was no longer any doubt—Koepka was tacitly encouraging fans to heckle DeChambeau. As far as anyone could tell, this was unprecedented in professional golf. (When I spoke to Paul McGinley about it, he called it a "catastrophic moment for our game.")

The fans obeyed Koepka, and the heckling began. For the rest of the summer, DeChambeau's rounds were populated by crowds of mostly young men shouting the word *Brooksy* at him no matter where he went. I got my first taste of the scene in early August in Memphis, when DeChambeau entered the back nine on Sunday at 18-under, just two shots behind the leader, Harris English, who was himself fighting for the biggest win of his career and a spot on the Ryder Cup team. Nobody else was closer than 16-under, and nobody would improve on that number for the rest of the round. Even par on a relatively easy course, for either player, would have been plenty.

What followed was one of the most dismal nine-hole stretches you could hope to see on the PGA Tour. On the one hand, you had English, one of the nicest players around, get caught under a handful of (justified) slow-play warnings, rush through the back nine in staggering humidity and swirling wind, and lose a lead that looked unassailable. On the other hand, you had his playing partner, the most controversial player on Tour, enduring what amounts to four-plus hours of bullying that had been openly encouraged by his rival. It was an ugly scene: poor displays of golf, worse displays of behavior, and two contenders who didn't collapse as much as they imploded.

For English, it was a disappointing end to what should have been the biggest win of his career. A year earlier, he quietly had one of the most successful campaigns on the PGA Tour. With his second-place finish at The Northern Trust that fall, and a fourth at the US Open a few weeks later, he moved back into the top forty of the world rankings after a long, agonizing period in golf's desert. The fact that he did it despite testing positive for the coronavirus in late June turned English's story from surprising to jaw-dropping. Entering the Tour Championship that year, he was the most unexpected name in the top ten, alongside players like Dustin Johnson, Justin Thomas, Collin Morikawa, Jon Rahm, Patrick Reed, and Bryson DeChambeau.

Just a year before that, his world ranking had been 369th, and when he could gain only conditional status for the 2020 season, it seemed as though everything was getting worse. But the conditional status mattered quite a lot, and he parlayed it into a spectacular fall season, stringing together four top-tens in six fall starts to mitigate some of the conditional stress. He still had to fight for sponsor's exemptions to some tournaments in 2020, but he gained entrance to others by virtue of his fall success.

In fact, that was the best stretch of golf English had played in years, and even a pandemic and a positive test couldn't stop the good times. His 2020 season represented the first signs of life for a career that began with the promise of something great.

English grew up in Moultrie, a small town in southern Georgia about forty miles north of the Florida Panhandle and Tallahassee. There was just one golf course in the entire county: an old-school track called the Sunset Country Club dotted with small, humpback greens, where English first played with his father at age six. Ben English played basketball at Georgia and recognized the high-level athletic instincts in his son. He made more than enough as a cotton broker, buying from the farmers and selling to the gins, to give Harris every chance to develop his game.

In the summers, English played at the Sunset Club with friends, and it wasn't long before he was traveling around the southeast to junior tournaments. He presents a calm façade to the world today, so it was almost hard to believe him when he spoke of his terrible temper as a child. It got so bad that he'd become angry if he saw his parents watching him play, and he forbade them to walk with him during his competitive rounds. Finally, at thirteen, when he "showed his ass" on the course one too many times, his mom sat him down and read the riot act: this is embarrassing, and it's not how I raised you. When she told him to watch Davis Love III and Fred Couples, and notice how their reactions looked the same after a good shot or bad shot, he began to improve.

English was a good student, and his parents knew that the education and athletic opportunities in southern Georgia's public-school system left a lot to be desired. When he turned fifteen, his mother suggested a boarding school where he could focus on academics and try to gain golf exposure with an eye on a Division I scholarship. They chose the Baylor

School in Chattanooga, Tennessee, and to ease the transition, his mother moved with him into a condo near the school so he wouldn't have to be alone. Ben visited on the weekends, and the competition at the school—Baylor sent golfers to big universities almost every year—pushed him to get better and better.

He made huge strides, and quickly became one of the school's best players. As a junior, at the Tennessee state championship, English hit a miracle forty-foot birdie putt and watched his opponent miss one from five feet to give Baylor the title.

He put together a solid college career at the University of Georgia, but left on a bitter note when he lost the final match of the national championship to Patrick Reed.

"Go back in history and ask Harris if there was one match that he wanted to win," Georgia coach Chris Haack said. "That was the match."

He recovered quickly in his early days on Tour, but by 2019, the shine had worn off, and English reached his thirtieth birthday toiling on the fringes, far from stardom.

He spent those years in the wilderness bouncing from teacher to teacher, and he searched a little too hard for the perfect guru to lift his malaise. In the spring of 2019, he finally found the right man in Justin Parsons, a teaching pro from Harris's home on St. Simons Island, Georgia, who has helped build up English's confidence in tandem with his game over the past year.

When you drill down into the numbers, Parsons starts to look like a miracle worker. In comments made throughout 2020, English continually referred to "going back to what I did well," and a look at the Tour's strokes gained statistics shows that while English remained one of the game's best putters, he grew by leaps and bounds in every other category, from driving to approach. One combined stat, "strokes gained: tee to green," tells the full story: in a single season, English went from 147th to 16th. With his driver and irons, he had been transformed.

In fact, the numbers in every category go beyond vast improvement. Up and down the list, they're even better than the prime years of 2013–2015. By almost every metric, English had done far more than return to his former glory; he was playing the best golf of his life.

That hot streak continued into 2021, when he won the Sentry Tournament of Champions in January and the Travelers Championship in the summer to break his long victory drought. He was fully back, better than ever, and Memphis should have been the first top-tier victory of his career. Instead, it all went to hell with a back nine 40 that handed the championship to Abraham Ancer.

* * *

DeChambeau, somehow, fared worse. By the time his back-nine nightmare was over, he had posted 41, and when he met his caddie and manager behind the eighteenth green, he swore angrily as he walked to the scoring area.

All throughout his round, fans pummeled him with shouts of "Brooksy," and while this may sound minor and even funny on the surface, in reality, when you follow DeChambeau for even half a round, and you see the faces of the people taunting him for a mean little thrill, it looks crueler and more intense than comes across on TV. It clearly made DeChambeau miserable, but he was locked into an unwinnable position where if he reacted, he looked thin-skinned. Staying silent didn't help either. After staring down several fans throughout the course of play on Sunday—a long glare, accomplishing nothing, before he marched away—he finally broke down on the seventeenth tee when a female fan shouted, yet again, "Brooksy!"

"Good one!" he shouted back. He looked bitter, tired, and defeated, and the only thing you could feel for him in that moment was pity. There is a marked difference between disagreeing with someone, perhaps even disliking him, and supporting the kind of psychological abuse that he began to endure at every single stop, which was so effective that it was nearly impossible to police. DeChambeau and his caddie even approached the literal police walking with their group on Sunday to complain, but the heckling showed no signs of abating.

"It's not real fair for them to call him 'Brooksy' a lot," English said after the round. "It kind of sucks, and obviously he hears it, and it affects him a little bit. He doesn't like it, and I think that causes them to do it more. It just sucks that that's out here right now, that they're trying to irk people like that. It's just unfortunate."

DeChambeau, of course, had to pretend that none of it bothered him, but as English noticed, and as everyone with eyes can notice, he was bothered.

A single bead of water, dropped on your forehead, isn't much of an imposition. But when the drip-drip-drip is ongoing, and endless, it can drive you crazy, especially when it's coming from those who wish you harm. It was depressing to watch that sadistic impulse play out in Memphis, and it was depressing to know that a powerful rival of DeChambeau's had helped encourage it. Whatever thoughts I held of DeChambeau privately—they were mixed on a good day, and particularly negative that week—the bullying was outrageous and unforgivable, and it seemed to be past the point where anyone could control it. But it would have been nice if someone—someone like Brooks Koepka—had tried.

Instead, the job of squelching the controversy in the space of a single month would fall on the reluctant shoulders of Steve Stricker.

CHAPTER TWELVE

2008, Louisville, Kentucky

Azinger, the American guru . . .
rebirth in Valhalla . . . the blessed pods

"If you want to bring the Ryder Cup team together, maybe you have to break it apart."

—Paul Azinger

You can explain men like Tony Jacklin by historical circumstance—when one side is desperate, that's fertile ground for the emergence of a radical—and you can explain all the strong European captains that followed as having evolved from the source. Ditto for the weaker American captains—without a centralized plan, it's no wonder that they floundered with divergent approaches from one year to the next. In that context, it's tempting to view Paul Azinger as a transformational figure that appeared almost from nowhere, a genius who laid the foundation for America's Ryder Cup future.

In reality, his trajectory matches Jacklin's to a tee. His record as a player was 5-8-3 in four Ryder Cups, and that record mirrored the average American experience—he was undefeated in four singles matches at 2-0-2, with victories over Seve Ballesteros and José María Olazábal, but a dismal 3-8-1 in pairs matches. The United States actually won two of the Ryder Cups he played in, but as time went on and his career came to an end, he could only bear witness as the situation grew worse and worse. Just like Jacklin, he brought his revolutionary ideas to leadership on the heels of humiliation—the dual 18.5-9.5 blowouts in 2004 and 2006—at a time when it seemed like the Ryder Cup was no longer competitive and losing value as a sports property. By 2008, the PGA of America was very ready to hear Paul Azinger's ideas, and very ready to stop losing.

As far as Ryder Cup strategies go, Azinger's began in a strange place. One day long before Valhalla, he watched a show about Gibson guitars on the Discovery Channel and was too lazy to change the channel when it was over. In a stroke of great luck for the entire American golf world, the next show was a documentary on the Navy SEALs. Azinger followed the story halfheartedly, but he perked up when an officer explained how they formed tight bonds between the SEALs by placing them in small groups.

Azinger was already geared to think about the Ryder Cup. For years, he and a few friends—Payne Stewart, Dave Stockton, Lanny Wadkins—would spend hours discussing strategy every chance they got, and the minute he heard about the SEAL teams, his brain went to golf. His wife came into the room, and he pitched the idea to her: What if you broke a Ryder Cup team into small units?

The more he turned the idea over in his mind, the more he liked it. He knew that European teams seemed to unite in ways that the Americans couldn't, and that apparent unity was one explanation people put forward as to why they won so regularly. Much effort had been expended trying to form that kind of bond among American teams, but maybe, he thought, that was the wrong idea. Maybe twelve players were too many for real bonding, and maybe the secret was to stop trying.

"Tour players are hardwired to beat the guys next to them," he remembered telling his wife. "Then, one week a year we think they should go against their nature and become a championship team."

He even began to wonder whether Europe's so-called chemistry was based on a tendency to cluster into smaller groups based on their nationalities. It was human nature, and as he looked back on his own playing career and the American teams whose personalities hadn't clicked, he saw nothing but a doomed effort.

Twelve was too many, but four might be perfect.

* * *

Azinger's attraction to a military philosophy was natural, considering that his father, Ralph, was a lieutenant colonel in the US Air Force. When the elder Azinger retired, he started a marina where Paul worked during the summers. After the family moved to Florida, Azinger started his college golf career as a walk-on at Brevard Community College, got a summer job at Bay Hill, and eventually won a scholarship to Florida State. He turned professional in 1981, and drove between tour stops in a motor home with his wife, Toni.

His career didn't take off until 1987, but when he hit his stride, he hit it hard. In the next six years, he won eleven tournaments, with the cherry on top coming at the 1993 PGA Championship in a playoff win against Greg Norman—a win that put him in consideration for a future Ryder Cup captaincy.

It was also the peak of his playing career. That December, doctors found lymphoma in his shoulder. He underwent months of treatment, and though he came back afterward and even won the 2000 Sony Open in Hawaii, he would never rise to his previous levels. He played the senior tour for exactly four events in 2010, but it wasn't for him, and since 2005 he's worked as a TV analyst for ABC, ESPN, Fox, and now NBC.

There are two other moments worth mentioning in his playing career. In 1987, in Scotland, he held a one-stroke lead over Nick Faldo with two holes to play at the Open Championship. It was a massive moment in his career, and a chance to launch himself into the stratosphere, but he bogeyed the last two holes to lose to Faldo by a single shot. Afterward, Faldo reportedly said, "Sorry about that," in a way that Azinger found deeply condescending.

Like Jacklin and Nicklaus, Azinger and Faldo's paths would cross again and again from that moment on, at the Ryder Cup as players, and later in their television careers. It was almost a foregone conclusion that when it was time for each man to take the Ryder Cup captaincy, they would face each other. The rivalry was forever tense—they fought to a halved match in their 1993 singles match at the Belfry, but despite the fact that the Ryder Cup had been decided by that point, Faldo refused to concede Azinger's six-footer at the last hole for the tie . . . even though he had talked Azinger into conceding his five-footer on the sixteenth. Azinger made it, and later, reviewing the match long after his treatment for cancer, he said, "Look at that . . . I had cancer, and he still couldn't beat me."

He had other victories against Faldo; he and Chip Beck beat Faldo and Woosnam in four-ball in 1989, and he and Mark O'Meara lambasted Faldo and David Gilford in 1991. But the fact was that Faldo rose to levels he could never attain as a player, including the world number one ranking, and Azinger knew it.

The rivalry continued long after their playing careers had ended. In 2008, months before the Ryder Cup, Azinger criticized Faldo in no uncertain terms to the newspaper *Britain's Mail*.

"Nick Faldo has tried to redefine himself," he said. "Some people have bought it. Some have not. But if you're going to be a prick and everyone hates you, why do you think that just because you're trying to be cute and funny on air now that the same people are all going to start to like you? The bottom line is that the players from his generation and mine really don't want to have anything to do with him."

(When the story came out, Azinger joked that he left Faldo a voicemail: "This is Zinger. Well, it's already started. I don't know if you've seen it, but one of those papers said I called you a prick and that everyone from your generation hates you. Even though you pretty much are and everyone pretty much does, I have more diplomacy than to say that.")

Oddly, though, there was a kind of unorthodox bond between them—an oppositional chemistry, and for the two years they worked together on ABC, viewers liked them. After Azinger's remarks to the British press, he called Faldo twice to offer sincere apologies. Of their short-lived TV partnership, Azinger said that he wished it would never end. Yet in the same interview, he admitted that he felt his own achievements had been "minimized" compared to Faldo's, including on TV, and that it was hard for him to brush off.

In terms of pure competitive Ryder Cup grit, Azinger was the heir to Lanny Wadkins—beloved of his teammates, loathed by the opposition—and his great rivalry in his first three Cups was not with Faldo, but Seve Ballesteros. It got so bad that Ballesteros once described the American team as "eleven great guys, and Paul Azinger," and the mutual dislike began in 1989. There, in the leadoff singles match on Sunday, Azinger vowed not to be intimidated by the great Spaniard. When Ballesteros wanted to change a damaged ball on the second green, Azinger demanded to see the ball, and then refused to let him swap.

"Okay," said Ballesteros, "if this is the way you want to play today, we can play this way."

The tension mounted, and on the eighteenth, Ballesteros questioned his drop from a water hazard, shouting, "No, no, no!" as he raced toward him. When Azinger won with a spectacular up-and-down bogey on that hole, Ballesteros was reportedly seen with tears in his eyes as he walked off the course. Later, he approached Azinger, put his arms on his shoulders, and said, "We were very hard on each other today."

"We sure were," said Azinger.

"It's okay," Seve said.

It wasn't okay in 1991, though, when Azinger and Beck met the super team of Ballesteros and Olazábal in alternate shot. Once again, the action began on the second hole when Seve hit a shot near a hazard, couldn't find the ball, and wanted a drop. Once again, Azinger wouldn't let him—a lost ball that can't conclusively be proved to be in the hazard means you have to re-tee. A long argument ensued, which the Americans won. When Seve hit a shot into the palmetto bushes two holes later, they found the ball a few seconds after the five-minute period was up, and once again Azinger stuck to the rules, trying to force him to forfeit the ball before an official overruled him. Olazábal hit his ball into the water next, and another argument ensued about the correct spot.

Later in the front nine, though, the Americans made a big mistake, using the wrong ball to drive off the tee on several holes. The Spaniards didn't bring it up until the tenth hole—some thought the delay was on purpose, hoping they could let them continue to screw up and then claim multiple holes—and a massive shouting match ensued. Everyone was irate, but the Americans admitted their error only when they learned that they couldn't be penalized (the challenge had to come earlier). Despite getting away with it, the Americans were rattled, and their 3-up lead at the turn vanished into a 2&1 win for the Spanish.

"It broke my heart to lose that match," Azinger told me. "And then I didn't want to play him that afternoon, in my head I didn't, and then we drew them again. And they got us again. I was so pissed."

"You had to watch him like a hawk," Azinger remembers now. "He wore white shoes, and he would early-walk your ass. He would clear his throat. It was just another element of how great match play is, and you have to take it to that extra level, and that's what happened."

Over the course of his Ryder Cup career, Azinger proved his bona fides as a battler, and his victory at the PGA Championship made him an obvious candidate for captain. He didn't want to do it overseas, especially in 2006 when it should have been the captaincy of his late friend Payne Stewart, but when 2008 came, he was ready.

Yet even after two consecutive blowouts, it wasn't totally clear that the PGA of America was ready for him.

* * *

It was M. G. Orender, a former PGA of America president, who told Azinger that the Valhalla captaincy wasn't a sure thing, and that if he wanted it, he should start lobbying. The problem for Azinger was that he knew "lobbying," in his case, meant making certain demands that other potential captains might not make. He was stuck between two desires. He wanted it badly, and even felt a responsibility to turn the American Ryder Cup institution around—"I don't think I could live with myself if I didn't try," he told his wife—but he didn't want to sacrifice any part of his vision.

In October 2007, he met with PGA of America brass at a restaurant in Orlando and laid out his plans. He wanted smaller, almost self-contained units of players—a concept that came to be called pods—and pitched it as something that would come as a relief, taking away all uncertainty about pairings early in the process. He also wanted four captain's picks, up from two, and he wanted to change the qualification process so that only events in the year of the Ryder Cup counted for the standings, rather than the two years before.

On this topic, Azinger had personal experience—he was playing terribly before the 2002 Ryder Cup, knew he didn't deserve to be on the team, and didn't win a match. He also wanted the points system to be based on money won, as opposed to the old "top ten finish" criteria, to better reflect how players fared in big moments. "I only choked for two things: cash and prestige," he told the executives, and this new change would reward pressure performances.

Roger Warren, the PGA of America president, was impressed, and the one piece of pushback he received was on the off-year qualifying—they still wanted people thinking about the Ryder Cup even a year early. Eventually, a compromise was reached wherein only majors would count for Ryder Cup points the year before the match.

Azinger got the job, and his pod system became clearer in his mind when Mickelson advised him to go with four players per pod, not three, so that if one pod was firing on all cylinders, no player would have to sit. Azinger invited every living former US captain to a dinner, ten attended, and he tried the idea out on them too. He knew he'd have to build coalitions everywhere he could in order to muster support for the massive change in how the team was run.

He assembled three vice captains, one for each pod, and dipped into the pool of former captains by selecting Raymond Floyd and Dave

Stockton; his friend Olin Browne was the third. As the months went on, he was inundated with media requests, and he took his job of establishing the team message seriously. One of his main talking points was that America would be underdogs at Valhalla. That became much more convincing when he got a piece of devastating news: following his dramatic victory at the 2008 US Open, Tiger Woods needed major reconstructive knee surgery and would miss the Ryder Cup. Azinger had looked at Tiger as his crutch, and now his crutch would be on crutches. The only silver lining—it wasn't much of one—was that nobody doubted him when he promoted his team as the underdogs.

His next move was to enlist the help of Dr. Ron Braund, a corporate team-building specialist. It was Braund who gave him the idea of constructing the pods based on personality types. Azinger's original plan was to match players by their game types—long hitters with great wedge players, for instance. But Braund warned him that even if two players' games were compatible, if they responded differently to stress, the bonds could break under pressure. Who wanted to be quiet when the heat was on? Who wanted to talk? Who needed encouragement? All of these questions became important to him, especially because the bonding time was so short—one week.

What convinced Azinger was thinking of Ballesteros and Olazábal, the greatest team in Ryder Cup history. On paper, it was a horrible pairing—they were wild off the tee but could scramble with the best, meaning they had the same strengths and weaknesses—but clearly, the personal chemistry they shared overrode those concerns. Together with Braund and others, they began to create personality profiles using systems like the Myers-Briggs indicator.

In the end, they created three pods: the "aggressive" pod, the "influencing/relaters," and the "steady Eddies" pod. His next great challenge, and perhaps his boldest choice as a captain, came when it was time to make captain's picks. Azinger knew he wanted to pick Steve Stricker, but that left three other picks. He even went so far as to take input from the media, and he came up with a list of about twenty candidates. It was

Dave Stockton who reminded him that he should be picking not just on skill, but for his pods. All of this led Azinger to make his boldest choice of all: he'd let each pod choose their own captain's pick from his list.

Nobody knew about this until much later—it was kept as a tight secret throughout the Ryder Cup—but Azinger empowered his team to such a degree that it was they, not he, who added the final three players.

In the "aggressive" pod, Phil Mickelson, Anthony Kim, and Justin Leonard chose Hunter Mahan. The "steady Eddies" pod, consisting of Stewart Cink, Ben Curtis, and Stricker, chose Chad Campbell. Finally, the "influencer/relaters" pod, with Kenny Perry, Boo Weekley, and Jim Furyk, added Kentucky's own J. B. Holmes. From that point on, it would be called the "redneck pod." He took a lot of heat for the picks—Johnny Miller said that he wouldn't have chosen *any* of them—but he didn't care.

His players loved it, because he had taken a sacrosanct principle of the Ryder Cup—players like predictability—and elevated it to the next level, investing them in their own strategy.

"The mind of the human being seeks certainty and calm, and we don't like surprise that much," Stewart Cink said. "So Azinger did a great job sort of taking that surprise and uncertainty down to an almost non-existent level, and it enabled us to just be comfortable with each other."

The players who appreciated this included one who would take careful notice of Azinger's tactics, storing them in case he ever found himself in a similar position.

"That was my first one," said Steve Stricker, "and I take a lot away from what he did. He really incorporated guys becoming owners of the team. I was a captain's pick that Ryder Cup, and the first thing out of his mouth after 'congratulations' was, 'Who else would you want to see on the team?' So here he's asking me, a captain's pick, and he goes through the whole pod system, and immediately puts his trust and faith in me."

Azinger had learned so much from the Europeans, and his next move was one that was long overdue in America: he would control the course. Once the makeup of his team became clear, he worked with Valhalla staff to cut the first swath of rough down to an inch, and the second cut—the "Azinger cut"—to three inches. He had a team of big hitters, so he made sure that the tees were in places where they would clear any danger and hit into wide landing zones. He even had a tree limb taken down at the last minute because J. B. Holmes thought it was in his line.

Nor was Azinger averse to a trick or two. In establishing his captain's agreement with Faldo, he gave Europe the run of the course on the Monday and Tuesday the week before the matches, and then he advised the superintendent not to mow the greens on those days, making them far slower than they would be when play began. Strangely, though, no Europeans even bothered to show up, and Faldo seemed to make no effort to get them together. That was the first moment when Azinger began to wonder whether something strange was afoot with that year's European team.

A trick that did work was moving the tees way up on the long even holes—sometimes as far as eighty yards from their practice locations—and back on the short odd holes, in order to confuse their alternate shot pairings. Azinger's tactic was so effective, and so infuriating, that it inspired a rule change, and today tee placements are known by both teams in advance.

His other big development came in how he communicated with his players. Azinger is a natural people person, and he knew that different personalities needed a different touch. Players like his "rednecks" could get down on themselves easily and needed to be encouraged, where someone like Anthony Kim was full of swagger and responded well to being challenged—on the first day of matches, Azinger actually confronted Kim, telling him, "You're not showing me squat!" Kim's response was to smile back and tell Azinger to relax. He came back to force a half point. But if Azinger had taken that approach with someone like J. B. Holmes, it could have been devastating.

When the team finally met, Azinger let them all in on the plan—the pods, the picks, the personality profiles, all of it. Now they had a secret, which bonded them and, Azinger thinks, even reduced the dread that veterans of the blowouts like Mickelson and Furyk might have been feeling. Then he asked them to embrace the crowd—to hand out lapel pins, and to attend a Thursday-night pep rally in Louisville that ended up with fifteen thousand people in attendance. Finally, he handed out a list of twelve questions that he thought they'd be asked by journalists—"What's it like not to have Tiger here?"—along with corresponding boilerplate answers, thereby reducing their stress levels in media appearances.

When the Europeans finally flew in, Azinger met them at the airport. Nick Faldo emerged from the airplane door holding the Ryder Cup, and Azinger found himself already on the verge of being pissed off. When photographers asked for them to pose with the Cup together, and Faldo jokingly held it far away so Azinger couldn't reach it, his temper got worse. When he left, he wanted nothing more than to beat Faldo, and though he never said anything about it to his team, they could tell—this meant everything.

*　*　*

As for Faldo, his captaincy can best be summed up by something that happened very early and has almost been lost to history. Paul McGinley, who had a piercing ambition to become Ryder Cup captain and ended up being one of Europe's best leaders when he got the job in 2014, was slated to have his first vice captaincy under Faldo. Very early in the process, in May 2007, he resigned. The most he'll say now is that Nick "was his own man," and wanted to do things radically different from the template they'd established. Knowing McGinley, he also had a keen sense of how his own future candidacy might be tarnished by the association. When I asked him point blank if he had sensed the impending failure a year in advance, he paused.

"It's easy to say that in hindsight," he said. But he didn't say no.

It's also worth mentioning that everything Azinger said about Faldo is true. Mark James, the 1999 captain, told Faldo that he wouldn't pick him with a captain's pick even if he was playing terrific golf, and when Faldo sent the team a good-luck letter, James threw it in the trash in front of everyone. When another captain, Bernard Gallacher, was asked to describe Faldo, he said, "Faldo brings you points." *Was that all?* came the follow-up. "Yes."

Still, Faldo had what looked on paper like the stronger team, especially compared to Azinger's collection of journeymen. There was a chance that abandoning the European template, going rogue, and not necessarily inspiring the love and devotion of his players might not matter in the end.

In fact, 2008 was perhaps the purest test of the old question: Did the captaincy matter?

* * *

On Friday morning, the US pods worked to near perfection, with two wins and two halved matches in the foursomes session. They were all tight matches, and after Azinger delivered his message to Kim, he encouraged a struggling Cink and Campbell in a very different way, by relaying a quote from the football coach Lou Holtz, who had spoken to the team and advised them to focus in each moment on What's Important Now (i.e., WIN). When they fought back against Poulter and Rose, and Campbell hit a brilliant shot to clinch the match on the eighteenth, Azinger told him that he had just given his newborn son a highlight to watch for the rest of his life. Walking up the fairway, Campbell had tears in his eyes.

In the final match of that session, J. B. Holmes was struggling to hit the ball straight, and Azinger actually called his coach to get some advice. He also remembered that Holmes had once said to him that he played better when he was mad. So when he relayed the coach's tip, he also stoked the flames, telling Holmes that Dan Hicks said on NBC that Lee Westwood was giving him dirty looks. This too had the desired effect, and the redneck pairing pulled off a half point.

In the second match that morning, Justin Leonard and Hunter Mahan beat Henrik Stenson and Paul Casey 3&2, and it remains Stenson's worst memory in a long and successful Ryder Cup career.

"I didn't feel like Paul and I had a great chance," he said. "We hadn't played practice rounds together, we played different golf balls, and all of a sudden we got thrown together in foursomes."

In afternoon four-ball, the electric Mickelson/Kim team won against the Irish tandem of Harrington and McDowell, and Leonard and Mahan earned their second win of the day by defeating Sergio García and Miguel Ángel Jiménez. The Europeans won their only session on Saturday morning to reduce the deficit to 7-5, and when the Americans split the afternoon, it was 9-7 heading into Sunday. A nice lead, but far from comfortable, particularly given the European strength.

That night, Azinger pulled off what might have been his greatest coup. His whole gambit had been to empower his players, and now, though he had a very specific singles lineup in mind, he wanted to make them think that they were choosing their own lineup. So he wrote down the list he wanted on a piece of paper, stowed it in his back pocket, then went into the team room holding up a blank piece of paper for everyone to see.

"Boys," he said, "we can go out veterans first and rookies second, rookies first and veterans second, we can go out willy-nilly, or we can go in the order of our pods."

By that point, the team loved the pods so much that by acclaim, they chose the pods.

"I think the aggressive pod should go first," he said, and the cheers were louder. Everyone called for Anthony Kim to go first, which was what Zinger had in mind.

"Who wants to follow him?" he said. "Hunter?"

Of course Mahan said yes.

"Why don't we anchor it with Phil?" he said, as though the idea had just occurred to him, and that too was met with support.

He looked at Kenny Perry. "What do you say we come at them with the rednecks next?"

The rednecks whooped.

"Kenny, can you follow Phil? Jim, can you anchor it?"

Which left the steady Eddies, who of course fell in the order he wanted. When it was over, the list he came up with in front of the team was exactly the same as the one in his back pocket.

To pull something like this off takes charisma and showcases another aspect that the best captains tend to have in their repertoire: a bit of positive manipulation, and the ability to dispense the right amount of information (and no more) to the right people at the right time.

On Sunday, Anthony Kim won his match in a rout against Sergio García, but the Europeans struck back in the next three matches. It was the rednecks who came through in the end. Kenny Perry won in front of his home state, beating Henrik Stenson 3&2, Boo Weekley took down Oliver Wilson—one of the lasting images of that day, and of that whole Ryder Cup, is Weekley riding his driver like a horse as he galloped down the fairway—and another Kentuckian, J. B. Holmes, beat Søren Hansen. Azinger had told Jim Furyk, the nonredneck of the redneck pod, that the Cup might come down to his match, and that's just what happened— with a 2&1 win over Jiménez, he clinched.

The last pod split their matches—often lost in the story of Valhalla is that even in the midst of a drubbing, the great Ian Poulter won 4 points—and the final score was 16.5-11.5.

It was the best kind of redemption for the Americans, beating a tough European team with what looked like one of their weakest teams yet. For Azinger, it was a brilliantly wrought captaincy just when his country needed him, and in the last act of his competitive life against Nick Faldo, he came out on top.

In the aftermath, Faldo handled himself poorly, even going so far as to call Sergio García "useless." It was an insult the Spaniard would never forget. Six years later in Gleneagles, when the European team was praising Paul McGinley in the victorious press conference and commenting on how he'd learned from past captains, García shouted, "Do you think he talked to Nick Faldo?" And four years after that, in Paris, when he became Europe's all-time points leader, Sergio couldn't help himself.

"I have passed some of my heroes today," he said. "And Nick Faldo."

*   *   *

Azinger had ambitions to captain again in Europe, but he waited too long to ask, and the PGA of America had already moved ahead. The 2010 captain, Corey Pavin, called Azinger exactly once, and didn't ask him a single question about his pod system. In rain-soaked Wales, the Americans lost what was a very winnable Ryder Cup. Two years later, at Medinah, Davis Love III had long conversations with Azinger, and adopted many of his ideas. It's a Ryder Cup the Americans should have won, but an unthinkable Sunday comeback by the Europeans resulted in another defeat.

In 2014, new captain Tom Watson had one short conversation with Azinger, to ask why he preferred four captain's picks to two. Again, he showed no interest in the pod system.

Stewart Cink later said that abandoning Azinger's approach was one of the strangest things he'd seen in his career, particularly after how badly things had gone before the pod system, but though it took some time for America to understand what Azinger had done, that recognition would come. After 2014, his name was referenced repeatedly, and his work at Valhalla played a seminal role in America's Ryder Cup future.

CHAPTER THIRTEEN

August 2021, Jersey City, New Jersey

Bryson's nightmare continues . . .
hurricanes in Jersey . . . Tony Finau's
brilliant Monday . . . one month to go

"Sometimes I think it's easier for me to just go work in the street."
—Jersey City police officer, on following Bryson
DeChambeau's group at The Northern Trust Open

Jersey City is a gray tangle of highways and high-rises, inhospitable by appearance, with all the anxious intensity of the bigger city across the Hudson River, but very little of the style and grandeur. When you park your car on Morris Pessin Drive and walk toward the media center by Liberty State Park, you see the startling green figure of the Statue of Liberty on your left, and beyond that the skyline of Manhattan. Exit the media center to the west, though, and it's just another parking lot, with scaffolding climbing up the side of a nondescript building. Up three flights of stairs, you enter a dingy, dark gray room, and then a darker hallway, and then another dingy room with an exit. Pass that threshold, and suddenly, on a plateau of grass that used to be a landfill, sits the world's most incongruous golf course: Liberty National.

This was the last Northern Trust, to be replaced on the PGA Tour play-off calendar in 2022 by Memphis, and it meant the end of top-tier professional golf in the New York metro area. In 2021, for the last time, it marked the first leg of the final stage of Ryder Cup qualification, at the FedExCup playoffs—a final testing ground for the Americans and Europeans vying for an automatic spot or hoping to impress their captain enough for a pick.

A week earlier, in Greensboro, North Carolina, there had been another kind of cutoff, this one for the playoffs themselves. In the intense heat and humidity of the North Carolina Piedmont, players unknown to the casual golf fan fought for every birdie as they struggled to finish inside the top 125 and retain their PGA Tour card, or inside the top 200 to give themselves a prayer at the Korn Ferry Tour finals. There were three thoughts on everyone's mind in North Carolina that week: the temperature, the playoffs, and the Ryder Cup.

On the last topic, the figures of most intense interest were Justin Rose and Tommy Fleetwood, both of whom needed exceptional weeks after below average seasons to sneak inside the top 125 and make the playoffs. Fleetwood didn't even come close, with a –1 finish, and he marched off into the parking lot when his last round finished, unwilling to talk about a disappointing end to a disappointing year. Unlike Rose, though, he was safely inside the cutoff in the European Ryder Cup standings, giving him a chance to reprise his 4-1 performance in Paris.

Rose's struggles had been greater, he needed the playoffs more, and he responded by nearly winning. After a birdie on the thirteenth hole on Sunday, he stood at 15-under, a score that would have been good enough to secure a playoff berth. Instead, he played his five holes in 2-over, finished tied for tenth, and was the odd man out in the FedExCup standings at 126th.

"Couldn't be a worse result, really," he told the media, gamely summing up the near miss. Rose would head back to Europe and finish T-6 at the final qualifying event, the BMW PGA Championship, but it wasn't good enough in Harrington's eyes, and he was doomed to miss his first Ryder Cup in eleven years.

The final big story was about the two Kevins—Kevin Kisner, who won in a six-man playoff (after Adam Scott missed an unthinkably short putt to win on the first playoff hole), and Kevin Na, who made that same playoff, and who was on the verge of catching fire and finishing third in the playoffs. Both would make Steve Stricker's life more complicated in the days to come.

* * *

Tony Finau still has a distinct memory of watching the 1999 Ryder Cup, the comeback at Brookline, in his apartment in Salt Lake City. He was ten years old then, and though he didn't watch much golf as a kid, the Masters and the Ryder Cup were two that caught his attention. A talented basketball player, he was drawn immediately to the team environment that was evident at Brookline as the US team stunned the Europeans. Playing in the Ryder Cup became a dream that day, and as a member of the Junior Ryder Cup in 2004, he was able to watch the thrashing at Oakland Hills in person. Like many of his American peers, the sight of Europe routinely celebrating victory after victory was both aggravating and motivational— among his other professional goals, he wanted to be part of the change.

The story of how he became a golfer is far outside the typical narrative of a well-off American learning the game culturally and having his dream financed by his parents. Kelepi Finau, Tony's father (he goes by Gary), was born and raised in Tonga, and golf to him was little more than a symbol of the social class he couldn't attain. "I hated the game," he said in 2015. "We were from the other side of the street."

Gary worked as a baggage handler at Delta Airlines, and he and his wife, Ravena, raised their nine children in a tough neighborhood called Rose Park in northwest Salt Lake City. Despite the broader national perception of Utah as a bland safe haven, the Finau boys grew up around gang violence, and were approached to join as kids. That's part of what inspired their mother, Ravena, to push them into a hobby. Her first idea was tennis, but in part because of Tiger Woods's win at the 1997

Masters, they opted for golf. The boys got their start beating balls into a mattress in the garage, and after that, Gary would spend hours with them at a nearby par-3 course called Jordan River. They stuck at first to the chipping and putting greens because they were free before the club pro noticed them and offered them free use of the course. Gary would "teach" them as best as he knew how—with help from a Jack Nicklaus book and instructional videos he checked out of the library—and Tony later said he had no idea that his father knew nothing about golf.

Finau was a talented athlete who could dunk a basketball from a flat-footed start, and he excelled at golf, along with his brother Gipper. They began to travel to play, and as a way of raising money, the family would hold fundraiser luaus in which the boys would perform a Polynesian tradition called "fire-knife dancing" (an art that Tony's uncle performed at a world-class level). At age twelve, Finau won the Junior World Golf Championships, and began to dream big. His mother refused to let him enter a different high school for golf purposes—she didn't like the idea of putting sports above family—so Tony started a golf team at Salt Lake's West High, recruiting a few friends, and together with his brother, they managed to win the 4A state championships his junior year.

His game continued to blossom, and he turned down basketball scholarship offers to turn pro at age seventeen, leaving high school before graduation. He finished second on the show *The Big Break* in 2009, but was destined to spend seven years on the minitours, living with his father and wife in a one-bedroom apartment.

In 2011, his mother, Ravena, died in a car accident. Devastated, Tony developed a bleeding ulcer and wanted to quit the game, and it was only his father's encouragement that kept him in golf. He stuck around, and graduated to PGA Tour Canada in 2013, the Web.com Tour in 2014, and, at long last, the PGA Tour a year later.

Finau won his first title in 2016 at the Puerto Rico Open, an alternate event, and this would later come to be seen as an anomaly as his career progressed in two paradoxical directions. On the one hand, his game continued to shine, and he rose inside the top one hundred, and then the top fifty, in the world rankings. On the other hand, the more he put himself in contention, the more he gained a reputation as someone who couldn't finish. By early 2021, he had notched thirty-six top-tens without a victory since his win in Puerto Rico, and the next best player in that category had just sixteen. Some of the near misses were ugly, and some were impressive, but taken all together, it seemed to speak to a competitive weakness when it came to crossing the line.

At the same time, it also spoke to a surprising mental strength. Finau told a story from childhood about a temper tantrum that led to a five-putt on the eighteenth green in front of his father, and how his father's silence in the aftermath chastened him. That lesson, plus his strong Mormon faith—when he twisted his ankle at the Masters, his family held a prayer service for him—gave him a kind of resilience in the face of his Sunday failures, and he managed to bounce back with incredible regularity even as the "Tony Finau can't win" narrative spread like wildfire.

Despite the apparent similarities between clutch play and the ability to bounce back, they are in fact not the same. The concept of clutch is more immediate and requires responding to intense pressure within the space of a few critical moments. Arguably, it says little about what kind of person you are in the broad scope of life and more about the accident of how you handle the chemical phenomenon of nerves. Resilience, in contrast, is more of a choice—an outlook that you adhere to regardless of temporary successes and failures.

That's what Tony Finau showed in the years without a victory, and it was that special courage that he brought to Jersey City and The Northern Trust.

* * *

On Friday in Jersey, Ian Poulter spoke outside the interview stage, bouncing a ball hard on the concrete, as he faced the likelihood of not making the top seventy and the next playoff event.

"Nobody died today!" he almost shouted, his eyes widening. Despite the intensity, he was in a good mood. "Nobody died today! I'll either go on next week, or I'll go home Sunday. It's irrelevant. It's irrelevant! Shit happens. The Ryder Cup is in a month. That matters! This doesn't matter."

When I found Lee Westwood outside the locker room, I asked him how often he was in communication with Harrington.

"I haven't seen him since the Open," he said, adding that there were no texts or phone calls. "He knows what I'm capable of in Ryder Cups . . . that's when the vice captain calls the player, and the captain talks to the vice captain."

"Do you talk to the vice captains?" I asked.

"No."

On Saturday, it became clear that Hurricane Henri was set to ravage the New York metro area, and Sunday would likely be a complete washout, so I used the calm before the storm to follow Bryson DeChambeau, who was paired with Zach Johnson, one of Stricker's vice captains. Johnson told me after his round that communication was constant at that point, between the captains, the PGA of America, and anyone involved in decision-making. Johnson, too, was attempting to communicate with DeChambeau on the course, to give him some comfort in the face of the heckling that the Jersey crowd laid on him as he navigated his third round.

The course was surprisingly attractive for a former landfill, full of honey locusts and cedars and blue spruce, but you can smell the remnants of the landfill when the wind is up, and the Jersey crowd didn't add much to the ambience. "Nice hit, you clown!" yelled one fan, who tossed in a "Doucheambeau!" for good measure and was promptly pursued by undercover police in the gallery. He was given a warning, but another fan was tossed for allegedly yelling "Brooksy!" at him. Others, because they were in packs or in the bleachers above the cops' reach, got away with it. Despite the spots of intensity, the scene wasn't as bad as Memphis, but DeChambeau looked equally miserable, and he shot his worst round of the tournament, a 72.

Back inside the concrete hovel used for interviews, word came down that Matthew Wolff had tossed a club into the woods, meaning that DeChambeau wasn't the only one who had a bad day. I watched Jordan Spieth sign autographs for a group of children who seemed too enthusiastic to me, as though they had been taught how to appeal for signatures, perhaps at the behest of some scheming adult in the background who would sell the memorabilia online later. As these thoughts entered my mind, I realized some kind of deep New Jersey cynicism had crept into my brain, and I had better get out before the hurricane blocked me in. As the first rains fell that night, I skipped town.

*   *   *

Play was canceled on Sunday, but the tournament finished on Monday, and Tony Finau, the man who supposedly couldn't win, played his back nine in 5-under, including an eagle on the thirteenth hole, to overtake Jon Rahm. Finau had formed a special relationship with the golfer Billy Casper as a child. They met in Utah when Finau was fourteen, and at the 2019 Masters, when he made the final group on Sunday, he even carried a special ball signed by Casper. They grew close enough that Casper gave him an inscribed copy of his memoir, and Finau attended Casper's funeral when he passed. As he played his final stretch in New Jersey, Finau remembered a quote from Casper's book: "The loudest noise in golf is the swift change of momentum."

Finau had it, and Rahm lost it. By day's end, only the Australian Cam Smith could match Finau at 20-under, but on the first playoff hole, Smith launched his tee shot out-of-bounds, and when Finau's approach found the green, he was able to enjoy the walk up to eighteen, secure in his impending victory.

"I've been thinking about that walk up to eighteen a long time," he said.

That day, he received thousands of text messages, and one of the first was from Tiger Woods, who told Finau he was proud of his fight and grit. Two days later, in Maryland for the BMW Championship, Finau admitted that the losses over the years had filled him with disappointment and frustration, and that it had taken every bit of his upbringing and his resilience to "take them on the chin."

Along with the money and the redemption, Finau had also managed to launch himself up the Ryder Cup standings. He would end up finishing seventh, just outside the automatic qualifying, but considering how well he had done in Paris—he was the only one of Furyk's picks who proved himself worthy of the choice, and the only American besides Justin Thomas to post a winning record—and considering how well his long game was suited to Whistling Straits, there was no longer any doubt that he would make Steve Stricker's team.

CHAPTER FOURTEEN

Interlude: Why Does Europe Win?

Diagnosing a forty-year disease

In the quest to explain Europe's dominance in the modern era, several theories have been advanced, and they came to the forefront yet again in the days leading up to the Ryder Cup. The Bryson-Brooks feud, in particular, seemed like the latest blueprint for American failure, a telegraphed signal of exactly how everything would go wrong in Wisconsin, and a symbol of the dysfunction that reigned over the years. Once again, the reasons for Europe's great forty-year Ryder Cup coup were on the tip of everyone's lips. Some theories are little more than stabs in the dark, and some are at least partially accurate, but none can explain the phenomenon completely. (As Henrik Stenson told me, it's a game of small margins, and if 2 percent of everything is true, it adds up to a significant advantage.)

In order to separate belief from fact, it's worth examining them all in detail.

Theory 1: The Americans Just Need to Play Better!

This is the theory that comes easiest to those who don't have the will or the desire to analyze Europe's 12-6 record between 1983 and 2018 on anything but a superficial level. It's not exclusive to Americans, but if you hear somebody say this, you are very likely speaking to an American. The idea goes that the Ryder Cup is a small sample size, consisting of just three days of play, and that random variation explains all of Europe's success. Typically, proponents of this theory don't believe it applies to the pre-European era. Americans won almost every match from 1927 to 1981, in other words, because they were simply better players, but when Europe started winning with lopsided regularity—every time at home, half the time in America—it was a function of luck.

The more America lost, the more this theory fell out of favor, likely because its proponents became too embarrassed to argue its merits publicly, especially in the last fifteen years. Still, it persists to this day. When fans espouse it, they have an interesting tendency to become angry when other ideas are promoted, such as a strategy advantage for the Europeans. Their attitude becomes defensive and dismissive, and they retreat quickly to the comfort of the "nobody's to blame but the players" perspective.

It's still a common theory among American players and captains. When the US team was beaten in 2014 at Gleneagles, Phil Mickelson took it on himself to spur a one-man revolution in the postmatch presser, but Tom Watson was steadfast.

"Well, the obvious answer is that our team has to play better," he said. "That's the obvious answer, and they do. I think they recognize that fact; that somehow, collectively, twelve players have to play better."

That word, *somehow*, does a lot of work there, as though it was just bad luck or perhaps a failure of will that cost his team the loss, and nothing deeper like his own tactics as a captain.

Before the 2021 Ryder Cup, at the one-year-to-go presser in October 2019, Steve Stricker seemed to lean in this direction.

"It's about playing better," he told the gathered reporters. "Bottom line is, they played great, and they outplayed us, and you know, we're going to have to come and be ready and make the putts that we need to and hit the key shots down the stretch that we need to hit to come out on top."

Patrick Cantlay may have given the most thoughtful discourse from this perspective on Wednesday at Whistling Straits, using a playing cards analogy.

"The matches are only played every two years," he said, "and golf is very chancy. So would it surprise you if the US went on a similar run to what Europe has been on for the next twenty years? Wouldn't surprise me. You go to Vegas, and you play roulette, and the chances are fifty-fifty but skewed toward the house a little, it could hit red six times in a row, but that's not abnormal."

Cantlay's eloquence is a credit to the argument, but in fact, though he's a very smart guy, Cantlay is dead wrong here. Yes, obviously "playing better" is the key ingredient, in the sense that Ryder Cups are decided by the number of points scored and a team wins those points by playing better golf than the opponent. But it's wildly reductive—it's not the kind of sound bite you'd accept from a basketball coach, for instance, but captains in golf get a pass because they come from the world of individual sports, and it's easier to ignore the fact that the Ryder Cup is very much a team event disguised as a collection of individual matches.

Europe's dominance is more than just a random hot streak, as anyone who examines the tactics and templates of the two teams can attest. The sample size of one Ryder Cup is indeed relatively small, but the sample size of eighteen of them, consisting of 504 matches across thirty-five years, is not.

In that time, facing more talented competition almost every year, Europe rolled up a massive edge. That goes far beyond statistical noise.

The "play better" argument, in fact, serves two purposes. First, it removes the need for accountability. If bad luck is to blame for the multiple losses, then nothing needs to change at the leadership level—you simply wait for the luck to swing around to your side. That's why so many American captains have taken comfort in the concept: it beats looking in the mirror and facing some difficult truths. From a media perspective, it's an alluring idea because it's the simplest idea, requiring the least amount of explanation. And from a fan perspective, it's a way of saving pride—if you're the victim of randomness, that means Europe isn't smarter or better, but has simply been the beneficiaries of a few abnormal coin flips.

At the risk of sounding insulting, this mindset is maintained today only by those who don't *want* to think about the true roots of the problem, whether out of self-preservation, laziness, or a lack of intellectual curiosity. It's an outmoded way of thinking, and as Paul McGinley confirmed for me when we spoke, European leadership absolutely loves it when they hear this line of thinking parroted by Americans. Luckily for the US team, despite some of his initial comments, Steve Stricker was absolutely *not* mired in that mentality in 2021.

In every bad theory, though, there is at least one kernel of truth, and the kernel here is that luck can absolutely play a part in an individual Ryder Cup. The US team would never have won in Brookline, nor the Europeans in Medinah, without incredible luck throughout their Sunday comebacks. In every close Ryder Cup, regardless of who wins, you can identify small moments in which the victorious team had fortune smile on them. This is true of any sport, but as we see with those two huge comebacks, luck has a way of canceling itself out over time, and with enough results, it ceases to be a determining factor.

Theory 2: Europeans Simply Play Better Under Pressure

Although this has been true in isolated Ryder Cups, it holds no water if you expand to the entire world of professional golf. Many of Europe's best Ryder Cup players, from Colin Montgomerie to Lee Westwood to Ian Poulter to Luke Donald, have never won a major championship. Others, like Sergio García and Justin Rose, have won just a single major, a disappointing total considering their abilities and accomplishments. When these players came close at the biggest individual events, they were routinely outclassed by Americans, and through the decades, players from the United States have won the most majors and put together the best individual careers. By any objective measure, the United States has the best pressure players.

It may be true that Europeans have excelled under pressure more often in the modern Ryder Cup than their American counterparts, but in order to explain this, you have to go beyond the idea that they're inherently better under pressure—that idea is easily refuted.

To go back to the kernel of truth, the salient idea here is that Europe has tended to react better to the pressures that come *off* the course in the Ryder Cup. Pádraig Harrington still laughs about 2010, at Celtic Manor, when rain pelted both teams and a controversy ensued over the alleged failure of the American rain gear.

"Nothing in this world would have kept that rain out," he said, which didn't stop several European players claiming they were totally dry, and which culminated in the US team spending thousands of dollars on different clothes. "It was like standing in a full, powerful shower. I don't know what the US expectations were. We had the greatest fun over that, but we all just kept our mouths shut. But anytime there's a bit of trouble or controversy, it tends to benefit Europe."

Theory 3: Europeans Just Like Each Other More

On the surface, there's a lot to like about this theory. American dysfunction has reared its head time and time again in the modern Ryder Cup era, from Trevino freezing out his players in 1985, to Nicklaus lecturing them after a loss in 1987, to Sutton's nightmares with Tiger and Phil in 2004, to the Mickelson rebellion in 2014, to the failed Reed rebellion and the DJ-Koepka fight in 2018. And those are just the ones we know about.

Then there are the match records since 1983—Europe enjoyed a 158.5-129.5 edge in pairs matches, whereas the singles were almost dead even, with America leading by a single point, 108.5-107.5. You look at that disparity, and it becomes obvious that Europe enjoys a huge advantage in teams of two. It's easy to jump from there to the concept that American egos are too big, the players are too selfish, and nobody likes each other, and thus Europe, with its tighter bonds, succeeds in a team environment where the US fails.

"If you take the PGA Tour, you've got maybe thirty different accommodation options for the week, and everyone's got their own car. Some travel with a team, some travel with a family, some travel alone," Henrik

Stenson told me. "On the European side, at least when you start out, there's one official hotel, everyone goes on the bus between there and the golf course, and it just feels like you maybe get to know the guys a bit more in the early days."

For further supporting evidence, you can look at some of the famous European pairs, from Ballesteros and Olazábal to Clarke and Westwood to, more recently, Tommy Fleetwood and Francesco Molinari, aka "Moliwood." In every case, there seemed to be a special bond there that isn't seen on American teams.

But while it's true that Europe has succeeded brilliantly in pairs play, and while the US team has had its chemistry problems, the plain fact is that Europeans *don't* all like each other. Sergio García and Pádraig Harrington have been famously at odds for years, and Paul Casey remembers how Colin Montgomerie and Darren Clarke would walk down the fairway arm in arm at the Ryder Cup, despite the known animosity between them. There was one older European player who, when asked to explain Europe's chemistry, offered this: "We get together for a week, we get along, and when it's over, we all go back to hating Monty."

For every American player who is unpopular with his peers, there is a European equivalent like Montgomerie or Nick Faldo. The idea that European golfers are best friends is a total myth.

It's also beneficial to contrast two separate incidents that came on Saturday night at a Ryder Cup, with one team holding a significant lead. At Medinah, with the US leading 10-6, Davis Love III and his vice captains decided to have a team-bonding session. It was described as a kumbaya moment, where the players went around a circle and described what they liked about each other. There's nothing inherently wrong with this, and it certainly doesn't explain what happened the next day, but there are some who still believe that the lack of intensity that night, the failure to prepare to finish the job with vicious clarity, contributed to a mindset that allowed the nightmare of Sunday's European comeback to play out.

In 2004, on the other hand, with the Europeans holding an 11-5 lead after Saturday's play, captain Bernhard Langer came into the team room and saw his players at their ease, drinking wine, laughing, and generally acting like the Cup was already over based on the huge lead they'd established. He sat down at a long table, the team joined him, and he stared at them for ten long seconds, not even a hint of a smile on his face. The silence became intolerable, and when the tension reached its peak, Langer brought his fist down on the table.

"Tomorrow," he said, "I want the fucking record."

The next day, he almost got it, tying the modern record with an 18.5-9.5 win, and on American soil.

What these two stories illustrate is that sometimes the Americans can be nicer and more supportive of each other than the Europeans, and in the past, it has arguably hurt them. Nobody would ever deny that the European Ryder Cup tradition invokes a special bond between players, but at heart, their relationships are no more precious than America's.

The kernel of truth: they may be better at hiding it.

"The grievances on the other side have been pretty public," Rory McIlroy said, when asked about the personality clash between Harrington and García. "Our thing, I think it was kept pretty private, and nobody else was involved."

And as Pádraig Harrington told me, there's more natural separation between European players who hail from different countries.

"Remember the difference between players is that all twelve American players are competing for the heart of one country," he said. "Whereas in Europe, we can have the number one English player, the number one French player, the number one Swedish player, and they could be happy being number one in their country and not necessarily have the same rivalry. In the States, they're all fighting for the same fan, and it causes more friction."

Theory 4: Europe Just Wants It More

If you want to make an American professional golfer mad, tell him he doesn't really care about the Ryder Cup. In John Feinstein's *The Last Major*, Davis Love III bristled when presented with this idea.

"If anything," he said, "our problem has been that we've wanted to win *too* much. At times, we've tried too hard."

This has even been true in American Ryder Cups, such as in 2004, when they were blown out at home and seemed, as a team, incredibly nervous while the relaxed Europeans laughed their way around the course to a record-setting victory.

There have been plenty of times when American teams have looked listless or discouraged through the years, but that's a function of losing, not desire. You can see the same dismal spirit in the Europeans in 2008 at Valhalla; it just so happens that Europe hasn't lost quite as often. Nor have the Americans lacked for emotional moments. Even peripheral figures like Brad Faxon in 1995 and Hunter Mahan in 2010 have wept after losing crucial singles matches, and the collective passion after Justin Leonard's putt at Brookline was so intense that the Americans briefly lost all sense of decorum. Plus, sadness and joy share the stage with bitterness—one of the rallying cries for the 2021 team was the unpleasantness of losing in Paris and having to watch the Europeans celebrate on the eighteenth green.

"I've met a few US players at the after-party over the years," Harrington said, citing Jim Furyk and Phil Mickelson specifically, "and I've seen it burn deep in their souls that they lost. I've seen them devastated. Absolutely devastated."

The kernel here is that for a certain generation of American Ryder Cup players, the tournament was not on their radar as young men. Davis Love III, who became the single figure most responsible for changing the culture in America, told me that making a US Ryder Cup team was never one of his goals. That's because he was born in 1964, and by the time the Ryder Cup became competitive in 1983, he was already twenty-one years old, and had not grown up watching an intense rivalry. It didn't matter much, though, because by the time he played his first in 1993, the fight was on, and he and his generational cohort cared deeply about winning. Today's American Ryder Cuppers grew up watching Europe defeat their heroes time and again, and the disinterest that Love may have felt in his younger days is no longer a feature of modern American players.

You can say the US has been agonizingly slow to respond to Europe's innovations, to the degree that it became embarrassing, but to fault them for a lack of desire is to misunderstand the low periods.

Theory 5: Europe's Political Culture Is Inherently More Group-Oriented Compared to the Individualistic United States

This is an incredibly seductive piece of sociopolitical analysis—Europeans grow up in countries whose governments and cultures are socialistic by comparison to the United States, whose purer form of capitalism emphasizes individual achievement. Concepts like community and team are a more critical part of European life, so they internalize it as children and are naturally better by the time they grow to become professionals. As supporting evidence, you have the fact that Europe succeeds in pairs sessions to a greater degree than singles (although, again, they still punch well above their weight in singles), and the United States has had the most success in modern Ryder Cups when they are separated into pods and aren't forced into the group activities that seem to come so naturally to the Europeans. Life on the PGA Tour, too, is more sequestered, largely due to the amount of money available. Players can bring their families or their team and live in relative isolation, while on the European Tour it's always been more common for players to hang out after rounds and between tournaments.

This theory is not provable—it's a purely intellectual idea you can't test in any practical way—and one way to refute it is to say that in other sports, America does just fine in a team environment. A counter to that would be that golf in America attracts a specific kind of individual—almost certainly politically conservative, and probably a loner—which makes that person more likely to be an extreme individualist who isn't naturally inclined to buy into a team game.

Is it true? Possibly. It strikes me as overly simplistic—European golfers tend to be more conservative and individualistic too—but there may be seeds of truth in there.

For one thing, when you observe European fan culture, it's noticeable how instantly and immediately they fall into a group mentality. Where American fans find it awkward even to get simple chants going, a group of strangers from the United Kingdom will actually sing together without a hint of self-consciousness—an act most Americans would find unbearable.

In team dynamics too, you can see a similar difference. Chris Solomon of *No Laying Up* had a front-row seat for the 2021 Solheim Cup—the women's version of the Ryder Cup—when Europe defeated the US team in Ohio.

"There's not an element of caring more or wanting it more," he said, "but the Americans want it *individually*. They're not willing to buy into this team thing, or to sacrifice themselves to be bigger than whatever they can contribute on the golf course . . . The American players are putting so much pressure on themselves, and not getting true support from a team aspect, and it's causing their golf to decline during the event . . . where the Europeans are so bought into this team thing that their play is actually elevated by having this ecosystem around them."

He described the European team room during the celebration, when a few of the introverted players were inclined to remain on the sideline, not dance, and not sing, and one by one the other players pulled them in, as though they were operating from a deeper instinct, refusing to let anyone exist outside of the critical team unit.

He contrasted that with the 2016 Ryder Cup, when the American collection of talent overwhelmed the Europeans, but the celebration when Ryan Moore hit the winning putt was strangely muted.

"What's the matter?" Rory McIlroy asked them. "Did you forget how to celebrate?"

Theory 6: Europe Is Intrinsically Motivated to Beat the Americans

Now, finally, we arrive at something indisputably true. This is a central reality of the Ryder Cup: America's superiority in the game, dating back to the post–World War I decade, when US golfers overtook their British counterparts. British and European golfers have felt like the underdogs ever since, and they've always been right, because America has never relinquished its top spot since those formative years, and likely never will.

This helps explain the great trick of the European Ryder Cup team: despite winning over and over, they still manage to be thought of as the inferior team, and they use that as motivation. How do you win and still keep that chip on your shoulder? Call it the magic of the perpetual underdog—a neat psychological trick in which you get the best of both worlds. You keep winning, and you keep a steady stream of inspiration as the team that *shouldn't* win.

"Because it's every two years, you lose what's happened in the last Ryder Cup," Stewart Cink said. "There's different players and there's turnover, and when you compare the teams, the media is always focused on world ranking and who's better on paper. Which is meaningless. Now, if they played a Ryder Cup every week, and this team was 9-3 in their last 12, you'd say, 'This team's the favorite.' But every two years, I think you kind of throw that out the window."

Both teams want to win the Ryder Cup, but there is a specific, unmistakable desire among Europeans to beat America that doesn't exist the other way around. For the Americans, it's never quite as personal—they're the reigning kings of the sport, they know it's not going to change, and it would never occur to them to have a specific grudge against the UK or Europe. They're simply too good.

This is a unifying reality for Europeans, who relish the chance every two years to prove themselves against the world's premiere golfing force. Whenever a player or a team took a point against Tiger Woods at a Ryder Cup, they considered this an enormous coup, but it wasn't just because he was the great Tiger Woods—it was because he was the very best America had to offer, and to beat him was to drive a stake into the heart of the American juggernaut and prove themselves as worthy adversaries in the process. That's the crux of the motivation here—the constant need to prove that you belong. America will never have it, because they're assured of their status, but Europe will always be able to put aside their small differences in service of that unifying goal.

"Who doesn't love beating the Americans, right?" Ian Poulter asked rhetorically. "In the era that I grew up watching golf, and the Belfry when I went to watch the Ryder Cup back in the day, the US were always super strong. Strength and depth have always been there in the American team. We've always been the underdogs. It's not like we're playing it down; it's on paper. You can see it for yourself."

When I asked Bernhard Langer to explain Europe's success, he sounded like he still had a grudge.

"We just love to show the rest of the world that Europe has good golfers," he said. "We've lost so many times in Ryder Cups, and the Americans were always the best players. Supposedly."

Pádraig Harrington went even further, resorting to a *Beverly Hill-billies* reference.

"We go to try to win the Ryder Cup, whereas the US tries not to lose it," he said. "Because they're favorites, because they *should* win, they're afraid, whereas we're the country cousins! We have a point to prove. Even if we did find oil in our backyard, we'd still have a point to prove."

The fact that they adopt this attitude means they're on the look-out for every slight. On the flip side, and just as importantly, America's strength routinely fools its supporters into thinking that they should win every Ryder Cup, sometimes with ease. That leads to casual arrogance. One example that the Europeans embraced before 2018 came in a Golf.com article by Alan Shipnuck making the prediction that America was too strong and would soon start winning Ryder Cups routinely. To an observer like me, it seemed tongue-in-cheek at best, and certainly not something to inspire any wrath. Shipnuck wasn't even a player! To the Europeans, though, in their perpetual fighting posture against the US, these were fighting words.

"Americans can't help themselves! You don't respect Europeans, and you overestimate how good you are, and you underestimate how good they are, and you do it every single time," Paul McGinley said. "If we'd scripted it, we could not have done a better job than Shipnuck did for us. I want to buy this guy a drink every time I see him; he could not have helped us any more than he did. The arrogance with which he wrote represented a lot of what the American media was, and the players are buying that because they're listening to it, and they're thinking, 'Yeah, we *are* great, thanks very much.'"

As far as America goes, I think he was slightly overstating the point—if anything, the American players sometimes greet the Ryder Cup with dread, traumatized by past results. At least in recent years, it has never struck me that the players themselves were arrogant, much less the captains. But his point about Europe is resonant—even a throwaway piece on the internet can motivate them, because they're always looking for signs that the United States is underestimating or disrespecting them.

The same thing played out in early 2020 when Paul Azinger made comments on TV about how Tommy Fleetwood wasn't a complete golfer until he could win on the PGA Tour. That created a tempest, with Europeans rushing to his defense, and it would have been a major storyline at the 2020 Ryder Cup if a global pandemic hadn't swept it away.

Theory 7: Europe Has Had Better Leadership

This has been the decisive factor, and the main thing Americans had to overcome in 2021. Whatever the motivations—saving the Ryder Cup, a special chip on their shoulder for the Americans, cultural solidarity—the situation that emerged in the early 1980s with Tony Jacklin is that Europe discovered a way to win Ryder Cups, established a template, and with few exceptions, stuck to this plan down the decades.

For a long time, Europe would battle-test its captains in the "Seve Trophy," a competition between the UK and continental Europe, and though that tournament went defunct in 2013, there is now a huge movement to resurrect it in order to reestablish a trial run for future Ryder Cup captains. The US has a ready-made analogue in the Presidents Cup, but because of the schism between the PGA of America and the PGA Tour, there was never a captain who led the Presidents Cup and went on to captain a Ryder Cup until Steve Stricker. Meanwhile, the Seve Trophy boasted captains like Colin Montgomerie, José María Olazábal, Paul McGinley, and Thomas Bjørn, all of whom went on to captain a winning team in the Ryder Cup.

That's just a small example of an area in which the Europeans had a leg up on the Americans. There are plenty of others: Europe embraced captain's picks before the US, Europe embraced vice captains before the US, Europe began controlling the course before the US, Europe thought deeply about pairings before the US, Europe jockeyed for lineup order advantages before the US, Europe embraced statistics before the US. There are even examples of structural edges that are out of America's control— because the European Tour controls the Ryder Cup on the European side, the Ryder Cup course is almost always played on the European Tour that summer, which means the European players get to compete on it before the Cup. Because the PGA Tour and PGA of America are different organizations, Ryder Cup courses in America are not on the regular PGA Tour calendar, and aren't overly familiar to the American players.

That's just the tip of the iceberg. The fact of the matter is that at every juncture, Europe has held some strategic advantage since 1983, and the US was painfully slow to catch up.

Put even more simply: Europe realized the Ryder Cup was a *team sport*, albeit one disguised as an individual sport, when Tony Jacklin took over in 1983. The Americans neglected the team element because they believed for far too long in the principle that winning Ryder Cups was simply about going out and playing better than the opposition when the time came. That belief was so extremely held that for decades, they treated the captaincy as a ceremonial position while Europe was using it as a strategic bludgeon, and their template was carried down throughout the years.

As an example of how organization and preparedness matters, take these two quotes:

"I thought _____ was an incredible captain from an analytical point of view. Had everything covered. He kind of knew the profile of each of his players, and he had a plan, and that plan was so in-depth. Every player knew what their role was even prior to the tournament starting. I think for me, that was the most clinical team that I've been on. Almost like the result was never in doubt."

And:

"There was just an unbelievable level of organization before, and there was no uncertainty about who you were going to play with and who you were going to spend your practice rounds with. There was a system that kind of paired up players together. There was just a lot of really in-depth personality matching and studies, and I think that led to us being very comfortable on the golf course, and we played like we were comfortable on the golf course, and we won."

The first quote is from Justin Rose, about Paul McGinley in 2014, and the second quote is from Stewart Cink, about Paul Azinger in 2008. In both cases, the hyperorganized captain won. The difference is that Justin Rose has won three Ryder Cups because Europe's captains always tend to be extremely prepared, and they learn from each other. Stewart Cink went 1-4 in Ryder Cups, because Azinger's captaincy was an aberration from the American norm of tactics that changed from year to year. Without knowing it, the Americans were desperate for a system.

Paul Azinger was the first American to recognize how to fix the problem, and he executed his vision perfectly. When he was done, he wanted to take his show on the road and captain the Americans again in Europe. He was rejected, and his ideas were forgotten. America lost two straight Ryder Cups, and it would take an absolute humiliation in 2014 to shake them awake.

CHAPTER FIFTEEN

2014, Auchterarder, Scotland

*The European guru at Gleneagles ...
the ultimate humiliation ...
Mickelson's revolt*

"*Here's the irony of it—the more I let these guys be individuals and do what they do on a week-to-week basis, the more unified they are. Just by leaving it up to them. I used to go down in the evening, everyone was in the team room, laughing and joking because they were there on their terms, they weren't forced to do it. That's how they became unified—they bonded naturally on their terms, not because the captain made them have dinner together.*"

—Paul McGinley

"*There's no doubt that Paul turned this into a full-time job. He gave probably three and a half years of his life to the Ryder Cup. And that puts a certain amount of stress and pressure on everybody following after him. You don't want to leave any stone unturned, and you don't want to be seen to leave any stone unturned.*"

—Pádraig Harrington

There's something about the 2014 Ryder Cup at Gleneagles that still captures the imagination, and it has very little to do with anything that happened on the course. The result was exactly what you'd expect—a strong European team playing at home, where they hadn't lost in twenty years, routed the Americans. No surprise there. There wasn't even a hero on the course, because Europe didn't need a hero.

What remains intriguing about Gleneagles is *how* the obvious result came to pass, in circumstances that were dramatic and controversial and frequently embarrassing. Yes, the US team was quintessentially itself, and yes, so was Europe, but they so thoroughly embodied the stereotypes of the past four decades—brutal efficiency through hyperorganization on the European side, and rank dysfunction on the American side—that the contrast demanded to be recognized. When the mess was over, it was no longer possible to say with any credibility that the Ryder Cup was simply a test of which individuals played better. The effect of management was so obvious that even the most dyed-in-the-wool stubborn American couldn't pretend everything was fine.

What was so intriguing about Gleneagles, and what remains so intriguing today, is that it's the Ryder Cup that broke the Americans.

And it's also the one that set them free.

*   *   *

There's an interesting irony around Gleneagles, and it stems from the fact that when you look closely, there were seeds of the American awakening in 2012 at Medinah. In that Ryder Cup, Davis Love III led his team to a 10-6 lead at home, and a combination of a few small mistakes, abysmal luck, and some major European heroics—Ian Poulter singlehandedly staving off disaster with five straight birdies to win his match Saturday night, for one—led to a Sunday meltdown that we now call a "miracle." In the aftermath, all of the positive leadership Love brought to the table when he outclassed his counterpart José María Olazábal over the first two days was forgotten, and the golf world understandably fixated on the comeback.

It's clear today that this wasn't wise, because any captain has a significant amount of control on Friday and Saturday and much less on Sunday, and ignoring that truth means reacting to the chaos of singles rather than building on the planned success of pairs. Medinah could have been a foundation for success, rather than a source of shame, but at the time, the American collapse seemed to feed into a few narratives. Most prominently, the thinking went, they just weren't tough enough; everyone was too nice and too soft, and they lacked the killer instinct and passion of the Europeans.

The order of the day at the PGA of America was change, and into this dynamic stepped Ted Bishop, the PGA of America president whose tenure was destined to become infamous. (Presidents serve for a single two-year term, and to put it mildly, *infamous* is not an adjective you want attached to your name in that role.)

With the challenge of facing a very strong European team in Scotland, Bishop felt that he had to make a bold choice, and that he had license to do so. The Medinah loss gave him a kind of mandate, and this freedom, paired with his natural penchant for standing out—borderline narcissism, to some—created the foundation for a maverick gambit. The natural choices for captain that year would have been someone like David Toms or Larry Nelson or maybe even Fred Couples, if the PGA of America could look past his stints as a Presidents Cup captain. Perhaps even Paul Azinger would have been considered for a reprise. But Bishop's instinct was to do something completely shocking, and in December 2012 he named Tom Watson as the next captain.

In some regards, it made a little bit of sense. Watson was the captain the last time the Americans won in Europe, in 1993, he was beloved in Scotland for his Open Championship wins, and he had a take-charge alpha male personality that some felt the Americans needed.

On the European side, it looked like Paul McGinley was the natural choice in the line of succession, and at least in modern history, he had the worst playing résumé of any captain from either side: no majors, no WGCs, and only four European Tour wins in his entire career. To put someone like Tom Watson against a nonentity like McGinley, one line of thinking went, would be a huge psychological blow to Europe, rattling their cages two years before anyone hit a shot.

Watson got the nod on December 13, and in the opening press conference, Bishop told the story of how the inspiration struck.

"I remember I got home, and I called Huber on Saturday," he said, referring to Jim Huber, a writer who had actually written a book about Tom Watson, "and I said, 'Jim, I have a really out-of-the-box concept I would like to throw at you just to get your opinion.' I said, 'What would you think of Tom Watson as a Ryder Cup captain in Scotland in 2014?' And there was this deafening silence, and Jim came back, and he said, 'You know what, that's a brilliant idea. That idea is absolutely brilliant.'"

This short exchange said a lot about Bishop—his need to stand out as an individual and his tendency to inflate himself in his own stories, in this case through the mouth of a third party.

Watson mostly said the right things, but when asked to pinpoint why Europe had had such success, he reverted instantly to the favorite preoccupation of Americans who don't want to think of the Ryder Cup as a team sport.

"Well," he began, "as Jim Colbert said in a players' meeting in front of Deane Beman a long time ago when players were complaining about certain things that were going on on the Tour, he got up in front of all the players there and said, 'You know what your problem is? Play better.' And that's essentially the same thing. The Europeans have outplayed us."

He also addressed his age—Watson would be sixty-five by the time Gleneagles came around—before anyone could ask.

"We play the same game," he said.

That much was true. But what became clear is that even though he played the same game as his younger charges, they lived in a very, very different world, and there would not be a lot of mutual understanding . . . to put it mildly.

This press conference also provided the first hint that their idea of "shaking things up" wasn't particularly sophisticated. It was mostly just

Watson being Watson, making decisions with his gut, knowing things that others don't, and commanding respect by sheer gravitas. They saw him as John Wayne, the quintessential American hero, beyond questioning, and to Ted Bishop especially, the great victory was in simply naming him captain.

As it turned out, that would not work, and in fact, none of their reasoning held up to closer scrutiny. Yes, Tom Watson was a great player, but as we'd discover again in 2021, there's very little evidence in any sport that being a great player makes you a great coach, or even a good one. In fact, the exact opposite is true—it's no coincidence that baseball has a cliché about backup catchers making great managers. Past greatness can even limit a coach—how do you explain genius to someone who isn't one?

The idea that his triumphs in Scotland would somehow win him the adoration of the crowd was also embarrassingly shortsighted. Sure, they would show him respect, but when it was time for the actual golf to happen, it wouldn't diminish the partisan nature of the European fans. Finally, the idea that Watson could motivate by the sheer force of his personality ignored the important fact that he wasn't dealing with peers who knew him on the course. The current Americans, from Jordan Spieth to Bubba Watson to Rickie Fowler to Phil Mickelson, were all extremely talented, with significant egos of their own, and maybe they'd look at Tiger Woods with a certain amount of reverence. But they didn't know Tom Watson the same way, and more importantly, he didn't know them. Nor did he take the time to try.

Finally, they completely underestimated Paul McGinley. With a little more insight, they might have asked themselves an important question: How does somebody whose playing career was so modest rise to the position of Ryder Cup captain? And if they thought about it, they may have concluded that he must have some pretty extraordinary skills. Instead, they thought they could blow him out of the water by appointing a legend.

As it turned out, the no-name leading Team Europe was a thinker, and he was going to prepare for the Ryder Cup like nobody had prepared before him. He would look at his captaincy the same way Steve Stricker would in 2021: this was his major.

He adopted a humble, low profile, content to let the Americans make all the news in the lead-up to the Cup, but beneath that quiet veneer, his brain was churning. Nobody on his team would be in awe of him, but he didn't need that—his strategy was entirely different. And when Tom Watson, beloved of the Scottish people, finally made his way to Gleneagles in the fall of 2014, he had absolutely no idea what was about to hit him.

* * *

If there's one thing to be said for Bishop, his selection of Watson really did unsettle the European powers. For a moment, they seemed to be occupying his headspace and worrying that McGinley was too underwhelming a figure to meet the great Watson. That worry manifested into two significant challenges to McGinley, and came extremely close to tanking his candidacy.

The first challenge was a surprise. Darren Clarke had long been in the line of succession for European captains, and likely had the inside track on Gleneagles. Then he won the Open Championship in 2011, the greatest triumph of his career, and it changed his focus. He sent a letter to McGinley telling him he didn't want the captaincy yet, that he would step back, and that McGinley would be in line for Gleneagles.

That had to have come as a major relief for McGinley. He and Clarke were good friends, and along with Pádraig Harrington, they were the three foremost Irish golfers of their generation. That said, Clarke and Harrington were significantly more accomplished than McGinley, and whether he liked it or not, that was a huge deficit when it came to securing a captaincy.

Growing up in Dublin, McGinley's primary focus was on Gaelic football, a uniquely Irish sport that resembles a combination of soccer and rugby. His dad worked with the Royal Merchant Navy and later as a TV repairman, and the family lived in a suburb called Rathfarnham—the same suburb where Harrington grew up. McGinley was a very good footballer, if not great, and he was constantly on the verge of playing for his county—a high honor in the sport—without ever quite getting there. At age nineteen, while practicing, he shattered his kneecap, completely wrecking the patella, and was told that he'd never play competitively again. Only then, very late in the game, did McGinley turn his focus to golf.

His professional career is considered unremarkable, but when you consider the fact that he was a 6-handicap at age nineteen and became a successful European Tour professional who played on three Ryder Cups, it starts to look more impressive.

"More than anything, it's competitiveness," McGinley told me by way of explanation. "I look back on my younger self, and what I see is not a huge amount of talent, but what I did see is ambition—a lot of ambition. Ambition to get out of Ireland, ambition to travel the world, ambition to be a noise."

Starting so late, McGinley was also unique in that the bulk of his life to that point had been in team sports. This gave him a different perspective from golfers who had been dedicated to an individual sport—and all the necessary selfishness that entails—from a much younger age. It also helps explain why he understood the team dynamic of Ryder Cup competition so intuitively. One way he tried to reach players was by emphasizing that they weren't playing for Europe alone—a big, impersonal entity—but for their country, their town, their golf club. He excelled at making things personal.

In terms of his own career, McGinley won his four European Tour events, played on the Walker Cup, and won the World Cup of Golf and a few Irish PGA Championships. He had just a single top ten in majors, a T-6 at the 1996 PGA.

"If I was more selfish, I would probably have been a better player," he told an Irish writer. "I didn't think I could win major championships. I wish I had more ambition and rawness and that 'fuck you' attitude . . .

My game got close enough to win major championships, but I don't think my mind ever did."

As his career progressed, he was caught and then lapped by the likes of Clarke and Harrington, leaving him in the shadows. He did, however, play in three Ryder Cups from 2002 to 2006, and was on the winning team each time. With Pádraig Harrington, he beat Tiger Woods and Davis Love III in 2004, and he etched a place for himself in golf history when he hit the Cup-clinching putt against Jim Furyk in 2002. All this may have been an early sign—put Paul McGinley on a team, and he's probably going to win.

He also forged a relationship with Seve Ballesteros, particularly when Seve captained him during the Royal Trophy, a match play event pitting Europe against Asia. Seve recognized a kindred spirit, sought his advice on pairings and other strategy, and told him he'd be a Ryder Cup captain someday. He compared McGinley to his old friend Manuel Piñero, for the way his pure ambition and energy, rather than talent, propelled him to the top of the sport. It was McGinley who had the idea in 2010 of getting Seve to speak to the European team, which was one of his last Ryder Cup acts before passing away the next year.

McGinley became heavily involved in the Ryder Cup after his playing career ended. He took the helm twice at the Seve Trophy—the now-defunct match play event contested between a Great Britain and Ireland team and continental Europe—and won twice, both times with the inferior team on paper. After his second victory in 2011, with a Ryder Cup vice captaincy under his belt in 2010 and another coming at Medinah, he was ecstatic.

"Fuck me," he said, "this is coming easy to me. I'm loving this. I can win a Ryder Cup because I've just proved it here . . . There's nobody more prepared than me to step up to the next level."

Despite having the inside track, McGinley's candidacy was almost smashed to pieces a month after the Ryder Cup when Darren Clarke changed his mind. Letter or no letter, he wanted the captaincy now. It was devastating news for McGinley to hear, both from a professional and personal standpoint. He and Clarke were friends—McGinley had missed the 2006 PGA Championship to attend the funeral of Clarke's wife—and Clarke's renewed candidacy felt like a betrayal.

Almost immediately, Lee Westwood came out in support of Clarke. But then, as if the whole thing wasn't strange enough, Clarke dropped out by January. It could have been a moment of great relief for McGinley, but instead, Clarke delivered the worst blow yet when he gave his support not to his friend, but to Colin Montgomerie. Clarke and Montgomerie didn't even like each other, and the decision mystified McGinley. It ended their friendship and put his candidacy very seriously on the rocks.

With the decision set to be made in January 2013, the tide finally began to swing back in McGinley's favor when Rory McIlroy tweeted his support, saying that the Ryder Cup captaincy should be a one-time honor (Montgomerie had been captain in 2010). Luke Donald, Ian Poulter, and Justin Rose quickly followed, and Thomas Bjørn—chairman of the committee who would choose the captain—told the media, "We don't have to react to Watson's appointment, as Europe's record in past years is pretty impressive." Just as quickly as it flared up, the opposition to McGinley faded away. The fever broke, and he was chosen.

A few months later, at a hotel in San Diego during a family vacation, McGinley was in an elevator when he met a man from Boston wearing a Medinah hat. They struck up a conversation, and the man was thrilled to meet an Irishman—he had Irish roots. McGinley asked him if he'd been to Medinah. He had.

"I've been going to Ryder Cups for twenty years," he said. "It's the greatest event of all time."

When they got off the elevator, McGinley asked if he was going to Gleneagles.

"Of course I am," he said. "We've got an Irish guy as captain—how could I miss it? Are you going?"

"Yeah," said McGinley, "I might."

* * *

From there, everything fell into place ... or fell into pieces, for the Americans.

McGinley was influenced by generations of European Ryder Cup captains, but he was also influenced by Paul Azinger. After Azinger released his book *Cracking the Code* about his own captaincy, McGinley devoured it, and then approached Azinger to compliment him ... and to call him crazy for giving away all his secrets. Among the many lessons he took from the American captain was the concept of messaging—how to communicate to players in ways that make them feel secure, inspire them, and also point them in the direction of the captain's vision.

There's a lot to write about McGinley's captaincy, but perhaps the best way to understand his singular tenure is to look at a specific strategy he employed with just two of his players, Graeme McDowell and Victor Dubuisson.

Dubuisson, to put it mildly, is one of the strangest men to ever play professional golf. He's faded from the limelight since 2014, but that year, he wowed America with his heroics from the desert at the finals of the WGC Match Play against Jason Day, a championship he'd lose in extra holes. He was on track to make the European Ryder Cup team on the strength of finishes like that, and it presented McGinley with a huge problem. Dubuisson was a quiet, retreating, skittish person, unfriendly by temperament and almost fearful of human interaction. (The one time I spoke with him, I had the sense that at any moment, he might run away.) This is sometimes misinterpreted as arrogance, which makes things even more difficult for him. It would be somewhere between difficult and impossible for Dubuisson to make friends with strangers, and that's even if he wanted to, which he clearly did not. From a personality standpoint, finding a place for him on the team was always going to be one of McGinley's foremost challenges.

He tackled it in a few different ways. His first big idea was that he'd pair Dubuisson with a veteran, and he knew the player with the brains and the perspective to take on the job was Graeme McDowell. Not only that, but as one of the first captains to embrace statistics, McGinley knew from the Johnnie Walker Championship at Gleneagles that the best correlation for overall success was to play well on the par-5s, and it happened that three of the par-5s, along with a drivable par-4, were on even holes. This coincidence gave him a vision of the powerful Dubuisson teeing off on those holes in alternate shot, with McDowell hitting irons into the green. Not only would it solve his Dubuisson problem, but it would solve a second problem by hiding McDowell's length deficiencies. For each hole he analyzed, the math worked—Dubuisson teeing off was McGinley's own way to crack the code.

But how to convince the Irishman? Rather than ask him directly, at first McGinley did something completely new—he approached the European Tour about controlling their tournament pairings on Thursday and Friday. He met immediate pushback, but he persisted, unafraid to take the matter to the highest levels. Finally, after months of arguing, they agreed. That allowed him to pair McDowell and Dubuisson together a number of times without them knowing it had been done intentionally. Afterward, he'd approach McDowell and say, "Hey, what'd you think of Victor?"

McDowell liked him well enough, the caddies got along, and for his part, Dubuisson was getting more and more comfortable with the Irishman, which was no easy feat for someone so naturally antisocial. Comfort, to whatever extent it could be established, was going to be the critical factor in determining Dubuisson's success. Meanwhile, McGinley worked on overcoming the innate suspicion of new people and new situations in order to build their own relationship. He found his way into Victor's good graces by virtue of the Frenchman's love for Formula 1 car racing. Eddie Jordan, a former team owner and BBC commentator, was one of McGinley's close friends, and Jordan was happy to help. They invited Dubuisson to Jordan's boat in Monaco, and Jordan even spoke privately to the golfer, imparting messages fed to him by McGinley.

Slowly, trust was building.

The difficult part came when he had to break the news to McDowell. Two weeks before the Ryder Cup, with the groundwork laid, they sat down together. McGinley is a big believer in giving each player only the information they need—an amount that differs by player. For McDowell, a thinker and an analyzer, it was a lot—not just about him, but about the entire team. He was already a trusted member of the inner circle when they began to discuss his role, and McGinley knew he was a likely future captain.

McGinley led with the news that McDowell would only play three sessions, and predictably, it didn't go over well. He was a US Open champion in solid form, and he thought he might go as many as five sessions. Next, McGinley told him that in both pairs sessions, he'd be with Dubuisson.

"You're fucking kidding me," McDowell said.

Worse, it was alternate shot, and McDowell liked four-ball best. McGinley explained about the par-5s, how they paired well together, and how he needed someone with the poise and maturity to handle the task. Still, McDowell asked if he could play a four-ball session with someone like Rose or Stenson as a bonus. The answer was no, but McGinley had a trump card.

"I want you to play number one singles on Sunday," he told him.

McDowell sat up in his chair. It's a tremendous honor to go out first at the Ryder Cup in the singles session, and he, like many others, assumed world number one Rory McIlroy would have the privilege. To be told it was *him* was especially poignant, because he and McIlroy were embroiled in a business feud and were not on speaking terms.

"What did Rory say?" he asked.

McGinley had already cleared it with Rory, explaining that the best player should never play number one singles, because expectations are crushing and there's nothing to be gained. (This was a lesson Darren Clarke didn't learn, playing Rory in the top spot after an exhausting week at Hazeltine two years later, only for Rory to lose his perfect singles record to Patrick Reed.) It mattered very little to Rory, who readily agreed. To McDowell, McGinley implied that he had chosen him over Rory, thus playing to McDowell's ego.

As for only playing three sessions, McGinley had an explanation there too—in most cases, the Americans had a tendency to put out their best player in the world rankings in the number one singles spot, or at least the one who had played best that week. What that meant, usually, is that the number one player was playing his fourth or fifth session, and was likely exhausted. By only playing McDowell twice, McGinley was keeping him fresh to lead the team against what should be an emotionally and physically fatigued American.

"These guys are trained," McGinley told him, "but they're not trained to do that kind of golf, to show that kind of concentration. Their battery is slow."

There was one last ingredient in his plan—by playing McDowell first, he could put Victor Dubuisson last, and when McDowell finished, Dubuisson would still be early in his round, which meant that McDowell could circle back and walk with Dubuisson for the remainder, adding that extra factor of personal comfort as the Frenchman attempted to earn what might be a critical point.

McDowell began to see the full picture emerge, and not only did he agree, but he bought in to McGinley's vision.

And what happened to Graeme McDowell and Victor Dubuisson at Gleneagles?

On Friday afternoon, they anchored the alternate shot session against Keegan Bradley and Phil Mickelson, won two of the three par-5s they played, and scored a critical 3&2 victory to cap Europe's dominant session. On Saturday afternoon, they met Jimmy Walker and Rickie Fowler, who were playing their fourth session. It became clear early that the Americans were exhausted, so McDowell marched over to Dubuisson on the fairway and said, "Let's show these guys how energetic we are. Let's show them how up for this we are."

The result was a 5&4 bludgeoning. On Sunday morning, Graeme McDowell met Jordan Spieth in the number one singles spot. As McGinley predicted, Spieth had played three sessions and was one of America's best players that week. He took a lead on McDowell of 3-up at the turn, and then crashed. McDowell won four straight holes starting at the tenth—it was the run that ended America's hopes for good—and won the match 2-up. When he was finished, he walked with Victor Dubuisson in his final match against Zach Johnson, which ended with another half point for the Europeans.

It was an intricate plan McGinley had constructed for the two players, and it worked to absolute perfection. What's truly remarkable, though, is that this was just one piece of an even more intricate puzzle. This exact process was happening with every single player on the team, in various permutations, and it was a process that took shape over two years. Nor would personal grudges play a part. McGinley surprised everyone when he picked Lee Westwood over Luke Donald, despite the fact that Westwood opposed his captaincy at every step and Donald had supported him. Westwood was better for the team, and that's all that mattered to McGinley. He paired him with Jamie Donaldson, another rookie, and, like McDowell and Dubuisson, they went 2-0 in their foursomes match, and Donaldson won the clinching point for Europe on Sunday.

McGinley had mapped it all out, right down to the motivational speaker (Manchester United manager Alex Ferguson, who had made a career of winning at home as the favorite), motivational posters, and even the blue-and-yellow fish in the fish tank. And he had done it without overcomplicating things for his players; the puzzle was pieced together in his head, but the players only had to be themselves.

Not every move worked out, and not every relationship on the course was infused with perfect chemistry. His pairing of Stephen Gallacher and Ian Poulter faltered, McDowell and Rory were still not feeling especially friendly, and vice captain Pádraig Harrington and Sergio García disliked each other so much that they couldn't be within one hundred feet. But with so much study and coordination, it worked well enough to ensure a thorough clobbering.

* * *

On the American side, absolutely nothing went according to script—mostly because there was no script. Watson had originally chosen Bill Haas as his third captain's pick, but famously answered text messages from Webb Simpson the night before and changed his mind—almost certainly after Haas heard the news that he had made the team. (To Simpson's credit, I asked him about the texting story in 2021, and he answered honestly. "I was so, I guess, anxious about making that team in 2014," he said, "and maybe it was good and bad that I texted him, but in that moment I felt like, I don't know Tom as well, I don't know if he knows how much I want to make this team.")

As if to prove that his instincts were right, Watson led with Simpson and Bubba Watson in the first match. Simpson had the first shot of the Ryder Cup, and he popped the ball straight into the air. It was downhill from there, and they lost badly to the Euro superteam of Justin Rose and Henrik Stenson. The rest of the session went surprisingly well for the Americans, though, highlighted by the new team of Patrick Reed and Jordan Spieth crushing Ian Poulter and Stephen Gallacher 5&4.

After that coup, the two rookies expected to go back out for the afternoon. Watson had told the team that the afternoon pairings would be based on how play went in the morning—two groups were set, in order to get everyone involved on day one, but the other two would be determined by performance. To their shock, though, he approached them and told them they were sitting. It was inexplicable, and their absence certainly contributed to the Europeans winning three matches and halving another in the afternoon to retake the lead 5-3. (Watson never explained why he hadn't played them, citing "private team details.")

Saturday was more of the same—the Americans played well in the morning, winning 2.5 points, but ran into the McGinley alternate shot juggernaut in the afternoon, going down 3.5-0.5. Amazingly, Watson had not played Phil Mickelson or Keegan Bradley all day, despite Mickelson trying to convince the captain using every avenue of communication he could muster. He didn't even offer an explanation. Instead, he played Zach Johnson and Matt Kuchar, two players who had not even practiced together, who got beat by Donaldson and Westwood, and he threw out Fowler and Walker for a fourth time, only for them to be bashed by McDowell and Dubuisson.

"I made the best decisions I possibly could at the time with the help of my vice captains and my guts," Watson said that night. He went on to criticize his players, but the most he'd criticize himself was to say, "If I had to second-guess myself, I think it was based on just that, a couple players getting tired. Might have done it differently if I knew they were going to be that way . . . I regret not understanding that they couldn't handle it."

Not exactly strong accountability. That night, he led the team meeting by saying, "You stink at foursomes"—an attempt at a joke that only made everyone on the team madder—and then proceeded to insult several of Team Europe's players as he read the singles matches. Again, it landed with a thud. Furyk then presented him with the team gift, a replica Ryder Cup trophy signed by everyone. Watson only scoffed, telling them it wasn't worth a thing if they didn't win the real one.

At that point, Phil Mickelson grabbed a chair, placed it in front of Watson—effectively cutting him off from his team—and addressed every player by turn. He had a story to tell about each of them, and his positivity shifted the mood of the whole team. It would not be the last big moment of the weekend for Mickelson.

* * *

On the European side of things, McGinley had a favorite phrase that appeared on one of his posters: "We will be the rock when the storm comes."

He had learned from Medinah, and he knew that a 10-6 lead could be overturned, even on the road. He had planned as well as he could, leading with strength to keep the Americans from gathering any early momentum, but he also knew that once the matches started, it was out of his control, and that if things became rocky, his players would have to endure. The Americans threatened, albeit briefly—at one point in the late morning, the scores on the board would have leveled things at 14-14—but McDowell turned around the top match, Rory romped in the number three spot against Rickie Fowler, and in the end Donaldson sealed the deal against Keegan Bradley.

The final score was 16.5-11.5, a blowout that felt even worse than the lopsided score. Sun Tzu wrote in *The Art of War* that "the highest form of warfare is to outthink the enemy . . . The great warriors of old not only won victories, but won them with ease; because their victories were achieved without apparent difficulty, they did not bring them great fame for their wisdom or respect for their courage. Being prepared for all circumstances is what ensures certain victory, for it means you are fighting an enemy who is already beaten."

McGinley had embodied that principle, and in the process turned in one of the greatest captaincies the Ryder Cup had known. He would get some credit, but, aside from a few people like me who obsess over this competition, probably not as much as he deserved.

Of course, he was upstaged just minutes after the celebration began—Gleneagles is most famous for what happened *after* the golf came to an end.

* * *

It happened in the US team press conference—the exchange that transformed the American Ryder Cup.

"Anyone that was on the team at Valhalla," asked a reporter, "can you put your finger on what worked there and what hasn't worked since?"

The only three players who had been at Valhalla were Hunter Mahan, who wasn't inclined to speak; Jim Furyk, who just had; and Phil Mickelson. Unsurprisingly, Mickelson took the microphone. He went into a long explanation of how wise Azinger had been, how similar tactics had worked in the Presidents Cup, and how invested the players had been, but how it had been a failure in the Ryder Cup.

"That felt like a pretty brutal destruction of the leadership that's gone on this week," the reporter said.

"Oh, I'm sorry you're taking it that way," Mickelson replied, feigning innocence. "I'm just talking about what Paul Azinger did to help us play our best."

He went on for a couple more sentences, and the obvious follow-up came: "That didn't happen this week?"

What followed was a long, pregnant pause. Even Mickelson, a bold player who enjoyed total respect and support among his fellow players, was hesitant to break golf's code of silence when it came to trashing a colleague. In the end, his frustration won through.

"No," he said. "Nobody here was in on any decision. So, no."

The words may not look dramatic in hindsight, but at the time, considering the culture, it felt like he had brought a sledgehammer down on Watson's head.

Some considered this an act of tremendous disrespect to a legend, but to others, it was a long overdue lambasting of an incompetent system. It's difficult to assess Mickelson's own motivations. On one hand, he clearly had an interest in fixing the US Ryder Cup situation, and he may have thought that he needed to do something dramatic and public to make people pay attention. On the other, his ego had definitely been wounded by Watson leaving him out all day Saturday, and there's no doubt that he has a vindictive side. This moment is sometimes portrayed as a selfless act from Mickelson, but it was also clearly an attack on the captain who had dared to insult him. But it came with a price, and he knew it would.

"I saw him after that," Pádraig Harrington said. "It was hard on him. Whether you think it was right or wrong, he felt the responsibility, and it was a burden on him. We all know Phil loves to talk, but he would have preferred if he didn't have to do that."

Whatever the case, and however it's interpreted, it had the effect of forcing the PGA of America to act. An eleven-man task force complete with players, captains, and PGA of America officials was formed to examine the issue, and the words *task force* sounded so self-important that the immediate reaction from almost every corner was mockery.

"What a massive pat on the back and confidence booster it is for Europe that Team USA needs to create a Ryder Cup task force!" Lee Westwood tweeted, in a typical response.

"It was a bad name," Love admitted in 2021, laughing. "But the PGA of America said, 'Something's not right. Let's all sit down in a room.' And we got that big group of guys together, and we said, 'How do we start over?'"

With the input of the players and captains, they made a serious attempt to establish continuity in order to repair the broken ship of state. The road map had been laid out by the Europeans, and it had taken decades for the Americans to admit its value, but with the creation of the task force, laughter from the outside didn't matter—when they met for the first time in Florida (Phil Mickelson even traveled from California on his own money), they were finally starting down the right path. They formed a permanent board of six people, consisting of three captains or future captains and three PGA of America officials, and that board would decide it all—captains, venue, statistics, everything. And at long last, they asked themselves some fundamental questions.

"We had Raymond Floyd in there. We had Jim Furyk. We had Stricker. Tom Lehman," Love said. "Trying to figure out, okay, why did Darren Clarke know in 2010 that he was going to be captain in 2016, and how were they preparing him? And besides what Europe is doing, what did we do well and what did we do poorly?"

They went around the room, remembering what they had liked and disliked from previous Ryder Cups, and from there, a new strategy was born.

"We never had a game plan before," Love said, but that all changed with the task force. The specifics were manifold, but the overall philosophy was simple: it was time to start learning from the past, it was time to incorporate a system, and it was time to get better every year. That's called "institutional memory," and until then, the Americans never had it.

Love is, in many ways, the pivotal figure of the US Ryder Cup trans-formation, in that he spans the lowest moment—the Medinah collapse—to the present, having won in Hazeltine and served as a vice captain since. He's at the center of everything, and he's content playing any kind of role, from leader to assistant. At one point at a team meeting during the Ryder Cup in Whistling Straits, Zach Johnson kicked him under the table to get him to speak up on some strategic matter, but he refused—he trusted Stricker, and by staying silent, he communicated to Johnson and Phil Mickelson that he also trusted the process they had initiated.

"At least we're trying," he said. "You know, we're just golfers. I'm not Nick Saban. I'm just a guy that got really good at golf. We're learning to plan ahead, and to be coaches."

I asked Love what motivated him—why he had given up so much of his life and his time to taking on this monumental prospect of reversing the historical tides, even when it meant time away from his family and suffering the heartbreak of loss.

"My wife asked the same thing," he said. "My dad and Harvey Pen-ick [the famous swing coach] . . . they were golf professionals. They make golf better for everybody else. They do everything with a servant heart. That's how I saw them. So I'm giving back to the game. And after being the captain in 2012, I sat in the basement of the hotel on Monday morn-ing, literally in tears, thinking, 'I don't want this to end. I want to help these guys win.'"

* * *

The process yielded dividends in 2016 with the American win at Hazel-tine, and the difference in attitude heading into Sunday morning was made clear by a quote Spieth sent to the team:

"Fate whispers to the warrior, 'you cannot withstand the storm.' The Warrior whispers back, 'I am the storm.'"

But in 2018, they took another step back when a challenging course in Paris completely stymied them, leading to another blowout European win. There was no captaincy controversy there—apart from having his hand forced into some tough picks, Furyk was liked and respected by his players, and he remained so when the event was finished. But it raised questions about the merit of what it meant to be "nice," or to be popular.

"Jim's a nice guy, everybody likes Jim, nobody says a bad word about Jim," Paul McGinley said in early 2020. "Nobody says a bad word about Stricker. But what does that stand for at the end of the day? Not a whole lot."

To prove that the task force was no fluke, Stricker and the Americans would have to do what they hadn't done since 1983—win a second straight Ryder Cup at home.

CHAPTER SIXTEEN

2016–2021, Various Battlefields

The number wars

"The Europeans have a system that started right around 1983 with Tony Jacklin, and it has been built upon and refined over time to the point where it's like a machine. In the US, I think it's fair to say that it had been an ad hoc approach, and there hadn't been a sense of institutional memory or organizational conscience. With the task force, it was huge towards establishing a coherent system . . . and what systems do, along with allowing best practices to carry forward, is they also create mechanisms for processing failure. So when you do lose, there is a place to ask, 'What happened?' And that's tremendously empowering, not just because you get an edge over your opponent, but also knowing that no matter what happens, we're going to be okay. We're going to be better next time."

—Jason Aquino

"Like all good stories," Jason Aquino told me, "the story of Ryder Cup analytics began in a Cracker Barrel outside Baltimore, Maryland."

It was a tremendous first line in our two-hour conversation, but in fact, the story truly began many years earlier, in Aquino's childhood, in

Bethesda. He's always been a golfer, but more importantly, he's always been a Ryder Cup obsessive. Simply *watching* the Ryder Cup was never enough for him—he'd go so far as to tape the coverage, the press conferences on the Golf Channel, and the highlight reels, and then he'd watch it all over and over again when he got home from school. (Early in our conversation, while illustrating a point about the benefits of local knowledge for European teams, he told a story about Ignacio Garrido and Jesper Parnevik playing the seventeenth hole at Valderrama in 1997—this knowledge runs very, very deep.) Everything about the Cup fascinated him, from the passion on both sides to the shot-making under crushing pressure. And he hated that the Americans were so bad.

"It gnawed at me, seeing the Europeans win so much in the '90s," he said, rattling off names like Oak Hill and Valderrama and the Belfry. "I got tired of seeing these press conferences where we were just so sad. I wanted to see what I could do to make sure we never had one of those losing press conferences again."

It got to the point where his fascination with the Ryder Cup became such an overwhelming drain on his time that he forced himself to throw all his old videos in the trash. Life moved on, he studied strategic research and analysis at Georgetown, and he became a military analyst consulting with the Department of Defense on long-range strategy projects. Specifically, he worked for the Office of Net Assessment in the Pentagon, and he describes his job as "thinking into the future." In his case, this meant the future of defense, and by extension the future of warfare. How might other countries fight against America in twenty years? What kind of weapons would they buy? How would it change over time, and what were the implications for the strategic advantage the Americans held?

On a given day, Aquino might have spent his time thinking and writing about the naval balance in the Pacific, or global nuclear competition. The reason his job existed is because it takes decades for the military to develop new capabilities, and Aquino played an instrumental role in helping imagine the challenges they'd face down the line so they could start preparing now.

Throughout this time, he never stopped thinking about the Ryder Cup. It was an obsession that wouldn't go away. One day, Aquino wrote a war games scenario that he considered especially good, but as he was reading it over, he had a startling realization.

"I had freakin' written this before," he said, "years earlier."

He found that disturbing—a sign that his life was going in circles—and he knew it was time to seek out new experiences. He believed the only way to become better as a strategist was to apply new lenses to problems, and he was stuck mining the same territory time and again. So in 2013, he broke out on his own and formed the Scouts Consulting Group, with the idea that he would bring his analytical skills and apply them to other fields, with other clients.

He didn't start out with the idea that he'd be working in sports, but after the American disaster at Gleneagles, an idea that had been brewing in his mind for years resurfaced: What if there was a Ryder Cup research program? Most professional sports franchises have research and development departments, so why not Team USA? He reached out to the head pro at his course, Bethesda Country Club, who introduced him to a PGA of America official living nearby. The process had begun.

Which brings us to October 2014 and the Cracker Barrel outside Baltimore. His timing couldn't have been better, and that meeting with PGA of America officials went so well that Aquino was then introduced to the entire executive suite. That started a fifteen-month process of discussions and negotiations, and during that time Aquino and his new staff had to perform what he called "proof of principle" work, to show the PGA of America that even though they hadn't worked in golf yet, they were capable of the level of analysis it would take to provide a real benefit to the team.

In late June 2016, Aquino met Davis Love III and Jim Furyk at the Quicken Loans National at Congressional, and that was when two parallel tracks converged—the work of the task force, which was pursuing more statistical research at the insistence of players like Phil Mickelson, and the PGA of America, which had been testing Aquino and his group since late 2014.

Love later told me that he and his vice captains actually had to decide between three different companies—"They didn't say, 'Do you want stats or not?'" Love remembered, laughing. "They said, 'Pick from these three'"—and it was Aquino who sold them.

"What are sports but warfare by other means?" Aquino asked rhetorically. And how could Love and the PGA of America choose anyone other than the war games analyst who couldn't kick his Ryder Cup obsession?

That initial meeting went well, and they established the foundation for how the program would work. Aquino was impressed when Love said, "Don't get too caught up in what you think we know as players." He found that to be a critically important message from Love, giving them the permission and the freedom to challenge the leaders and present controversial ideas. In other words, Love was thick-skinned, and wouldn't react defensively to any information that went against their prior convictions. In 2016, it paid off in helping the Americans to a dominant win at Hazeltine.

"They're invaluable," Love told me. "On alternate shot, we would just think about who hit on odd and even holes, or who drives on par-5s, but they were breaking it all the way down to whether the hole was dogleg left or right, who hits the best wedges from certain distances. It's Moneyball. They're helping us with situations that we would never even dream."

One of Scouts Consulting's best tools is risk profiles—they present pairings, for instance, as high-risk or low-risk based on the output of their models, and they're always ready to translate that output into legible analysis. In other words, despite the density of the numbers, they can always answer the question of, "Why?"

One way Aquino measures his success with the team, albeit slightly tongue-in-cheek, is how close he's gotten to the captains in each successive Ryder Cup . . . as in, how *physically* close. They've had an office for all three Cups, but they didn't sit near any of the team areas in 2016 and weren't participating in meetings, although there was a constant flow of text messages and emails along with the standard reports and on-course shot tracking. They were moved closer to Jim Furyk and his vice captains in Paris, very near the team area, and they felt more like an active sounding board. Finally, in Whistling Straits, they were in the clubhouse, in the thick of the action.

The volume of communication increased with the proximity—to hear Aquino tell it, so did the quality of their analysis—and it was clear that the mutual trust had grown. When I spoke with Love, he mentioned that he was trying to get them involved for the Presidents Cup—to this point the American side has never used an analytics group.

* * *

There was another parallel story here, and that was the rise of golf analytics in Europe. As with many other elements of the Ryder Cup, Paul McGinley led the way, operating as a sort of lone wolf stat-head. He used a site called strokeaverage.com in 2014 to help him plan partnerships and alternate shot strategy, and he was often seen carrying around stacks of paper loaded with data as a vice captain in 2010 and 2012.

Darren Clarke had watched what Paul McGinley accomplished, and he had ambitions to take that to the next step. Through a friend, he heard about the work of analysts known today as the Twenty First Group, which was founded in 2013 and at that time mainly worked in advanced analytics for English soccer. They became Clarke's consultants, poring over all the data they could gather, but quickly realized there was a dearth of statistical "ingredients" in European golf. They knew they were capable of providing the guidance Clarke needed, but the European Tour had no Shotlink system like the one in use on the PGA Tour, and thus no granular data to crunch.

Shotlink is tremendously expensive, and is run in America with the help of a volunteer base that simply doesn't exist in Europe, so the Twenty First Group got creative and worked with the European Tour to develop an entirely new system. With the help of caddies, who logged shot-by-shot information after rounds, they were able to compile more advanced statistics, which then paved the way to giving Clarke and future European Tour captains the insights they needed. (Today, in partnership with IMG Arena, a GPS-powered Shotlink-like system is used on the European Tour.) The solution was so clever that the LPGA decided to implement something very similar this past summer.

In 2016, the two stats crews, Scouts Consulting and Twenty First Group, went head-to-head for the first time at Hazeltine. Unfortunately for the Europeans, they lost, in no small part because Darren Clarke's team was loaded with unprepared rookies.

Two years later in Paris, though, Bjørn and Twenty First Group had control of their own venue, and he'd relied on them for support from the start. They'd been working with him for almost two full years, feeding reams of statistical insight in person and through an app they built called Captain, all the while slowly building trust with a man who was remarkably open to the new approach they offered, but who was also steeped in the tradition of a sport that has been one of the slowest to embrace the analytics revolution. If their recommendations didn't yield actual on-course benefits, they knew too well how quickly they could lose the foothold they'd worked so hard to attain.

They were the ones who showed him that Sergio García's rough season didn't look so rough when you drilled down into the data, opening the door for Bjørn to select him as a controversial fourth captain's pick (Sergio went 3-1). They were the ones who recognized that unlike most courses, Le Golf National put a premium on driving accuracy rather than driving distance, and they helped Bjørn set up the course and his pairings for four-balls and alternate shot in accordance with the course profile. Their models even suggested the Molinari-Fleetwood pairing that would prove to be fabulously successful.

The most nervous moment for the Twenty First Group in Paris came after the very first session on Friday morning, when the Americans took a 3-1 lead in four-ball. These were competitive nerves, but they were also professional nerves, and perhaps even existential nerves. The plan they'd formulated for alternate shot was at risk, and in the back rooms of Team Europe, there was talk of diverging. The prospect had to be heartbreaking—as Dan Zelezinski, Twenty First Group's chief commercial officer, told me, alternate shot is the Ryder Cup format in which an informed statistical approach can provide a significant edge.

"You're identifying who complements who," he said, "not only through that simple layer of aligning individual player attributes, but in the context of this style of golf course and the specific challenges they're going to face. So it's multifaceted, but it's fair to say there's a lot of value to be added."

The analysts at Twenty First Group were excited about what was supposed to come next; the pairings that had been suggested for the afternoon were not just about meshing personalities and not even just about course fit, but going as deep as which players should tee off on which holes and how they should approach each hole strategically to optimize their advantage.

In the end, they had gained enough trust with Bjørn to convince him to stand strong—"Stick to the plan!" became a kind of team war cry, according to CEO Blake Wooster—and not only did Europe win all four matches, but none of them even went to the seventeenth hole. It was a thorough drubbing, and so was the rest of the Ryder Cup, with the Americans looking increasingly befuddled. When it was over, Bjørn credited his stat-heads for playing a "vital role" in the victory, just as Love had done with Scouts Consulting in Hazeltine.

In fact, it wasn't just for the Scouts Consulting's statistical merit that Love wanted them involved in the 2022 Presidents Cup. He knew first-hand that the Twenty First Group were promiscuous—in Melbourne, Ernie Els had used them to give a vastly superior American team an unbelievable scare, and Love has no interest in being the first US captain to lose the Presidents Cup at home.

*   *   *

If you ever want to feel like you're asking a CIA agent for state secrets, I recommend talking to a Ryder Cup analyst. Aquino and I spoke for a long time, but he warned me right away that if I sensed any awkward pauses, it was him deciding what he was allowed to tell me. If anything, Zelezinski on the European side kept things even closer to the vest. They are both war gamers at heart, intelligence is one of their currencies, and it's not a currency they're willing to give up easily. As both sides acknowledge, part of their job is trying to decipher what the other side is doing, and how they're utilizing their statistical models, in order to guess what strategies they might pursue and perhaps even to reverse engineer the model itself. So although I found my conversation with Aquino enlightening, it also included moments like this:

"What were the lessons you took from Paris?"

"Um . . . lessons from Paris . . . um . . . I'd rather not really talk about that."

"That's fair. You don't have to answer this either, but is that because you don't want to overstep what you see as your auxiliary role within the team, or you don't want to give away secrets?"

"Both."

Aquino and Zelezinski were also emphatic about giving full credit to the players and captains, and made sure to remind me over and over that they functioned only in a support capacity—providing information that was meant to be used as a supplement to the captains' knowledge and instincts. They are extremely sensitive about taking too much credit, or being seen as second-guessing their captains. This likely stems from the fact that golf has only lately broken into the statistics game, many of the men on both sides who have served or may serve as captain start out neutral or skeptical about their worth, and arrogance would be a bad look. (The one moment of true awkwardness in my discussions with Zelezinski came when I suggested that Harrington hadn't been listening to them when he reduced the number of captain's picks. They were deeply and immediately concerned about this claim, and though it seemed reasonable to me, they wouldn't give an inch.)

That said, it's not just self-preservation. Both groups have a keen respect for the intuition of professional golfers, and Aquino even tells them not to let all the information override their golfer brain. He cited a concept—a favorite of Napoleon's—called a *coup d'oeil*, a coup of the eye, which he defined as "the ability to look at any tactical situation and immediately assess where the battle's going and what is needed to win." And he would never claim that what he does is more important.

Because of these factors—secrecy and humility and perhaps a dose of self-preservation—you won't get many specific details about their contributions even after a Ryder Cup is over. Therefore, it's possible to know broadly that their analytics programs go extremely deep into the available data to predict which pairings will work, which might not, and which format suits each player best. In addition, that data allows them to advise captains on everything from tee placement to the length of rough to the width of the fairways to pairings orders on any given day.

Their work, however, starts long before the Ryder Cup begins. Zelezinski even told me that he considers his work 90 percent done by the time they arrive at the course. Both teams present models that forecast the likely automatic qualifiers months in advance so the captains can think about potential pairings much earlier, and they're on hand when it's time to make captain's picks with reams of data showing which players are better suited to succeed at the host course. In addition, they can function as pure researchers for historical questions that may serve the team. (Aquino offered a hypothetical that might interest a captain: How far down the points standings has a US team gone to use a captain's pick on a rookie?) Scouts Consulting even had a role in preparing the questionnaires that were sent out to American players to help determine which personalities would mesh or clash.

It's impossible to overstate how deep it goes, and although you wouldn't notice the foot soldiers if you weren't looking, I saw firsthand how ubiquitous the mathematical infantry from both companies were in Wisconsin, even taking data on player performances during practice rounds to feed back to the captains.

At Whistling Straits, while the focus of the golf world would be squarely on the play of Team USA and Team Europe, the third straight duel between the stats gurus, Scouts Consulting versus Twenty First Group, was set to be waged off-air. After two straight home blowouts, it was tempting to believe that home course advantage is too difficult to overcome for either side, but Zelezinski, while acknowledging the enormous benefit of a home crowd, noted that today's players are playing global schedules and that course setup isn't quite the weapon it had been years ago.

He might have been optimistic—when you have two teams committed to listening to the numbers, the side that gets to set up the course and choose the format inevitably will heighten their advantage. There is some talk of taking away the home team's right to manipulate the course, and though these are now just whispers, they've grown louder in volume in the past three Ryder Cups precisely because men like Aquino are so good at their jobs.

Clearly, Zelezinski and his team faced a harder exam. The outcome would be decided by the players on the course, but there was no doubt that it would be influenced—significantly, if you believe the words of the last two victorious captains—by the data wars waged behind the scenes.

CHAPTER SEVENTEEN
September 2021, Atlanta, Georgia

Last stop before Wisconsin . . .
Patty Ice . . . Reed's near-death experience

On the Wednesday before the Tour Championship in Atlanta, the final playoff event before the Ryder Cup, Patrick Cantlay became the latest in a long line of players asked to give his thoughts on the heckling of Bryson DeChambeau. His answer was so long, thorough, and smart that it became instant fodder for golf writers (myself included). In what amounted to a seven-hundred-word essay on the state of the game, Cantlay made the point that seeking attention on social media can lead to those situations, and that golf shouldn't tolerate that level of heckling because, unlike a player wearing Yankee pinstripes in Boston, there's no "armor" for the golfer, no home field to return to when the hard hours are over.

"If you only have 2 percent of the people against you because you're polarizing and you're attention-seeking," he said, "then you're kind of dead, because those people are going to be loud, and they're going to want to say something to get under your skin."

The response was sharp enough that one writer asked him if he'd read it—"No teleprompters here," he said—and I was convinced afterward, and still am, that he had prepared and maybe even memorized it beforehand. For many fans and writers, it was an introduction to how thoughtful and eloquent Cantlay could be, a trait that only became more apparent over the next three weeks as he waxed philosophical on various issues in his deadpan, almost plodding voice.

And he was in position to have great perspective on DeChambeau, because the previous Sunday, at the BMW Championship at Caves Valley Golf Club, he had dueled him for six playoff holes before prevailing in the most thrilling finish of the PGA Tour's season. His chances seemed dead on the seventeenth when, trailing by a stroke, he hit his tee shot into the water on the par-3. But an up-and-down from the drop zone, and a stubbed chip from DeChambeau, kept him just one shot off the lead, and he made up that shot with a twenty-two-foot birdie on eighteen that gave him an astounding 14.58 strokes gained putting on the field for the week, a PGA Tour record. His red-hot putter had saved him all day in the face of DeChambeau's onslaught, even as he was being outdriven by fifty yards on most holes, and now it had landed him in a playoff.

At that point, the crowd in Maryland, which had been riding DeChambeau all day, began to treat Cantlay like Rocky Balboa, punching above his weight against a rocklike opponent. The eruption when he drained his birdie putt, contrasted against the disappointed hum when DeChambeau made par, said it all, and it also reflected a bit of tension between the two players. They had barely exchanged two words the entire round, and the exception came when DeChambeau asked Cantlay to stop walking while he was addressing his ball for an approach shot on the fourteenth hole.

The duel was on, and it continued through spectacular par saves, more long putts by Cantlay, a birdie from both players on the seventeenth hole, and a twenty-foot birdie putt by Cantlay on eighteen to seal the victory on the final playoff hole. With that win, he clinched the sixth and final Ryder Cup automatic spot and surged into first place in the playoff standings before the Tour Championship.

The stress and disappointment of the whole scene, and the whole summer, led DeChambeau even closer to a breakdown. ESPN's Kevin Van Valkenburg had the good sense to follow him in the aftermath, and while he was trudging up the hill toward the clubhouse, a lone fan shouted, "Great job, Brooksy!" DeChambeau stopped in his tracks and walked toward the man.

"You know what?" he shouted. "Get the fuck out!"

The interaction ended there—a cop was summoned to deal with the heckler—but for a moment it seemed to be on the verge of exploding into something worse.

"I would say it's pretty tough to be Bryson DeChambeau right now," Rory McIlroy said later, while acknowledging that DeChambeau wasn't blameless for everything that had happened.

The PGA Tour had long realized it had a problem on its hands, and the next week, commissioner Jay Monahan said that shouting "Brooksy" at DeChambeau would be classified as harassing behavior—grounds for expulsion from a tournament.

And beneath the worsening chaos, the hope remained that maybe the Ryder Cup could be the start of a journey in the other direction for DeChambeau, buoyed by the support that he'd receive from the home crowd.

*　*　*

The biggest story at the Tour Championship was not Patrick Cantlay's win, though, or even DeChambeau, but a different Patrick: the familiar figure of Patrick Reed.

Reed had dropped out of The Northern Trust two weeks earlier, but nobody knew exactly how bad it was until he told his story at the Tour Championship—he had been in a Houston hospital for five or six days with pneumonia in the lower lobes of both lungs.

"The only thing going through my mind was, I'm not going to be able to tell my kids goodbye," he said. "I'm not going to be able to tell them I love them."

According to him, hospital officials told him to text his family often, because he might be close to death.

Of course, this being Reed, the situation quickly turned confusing. The obvious question was whether he had tested positive for COVID-19 (and by extension, whether he was vaccinated), and contradictory details emerged. According to a piece by Rex Hoggard at GolfChannel.com, Reed told Todd Lewis in a text that he was positive for COVID-19, but he later said that he was not tested for the virus when he was admitted to the hospital. According to him, he was only tested on release, and that test came up negative. This seemed extremely strange, and when I contacted the hospital, Houston Methodist, to clarify, a PR official wrote back, "You're correct that we cannot comment specifically due to HIPAA. But this seems very odd because we require COVID-19 testing of all patients admitted to the hospital. So what you describe is not our practice."

The idea that Reed could have been in the hospital for five or six days with lung issues without being tested until he left is beyond ridiculous, but that's the story he stuck to as he prepared for the tournament, monitoring his oxygen levels during practice rounds.

He played well, all things considered, even shooting a 66 on Saturday, but ultimately, he finished in twenty-fifth place out of thirty spots, and if Stricker needed a reason not to pick him, he had it.

The topic of COVID-19 and vaccines was constant in Atlanta, but there was very little concrete information about what the various players had chosen for themselves. Stricker had asked the members of his team to tell him their vaccine status earlier in the season, but it doesn't appear that anyone in his group or the PGA of America ever acted on that information.

"I'm vaccinated," Rory McIlroy said that weekend to a small group of writers. "It makes my life easier. Europeans do what we're told to do. We follow the rules. It's not the liberty, freedom stuff like over here."

* * *

At the Tour Championship, the scores of each player are staggered based on their standings, which meant that Jon Rahm would start at 6-under in fourth, DeChambeau would be at 7-under in third, Tony Finau in second would start at 8-under, and Patrick Cantlay would lead them all at 10-under.

At first glance, Cantlay's background in golf reads as typical as Tony Finau's reads strange—born in Long Beach, California, to a father who grew up playing golf; schooled in the game at a country club famous for producing touring pros; and raised by parents who made their money in real estate. It's Cantlay's attitude, the intensity and seriousness of it, that sets him apart. As early as junior high, he was interviewing golf coaches at rival high schools to see where he wanted to play, and at every moment he was pushing those around him for help, for information, for tips on all aspects of golf.

He became a star at UCLA, won various player of the year awards, set a record by holding down the number one amateur ranking for fifty-four weeks, and turned professional following his sophomore year. His success was instant, and he was leading the Web.com Tour and on the verge of making the PGA Tour when he fell prey to a back injury that was eventually diagnosed as a stress fracture in his L5 vertebrae. It dogged him for three years, and he didn't play a single event in 2015 or 2016. He was limited to rehab, physical therapy, and playing gin with the old men at Virginia Country Club in Long Beach. In February 2016, his life took a tragic turn when his caddie and longtime friend, Chris Roth, was struck by a car at an intersection in a hit-and-run accident. Cantlay was walking a few feet behind him when it happened, and Roth lay dying in his arms as they waited for the ambulance.

Somehow, after all of this, Cantlay made it back in 2017, regained his Tour card using medical exemption starts, and won his first Tour event at the Shriners Hospital Open that fall. More wins followed, at the Memorial in 2019 and the Zozo Championship in 2020, but heading into the Tour Championship, it had already been his greatest year yet. His win at the Memorial was perhaps slightly tarnished by the fact that Rahm had held a huge lead before the COVID-19 test had forced him to drop out, but his win against DeChambeau was iconic, and raised his profile to greater heights than ever before. He gained the nickname "Patty Ice," an homage to Falcons QB Matt Ryan, and that played particularly well in Atlanta.

To win the final leg of the playoffs and earn the $15 million prize, he'd have to hold off all the familiar faces, including ones he'd see again—on both sides—at the Ryder Cup. On Sunday, shocking nobody, it came down to him and Jon Rahm. The Spaniard had had the better weekend, but he needed to gain four shots on Cantlay, and heading into the back nine on Sunday, Cantlay was stubbornly holding on to a slim lead as Rahm made his charge.

At that point, perhaps fatigued at the end of a long season, both players hit a wall. It was nothing but pars for both of them from holes ten through fifteen as Cantlay clung to his one-shot advantage. The American broke through first on sixteen, hitting his approach on the par-4 to within five feet and converting the birdie, while Rahm missed his longer putt by six inches. Cantlay courted disaster on seventeen, hitting his drive and approach well right, and in what looked like a burgeoning collapse, his third shot came up short of the green. He pulled off an excellent up-and-down to save bogey, and Rahm missed yet another birdie putt. The lead was back to 1 heading to eighteen, a par-5, and the tournament came down to Cantlay's first two shots. His drive was a gargantuan 361-yard blast down the right side of the fairway, and needing just one good shot to clinch the title, he hit his second from 218 yards to 11 feet. Rahm failed to make his eagle chip, Cantlay two-putted for birdie, and in the last tournament of the season, he became the PGA Tour's only four-time winner.

He celebrated by taking a well-earned vacation with his good friend Xander Schauffele and their wives to Napa Valley wine country, where they'd cement their bond, relax, and prepare for a reprise of their Presidents Cup pairing.

On the strength of his win in Atlanta, Cantlay won the PGA Tour's player of the year in a result that was, charitably, a stretch—Rahm had the best stats of anyone in the game, by far, and had won a major. Rahm had also tied for the lowest score of the week, and the man who tied him, Kevin Na, was bullish on the Ryder Cup in the aftermath.

"I have two runner-up finishes in the last six starts, another top-one at a playoff event, and maybe win or second here," Na said, before Rahm had finished with the same cumulative score. "From where I started, to finish third in the FedExCup, eight shots back, I think I'm looking strong for a pick. I'm definitely going to probably text Captain Stricker. I haven't texted him, but I'm going to text him and see what he thinks."

There was one big thing working against Na, though, and it had been hinted at earlier in the week by Daniel Berger, who was in the midst of a so-so performance that he'd rescue with a Sunday 64.

"I've talked to Strick a bunch of times this week," Berger said. "His thoughts were that this doesn't make a difference in terms of making the team or not. It'd be nice to have a really great week, but at this point in the season, it's tough. Your body starts to break down, you've played twenty-five events. It's tough to mentally stay in it, that's kind of the battle I'm dealing with right now . . . His message has been that he wants me on the team."

In other words, Stricker had a plan in place, the preparation was complete, and a few hot days (or a few cold ones) in the last event of the year were never going to be decisive.

The season was over, and there were exactly twenty days left until the Ryder Cup began.

CHAPTER EIGHTEEN
September 2021, Whistling Straits

The Ryder Cup

"My favorite question is, 'Would you have done anything different?' I laugh. How much of an arrogant asshole would you have to be to say, 'No, I'd do it the same way'? Of course I'd do things different! For the first year, year and a half, there wasn't a week or sometimes a day that went by when I wasn't thinking, 'This is what I would have done.'"

—Jim Furyk, on captaining the losing
Americans in 2018

"They do everything we've learned. We've taught them a thing or two over the last twenty years. They've caught on. Every little bit of innovation that Europe has introduced to make an edge, they have now."

—Pádraig Harrington, on captaining the
losing Europeans in 2021

The measure of a Ryder Cup captain so often comes down to what he's learned from the past. That's especially true today, when he has forty years of results to study, and those results encompass every kind of scenario: blowouts at home, blowouts on the road, close matches everywhere, comebacks, near comebacks, and all sorts of permutations of pairs and singles success. A captain's job is endlessly complex, and involves details as minute as picking out the team's clothing, but its essence can be boiled down to this: they must have a plan that stands up to history, and because there's so little time to adjust in the heat of battle, they must have backup plans in case the first plan fails, and those plans must also align with what worked in the past.

In Europe's case, "learning from the past" often just means repeating what has been done before, with new innovations here and there but operating on the same basic template. Nick Faldo deviated from the "if it ain't broke" motto because he was too egotistical to follow somebody else's plan, and despite coming off three straight victories, Europe was pasted in Valhalla. Mark James in 1999 threw in his own wrinkle of sitting three different players through the first four sessions, thinking that otherwise his team would be too weak to compete. It failed, and now nobody does that anymore. Where Faldo's "plan" was clearly a bad one, cementing the need for continuity, James's plan was an addition to the template. Nobody knew it was bad until he actually tried, and despite the loss, he contributed to Europe's body of Ryder Cup knowledge.

To America's too. That's the rub here—so much information emerges after a Ryder Cup that any captain who is willing to study can learn not just from his country, but also from his opponent. Paul McGinley learned from the American loss at Medinah that when you hold a big lead heading into singles, you should lead with strength. As it happened, Davis Love III learned from this too, and so would Steve Stricker.

America's learning process is trickier, because until Azinger came along, they never established any kind of system that would feed them information on a year-to-year basis, depriving them of the foundation from which they could tweak and hone their approach. By veering wildly from one captain and one philosophy to another, they granted Europe an advantage that was exploited across the years.

By 2021, there was no longer any reason for that to be true. Azinger had shown a path, and though that was ignored for two of the next three Ryder Cups, the formation of the task force ensured that the learning process would begin in earnest, and that each successive Ryder Cup captaincy would benefit from the inherited knowledge of all that came before.

The advances of the task force are not necessarily profound when you say them out loud. Some remain a secret, but others are plain as day: establish a captaincy succession plan, so that current captains have previously served as vice (and in Stricker's case, have captained a Presidents Cup team), and be sure that at least one recent captain serves as a vice; embrace statistics and the edge they provide; foster chemistry through small pod groups; reduce stress on the players as much as possible; take as many captain's picks as possible, and choose players whose games fit the course; invest the players in the process of forming the team to whatever degree you're able.

They may not sound like earth-shattering ideas now, but it's important to realize that it took Europe decades to get there in order to finally discover an answer for American dominance, and then decades more for America to catch on. What may look like foundational elements for any team sport, or even a business, are plainly *not* obvious in an individualized sport like golf. To arrive there takes insight, and it takes a visionary figure who others can follow. Tony Jacklin and Paul Azinger were those figures, but they came around thirty years apart.

After the 2021 Ryder Cup was finished, Pádraig Harrington told me that he considered Jim Furyk something of an unsung hero to his team, just for the mere fact of being present in Wisconsin after being so thoroughly defeated in Paris. Furyk himself admitted that he compartmentalized that experience, put it aside in a corner of his brain, and somewhat forgot about it, or at least stopped thinking about it actively. The price of helping Stricker and the American team again in 2021 is that this defense mechanism shattered.

"For about a year, I just put it away," he told the AP's Doug Ferguson. "I forgot things, you know . . . and as soon as they opened that one door, my mind went, 'Oh, my God. There it is.'"

Furyk had been unlucky in two respects. First, he was an away captain in an era when the home team had won six of the last seven Ryder Cups, often by huge margins. In Paris, particularly, it also meant that there was very little chance he could get his players to visit Le Golf National unless they played in the French Open. Seven of the twelve members of the European team played there that year, and of those who hadn't, most had played multiple times in the past; from the US team, only Justin Thomas played in the Open, and he wound up with a 4-1 record that week and was far and away America's best player. The rest of the team was unprepared for the test.

Furyk's second piece of bad luck was that Bryson DeChambeau and Tiger Woods caught fire just before the Ryder Cup, winning three of the four FedExCup playoff events, which meant his hands were tied in terms of captain's picks. He would have liked to pick players like Kevin Kisner, Matt Kuchar, and Zach Johnson—shorter but more accurate players whose games would be perfect for Le Golf National—but their form wasn't as strong, and he had no recourse. Woods was plainly exhausted after winning the Tour Championship, and DeChambeau's game wasn't well suited for the narrow fairways and thick rough of the course. Likewise, another captain's pick, Phil Mickelson, had cooled off at the wrong time, but Furyk felt his performance had been too strong throughout the year to pick against him. Combined, these three picks posted an abysmal 0-9 record, which arguably doomed the Americans from the start.

Which raised the first question of the Stricker captaincy: Would he learn from his most immediate predecessor, and the man serving as one of his vice captains?

* * *

It's very difficult for an outsider to know the quality of a Ryder Cup captain before he makes his captain's picks, which meant that all eyes were on Steve Stricker on September 8, when the time came for him to announce his six selections.

Already, it seemed as though he had possibly outmaneuvered Pádraig Harrington simply by accepting so many picks. Stricker started with four, the accepted maximum, but when COVID-19 hit and it looked like the Ryder Cup might be held in 2020, six picks were offered to both captains. Stricker seized the chance, while Harrington stuck with just three. In fact, Harrington had actually *decreased* the number of allotted picks on Team Europe, from four in 2018. I had asked him about this in October 2019 at Whistling Straits, and the question seemed to annoy him just a little, which made me think it wasn't the first time he'd been asked.

"The logic is, basically, anybody you pick is under pressure," he said. "More pressure, more stress, than a player who is qualified."

It was one of those sentiments that felt plausible at the time, but as I came to learn, Team Europe's own statistical gurus, the Twenty First Group, had found in 2018 while working with Thomas Bjørn that captain's picks routinely performed better than the players who qualified at the end of the automatic list.

"We strongly recommended that he should take the maximum number of selections," Blake Wooster wrote afterward, "not only because captain's picks tend to perform better than the guys who qualify in the last couple of automatic spots, but also because we felt it made sense to give himself as much flexibility as possible."

Bjørn listened, taking four picks, but clearly Harrington had not. It's easy to overstate the importance of a small maneuver like this, but it was worth noting that Harrington had been privy to the same information as Bjørn, but still stuck stubbornly to his own logic about "pressure" on captain's picks, even when presented with data to the contrary.

Stricker, by contrast, was almost certainly hearing the same thing from Jason Aquino and Scouts Consulting, and he took the maximum number of picks, expanded it to six when he had the opportunity, and then, when the Ryder Cup was delayed and he had the opportunity to reduce the number of picks back to four—there would, after all, be a full season of points accumulation—he declined, staying with the full six.

"We just thought that it was in the best interests of the team to put our best team forward to give us that flexibility to get the pairings that we feel are best," he said in August 2020. "To get the guys that suit the course better than some other guys. It just gives us a tremendous amount of flexibility."

In addition, he had preempted any debate about whether Mickelson would get a captain's pick by naming him a vice captain a week earlier. After his win at the PGA Championship in May, Mickelson's best finish had been a T-17 in the reduced field at Memphis, but most of the results had been worse, and most recently he had missed the cut at The Northern Trust and finished T-66 in a seventy-person field at the BMW. On some level, he had to know he didn't deserve a spot on the team, and he took it in stride, tweeting that he was "humbled and honored" to be named vice captain. For someone so competitive, it had to sting to not be picked in a year when he had won a major, but publicly he was totally committed.

Stricker wound up picking numbers seven through ten on the points list, then number twelve and number fourteen, skipping Reed at number eleven and Webb Simpson at number thirteen. Which means that, technically, his picks could have been the same even if he had only been allotted two picks. The counterargument here is that perhaps it's easier to skip over number eleven when you have a full six picks than if you only had two or three, especially if number eleven is a known strong match play golfer. Whether you endorse that or not, the contrast here between the two captains is most notable for their *attitudes* rather than the specific outcome. Regardless of how it played out, Stricker was making a strategic decision based on a history of results, while Harrington couldn't be shaken from a conviction that had little evidence to back it up.

At Whistling Straits on September 8, Stricker selected Jordan Spieth, Xander Schauffele, Tony Finau, Harris English, Daniel Berger, and Scottie Scheffler. None of it was particularly surprising—three of the picks were an absolute lock, Harris English seemed all but certain, and Berger had seemed so confident at the Tour Championship that, perhaps incorrectly, many of us in the media felt he was a sure thing. Scheffler, in the last spot, was the only piece of the puzzle that wasn't clear beforehand. In his remarks on each player, Stricker emphasized in various ways that the three major criteria for choosing his captain's picks were chemistry, course fit, and how well they paired together, with course fit the most important of all.

"His stats across the board are very solid from top to bottom," Stricker said of Scheffler, "and the guy makes a lot of birdies, which should do us very well going around Whistling Straits."

In the end, Stricker had a team of six rookies. Darren Clarke had the same number in 2016, and the stage appeared too big for them, but Paul Azinger also had six rookies for his home Ryder Cup at Valhalla, and four of them went undefeated (the only one with a losing record was Stricker himself). It didn't concern Stricker, particularly because three of the rookies, Xander Schauffele, Patrick Cantlay, and Harris English, were already very accomplished on Tour—Schauffele and Cantlay had already proved their merit as a pair in Melbourne—and a fourth, Collin Morikawa, was a two-time major champion who seemed almost nerve-proof. Tony Finau put it best when he said that he had been one of the youngest players in 2018, but now, just three years later, he was one of the oldest. (As for Europe, they were an incredibly old team by Ryder Cup standards, with four players over forty compared to none in that age bracket for the US team.)

There were a few things Stricker valued in Scheffler beyond his statistical suitability for Whistling Straits. His victories over Jon Rahm and Ian Poulter at the WGC Match Play proved his toughness against two of Europe's legends, and he had finished in the top ten of the last three majors of the year. Plus, he had found something favorable in the statistics department: he paired well with Bryson DeChambeau, and Scheffler had written in the team questionnaire a year earlier that he wanted to play with DeChambeau. Stricker envisioned what felt like the perfect role for the rookie: partner with DeChambeau twice in four-balls (the stats even showed they could play alternate shot, if necessary), and then come out as a secret weapon in Sunday singles. It felt McGinley-esque in the way all the puzzle pieces fell into place, and as the last player picked, Scheffler would be thrilled to be on the team in the first place, and wouldn't dread playing with DeChambeau. Even better, his personality was so even-keeled beneath the tough exterior that everybody liked him, DeChambeau included—the two had known each other in college.

Stricker had a great excuse not to select Patrick Reed for the team. There's no real explanation necessary when a player has just been close to death in a hospital and hasn't shown a full recovery. But it became clear that even if Reed had been perfectly healthy, it's unlikely that Stricker would have selected him, a fact he made clear while discussing Scheffler a month after the Ryder Cup.

"We thought he'd be great in the team room," Stricker said. "He gets along well with everybody . . . We just thought it was a really good pick to make a team. There were . . . there could be . . . yeah, I guess that's all I'm going to say, is that we just thought it rounded out our team really well. And I mean *team*, you know? You know what I'm trying to say? And everybody at that level, whoever we would have picked, are very talented, so you're splitting hairs when it comes down to those picks."

"You can tell me to stop pushing if you want," I said, "but what I'm hearing is that all else being equal, when the talent is similar, you're going to get guys that other people like . . . chemistry is going to be a big factor."

"Yup," he said. "And moving forward, I can see six picks being the norm just for that reason."

In a golf world where these things aren't stated outright, especially by someone like Stricker, it was all the indictment of Reed I needed to hear. Stricker remembered what had happened in Paris and Australia, and he saw no reason to give him a third chance.

Of course, after polite words from Stricker publicly about how Reed handled the news—that he took it "like a true champion"—Reed's official Twitter account went on to like more than a dozen tweets that were critical of Stricker for not selecting him, including one that called

Stricker a "coward." If Stricker needed confirmation that he'd made the right choice, he had it. (In December, I attempted to put the question to him directly via text message—if Reed hadn't gotten sick, was he a potential pick? Or had the decision already been made not to? Stricker's reply came with a smiling emoji: "I'll pass on that one.")

It was abundantly clear that Stricker was listening very closely to his statistics team, as well as the players who made the team automatically, all of whom were consulted about captain's picks.

"My message from day one has been to outprepare the other team," he said, and it was easy to believe him.

Four days later, at the conclusion of the BMW PGA Championship, the European Tour's flagship event, Lee Westwood and Bernd Wiesberger had earned their way on to the team on a dramatic final day of action—Westwood by the skin of his teeth, after shooting 77. Shane Lowry was the odd man out, but Harrington rescued him with a pick, and he opted for Sergio García and Ian Poulter as his other two captain's picks. There was nothing wrong with those picks—they were unsurprising, particularly after the fallout—but it's interesting to wonder what might have happened if he had four picks. Using the same system as 2018, that would have excluded Lee Westwood, which would have allowed Harrington to pick Poulter, García, Lowry, and someone like Alex Noren, whom Harrington mentioned by name, or Justin Rose and his lifetime record of 13-8-2. It had been a disappointing year for Rose, but he had capped it off by nearly winning the Wyndham Championship and finishing sixth at the BMW PGA. Westwood, meanwhile, hadn't managed a top-ten finish in five months, and he was forty-eight years old and staring down a tough walking course in Whistling Straits.

Already, there was a crispness of purpose to Stricker's plans, while the European process seemed just the slightest bit shaky, and may have cost them a chance to dump the man who looked like their worst player.

* * *

The second lesson from Paris that Stricker needed to learn was course preparation. The US team didn't start "manipulating" courses to its advantage until Valhalla, but the Europeans had been at it for decades, and Le Golf National represented the next evolution in that process. "They had us over a barrel," Davis Love said, and the better team on paper was lambasted.

From the start, everyone had been telling Stricker that Whistling Straits was a good venue for the Europeans. This was at least half wrong, because the course only *resembled* a links track, but he knew that familiarity would be crucial regardless, especially because it would allow his players to prepare for the Ryder Cup with Whistling Straits foremost on their minds. When we spoke back in 2019, it was already a huge priority.

"Really, my number one goal is to get everybody there together after the twelve guys have been picked," Stricker said. "We have a three-week period in there that may allow us to do that. A practice situation is high on my list, and I've got to try to figure out a way to get everybody there."

He figured it out. There had been Ryder Cup practice sessions before, but never so close to the event, and no captain had managed to get more than nine players together at the same time. Stricker booked Whistling Straits for Sunday, September 12, and Monday, September 13, and eleven players showed up with their caddies—it was important to Stricker that they were included—along with all five assistants. The only exception was Brooks Koepka, who was still nursing a wrist injury and rehabbing with the hope of playing.

Stricker's secret to getting everyone on board was nothing more complicated than sheer persistence. He raised the issue again and again, starting with the veterans, and brought it up so often that by the time the week came around, it would have been almost impossible for anyone to refuse. Here, too, circumstances helped him—there were three open weeks between the Tour Championship and the Ryder Cup, which is not always the case.

Stricker's secondary goal, after course familiarity, was to get the group dynamic established before the week of the Ryder Cup. Despite being a markedly unsentimental captain, Stricker did conduct a team-building exercise, and when I asked him what the exercise was, he responded in his favorite way.

"I'm not really going to tell you about it," he said. "It was something we did together. It was emotional for me . . . I get moved pretty easily . . . and like I said, I can't really delve into what we did there, just because I don't want to."

"I've never seen a team get along so well," Love remembered. "And they were as disciplined and organized as any team I've ever seen. We keep talking about it."

"I thought it was huge, personally," Tony Finau said of the meetup. "Just to get us familiar with the golf course. Whistling Straits isn't a course that's right in front of you. You have to play it a handful of times, and in different winds, before you really understand. And not only that, but to get familiar with some of the guys. It's a real intimate type of feeling."

Finau played with Harris English that week, someone he considered a "hi-bye friend" on Tour to that point, but he got to know him well during the practice rounds and at the team dinner Sunday night at the American Club. They stayed in touch, and Finau now considers English a good friend.

Along with the benefits of team bonding and course familiarity, there was an accidental piece of good fortune that came from this two-day session.

"They got a practice round in the wind of the tournament," Pádraig Harrington said afterward. "That was a big deal. We obviously practiced in the wrong wind through no fault of our own Tuesday, Wednesday, Thursday, but the wind completely flipped for the tournament. So that shows their preparation, fair play."

As for the missing player, Koepka, he represented another issue for Stricker, and in more ways than one.

* * *

Earlier that summer, Stricker had admitted he was concerned about Koepka and DeChambeau.

"It's not making my job any easier, you know?" he said in an interview. "I haven't talked to either one of them. I will have to at some point . . . you can't have an outlier making trouble for everybody else."

That moment came in late August, when Stricker called both of them and received reassurances that it wouldn't be an issue. At the Tour Championship, Stricker held a dinner for the six automatic qualifiers and his vice captains, and the two sat together at the same table.

"I sat right beside Brooks," Davis Love remembered, "and when I saw them, I knew it was fine. Everybody in that room knew it was fine. And more importantly, Brooks and Bryson knew it was going to be fine."

It was so fine that both of them told the captain that they'd go so far as to play together if he wanted. It was a measure of Stricker's wisdom that he considered it, and he even thought it might be a dramatic ace to have up his sleeve in a situation where he was trailing late on Saturday, but ultimately he decided against it because it would focus too much attention on two personalities. Again, this was evidence of what he'd learned—he saw what had happened when Hal Sutton paired Tiger Woods and Phil Mickelson, and how what might be seen on paper as a thrilling combination could potentially backfire in unforeseen ways.

On September 14, just ten days before the start of the Ryder Cup and less than a week before the media blitz began in Whistling Straits, an interview with Koepka was published on *Golf Digest* that was a potential landmine for Stricker. It wasn't about his feud with DeChambeau, but his feelings on the Ryder Cup generally. Koepka didn't hold back.

"It's different," he told Matthew Rudy. "It's hectic. It's a bit odd, if I'm honest. I don't want to say it's a bad week . . . There are times where I'm like, I won my match. I did my job. What do you want from me? . . . You go from an individual sport all the time to a team sport one week a year . . . There are meetings and team building, and you're whisked away for a lot of things like pictures and all that. It's more demanding than

I'm used to, and there's a lot of emotion there, so by Sunday, you're just dead . . . It's just maybe not in my DNA, the team sports thing."

It felt like history repeating—in the lead-up to Ryder Cups, it seems there is always some distraction that threatens to undermine the team, whether it's as minor as Mickelson changing equipment manufacturers in 2004 or as major as Danny Willett's brother writing a funny but ill-timed anti-American screed in 2016 and essentially ruining his week.

Predictably, Koepka was trashed in the press, with Paul Azinger saying what many people thought, which is that if he doesn't love the Ryder Cup, he should give up his spot, particularly because it would prevent him from having to deal with DeChambeau in close quarters.

Stricker was worried enough about the interview that he called Koepka, but what he heard in those conversations was wildly different from what was printed in the interview, or so he claimed in a press conference at the Ryder Cup.

"What I have personally seen in the team room does not jive up to what I was reading in those articles," he said, while affirming to the press that the Brooks-Bryson feud was a "nonissue."

The true measure of how a captain handles these controversies is not necessarily how players like Koepka and DeChambeau *feel*, but how they act that week, and how thoroughly the captain and his team can snuff out the story leading up to the event. At the Melbourne Presidents Cup, it had proven impossible for the team to escape the Patrick Reed incident, but that occurred just a week before, and this had been going on so long that Stricker had time to prepare.

For a man with a personality that doesn't come across as forceful, Stricker once again proved that he had complete command of his team. He was able to get DeChambeau to speak to the print media, which hadn't happened in over a month, and taking a page out of Azinger's book, he seemed to have everyone prepared if they were asked about the two. On Tuesday, Koepka approached DeChambeau on the range for a quick chat, and the Ryder Cup USA account and the official website were sure to be there to take video and run stories on the innocuous meeting. And while that may have felt forced, it made a point: there would be no fighting.

The team was so successful at shutting down these narratives that by Wednesday, nobody was really asking anymore—it had been done to death, and even if Brooks Koepka hated DeChambeau and the Ryder Cup in his heart of hearts, there was no fuel for the fire. It wasn't just a performance for the media, either—Scottie Scheffler remembered that on the first night at Whistling Straits, DeChambeau was sitting with Koepka and his fiancée, Jena Sims, at dinner, and he and his teammates assumed from signs like that that the story was over.

Before the pandemic hit, McGinley said that Stricker's captaincy would be defined by how well he handled four specific personalities: Reed, DeChambeau, Phil, and Tiger. Circumstances forced Tiger out of the Ryder Cup, but the American captain had effectively incorporated Mickelson as a vice captain (and somewhat sidelined him in the process), excluded Reed without much in the way of pushback from any arena but Reed's Twitter account, and solved DeChambeau, plus Koepka to boot.

* * *

Despite assuring the press that Koepka did indeed "love" the Ryder Cup, Stricker also took his words to heart. In fact, the concept of being worn out by Ryder Cup week was not unfamiliar to him—or to the other players. Long before we knew about the pandemic, Stricker told me that he was "trying to reduce the amount of fluff" that comes with the event.

"I want to just make it about being together as a group, and the golf," he said, "and to me, that's all there is."

In his time playing in the Ryder Cup, Stricker had experienced first-hand how the obligations could wear the players down, and he knew that if Koepka was saying it out loud, other people were thinking it. Golfers are a selfish breed; they thrive on certainty and routine, and if the goal is to get them to play their best golf, then Stricker knew that reducing the number of galas and autograph obligations and everything else would be an important part of his job. As it turned out, COVID-19 would hand him a major assist in this regard. He was prepared to fight to limit the obligations, but he never had to, and the responsibilities that week in Whistling Straits consisted of team dinners and not much else.

In the week leading up to the Ryder Cup, there's a good deal of hype around speeches and videos and other motivational elements. Stricker never felt particularly impressed by anything he'd seen in that regard, and he knew that speechmaking would be his worst attribute as a captain—he was dreading his opening ceremony speech as early as 2019, and rightly so, as he would manage to get the home crowd to boo him. In his lone attempt at what Davis Love III called a "tough guy" speech to the team at Whistling Straits, he managed to get a few seconds in before he began crying.

"I wasn't going to cry on this one," he said.

"We *know* you're going to cry," they reassured him.

On his distaste for speechmaking, he was in sync with the rest of his team. The American golfers, even the youngest rookies, all had egos and wanted to win. They didn't need to be fired up—the most that was said in terms of motivation, according to Scottie Scheffler, came at the team dinners when the players who were in Paris conveyed how awful it had been to watch the Europeans celebrate on the green. (On that note, the procedure changed for 2021, in that the losing team no longer had to stay by the eighteenth green for the winning team's trophy presentation. When it was all over, Tony Finau remarked on the change, and seemed disappointed that the Europeans hadn't been forced to watch them.)

In fact, what was required of a leader was organization and preparation, and it was clear from the beginning that Stricker had delivered—"It seems, wow, these guys didn't even need to have a practice round, and they've got a lot of it figured out," Jordan Spieth said on Tuesday. Some media elements sought to discover the beating heart of Team USA, whether it was a secretly eloquent Stricker, or Phil Mickelson leading behind the scenes, or a player like Justin Thomas, but they were routinely disappointed—it wasn't a role that needed to be filled. And even though it was Stricker's natural inclination to stay silent, this too had been modeled for him in his first Ryder Cup as a player.

"During the week itself, I was a man of few words," Paul Azinger—a much more gifted speaker—told me. "I didn't say jack. No talking, nothing. There were no motivational speeches, none of that."

Davis Love was astounded at how little was said to the players, which marked a difference even from how Stricker ran his Presidents Cup team in 2017, when each night there were team meetings (though Furyk did most of the talking at those).

"He was so prepared when he got there," he said, "and the guys were so prepared that we had this big, beautiful table with a flag on it, and we got the whole team in there maybe once during the week. He did his team meetings at the golf course, and he did them quick."

Everything was broken into smaller units, right down to the group text messages. There was one between him and the players, with no vice captains, one between all the vices, one for each vice captain and their pod, and so forth. On this front, he was a devoted student of Azinger.

It was different in the European locker room. Catriona Matthew, the winning Solheim Cup captain, was the motivational speaker. A series of videos were released during the week, complete with sprawling seaside landscapes and stirring music, celebrating the history of the team and attempting to inspire the current players. The most famous of these made the point that fewer men had represented Europe in the Ryder Cup—164—than had been in space. A series of former players and captains urged the current crop to "make it count," and while the video struck me as corny, several European players, including Ian Poulter, remarked on how meaningful it had been. To say it would have fallen flat on the American side is a massive understatement, but the Europeans have always been more sentimental, and for them it was a success.

"The difference is, they operate in four pods of three," Harrington said, misstating the math slightly. "We operate in one pod of twelve. I was very keen that everybody on the team got the team experience with everybody. In the US, they clearly have issues in terms of, they want to keep private pods, because they've struggled in the past with that, haven't they?"

"Personality clashes?" I asked.

"Yeah, yeah, yeah."

Which is possibly why the American perspective is far less romantic. For so long, American captains attempted to copy the European system and engender a kind of brotherhood during Ryder Cup week, but what Azinger learned, and what men like Stricker had internalized at last, is that you can't have a European solution for an American problem. Professional golfers in the United States are the best in the world on their individual merits, and the way to get them to play to their level at the Ryder Cup is to preserve that individuality by any means necessary.

* * *

For those who didn't know, the practice round pairings made it abundantly clear early in Ryder Cup week that Stricker was operating on a pod system. On Tuesday, he put out Thomas, Spieth, Scheffler, and DeChambeau in the first pod; followed by Schauffele, Cantlay, Johnson, and Morikawa; and Koepka, Berger, Finau, and English in the third. There were slight differences on Wednesday, but on Thursday the same exact lineups were used, right down to the order in which they took the course. In fact, of the sixteen pairs matches that were played on Friday and Saturday, all but two came from these pods. One of the others, Cantlay-Thomas, was hinted at in the Wednesday changes, and only one, Koepka-Spieth on Saturday afternoon, seemed to come completely out of left field. Afterward, Pádraig Harrington lamented this element of Stricker's preparation.

"Very early in the week, he told them who they were going to be playing with and whether they would play foursomes or four-ball," he said. "We did the same thing in Europe, and that clarity is massive for players. One of the big stressors for US players in the past has been the doubt. But they got a lot of notice, and they clearly bought in to the fact that they wouldn't necessarily be playing foursomes or four-ball even if they were one of the best players on the team."

"One of the things I voiced to the captain was, 'I don't care what you have me doing, just give me an idea of what you see me doing so I can be prepared for it,'" Scottie Scheffler said. "That was kind of the theme of the whole week, that we're going to be as prepared as possible so there are no surprises and you can go out and play good golf."

This was not uncommon. Two years earlier, Henrik Stenson told me how he demanded that Ian Woosnam let him know on Thursday whether he'd be playing at all on Friday after he found out he'd be sitting in the morning session.

"Someone else might be like, 'Yeah, that's cool,'" he said of learning about a match at the last minute. "I'm pretty sure DJ would be like, 'Yeah, I got my clubs here, I'll be fine in an hour and a half.' But I want to be able to plan my day."

As early as Monday night, Stricker sat the team down and told them what the Friday pairings would be, as well as a blueprint for Saturday that was subject to change based on the results up to that point.

On the European side, the practice round pairings were an inscrutable puzzle. I felt like John Nash in *A Beautiful Mind* as I documented the foursomes from Tuesday through Thursday, and I couldn't make any sense of what I was seeing. This was just as true after the Ryder Cup as it was before. Sergio García, for instance, played with Lee Westwood in each practice round, and with nobody else even twice, but he never played with Westwood once in the Cup, and he played with Jon Rahm in each of his three pairs sessions.

Up and down the list, there was very little rhyme or reason to the teams Harrington was putting on the course, and it becomes even stranger when you learn that he, like Stricker, had established his Friday pairings early on. When the lineups came out on Thursday evening, none of the pairs had been together more than once in the preceding three days—in fact, only six of the sixteen European pairs would have seen each other more than once in the practice rounds—and when I asked him why, he gave a somewhat surprising answer.

"You don't want to get bored playing with a guy," he said. "Honestly, I've had it in tournaments, you play three days with somebody, and then you're playing with them the next five, four rounds of golf . . . I wanted everybody on my team to play with everybody on the team, and not turn up on a week like this and by the end of the week go, 'I never experienced that player.' . . . I know I'm probably the first captain to do it like that, but certainly every captain has to bring their own personal experience. You just want to turn up on Friday and still have that freshness and enthusiasm and excitement and I suppose a little bit of intrigue."

The charitable reading of this is that it's a novel idea. The uncharitable reading is that his team already had less preparation than the Americans on a course that rewarded repeat exposure, and now he was depriving his players of a chance to become familiar with each other's style in the limited time available before the high stress of the match itself.

On Wednesday, another bit of drama occurred when a player on the European team expressed that he was having trouble with his Friday partner's ball, and that he wanted a change. Reports indicated that it came from the Westwood/Casey/Fitzpatrick/Hovland group, where the balls hadn't meshed as originally expected, even though all four play Titleist. Later, it emerged that the player who was bothered was Matthew Fitzpatrick, and based on the practice pairings on Wednesday, it's clear he was originally slated to go out with Viktor Hovland, while Lee Westwood was supposed to go with Paul Casey. The last-minute switch meant that Westwood would be paired with Fitzpatrick and Casey with Hovland on Friday morning.

Harrington told me that none of this was as big a deal as the press made it sound—he was frustrated that it became a story—and that he and his vice captains had considered the balls beforehand, but that with so many players playing different balls, it was impossible to find a perfect solution anyway. It occurred to me as he said this, though, that if Fitzpatrick had been with Hovland on Tuesday—if Harrington hadn't been set on playing everyone with everyone—they would have identified the problem at least a day earlier, and I also sensed, for whatever minimal impact it might have had on the overall outcome, that one way or another, Steve Stricker would have sussed out this issue far earlier.

In fact, Davis Love said something to me—without meaning to reference Harrington—that hinted at this exact issue.

"In 2002, on Friday night, I'm out hitting Tiger's extra golf balls up and down the edge of the range to see if I can play it for him the next day," he said. "No, no, no, no. We're not ever doing that again."

In fact, Love said he got his hands on the list of balls every player used, and had it saved on his phone so that they could plan pairings well in advance.

* * *

To illustrate Harrington's personality, Paul McGinley told me a story from a dinner they shared together in August with their wives, just two weeks before the Ryder Cup. They were watching the US Open women's tennis final, cheering for the surprise British player Emma Raducanu. Halfway through the first set, she hit a first serve into the net.

"That's interesting," said Harrington. "She's not OCD."

When McGinley questioned him, he pointed out that after netting the serve, she had used the ball again after it bounced back. His wife, Carolina, said that maybe she *was* OCD, and maybe using the same ball was her ritual.

"No," said Harrington. "That's the third time it's happened, and the two times she used the same ball, but the other time she tossed it away."

That's what McGinley meant when he told me that Harrington was a lateral thinker.

"That's the shit he notices that went completely over my head," he said. "That's the world Pádraig Harrington lives in."

McGinley and Harrington are good friends, and like any close friends, they defend each other but also have a way of seeing each other's flaws. When I first spoke to Harrington, he referenced how ambitious McGinley had been in pursuing the Ryder Cup captaincy—"I'm trying to say this in a nice way . . . he *lobbied* for it"—and spoke about how the time and effort McGinley put into the job turned it into a full-time affair and put a certain amount of stress and pressure on everyone who followed.

McGinley, for his part, had his own quiet reservations about Harrington, buffered as they were by compliments on his intelligence.

"How are we different?" he said when I posed the question. "Ah, fuck me, who's the same as Pádraig? This guy's thinking on a different level than 99 percent of people, particularly golfers. Nobody is on his level.

"He was the youngest of the bunch," he added, speaking of Harrington's place in a family of five boys and a policeman for a dad. "He had to learn to survive, and he learned by being clever, and he *is* clever. He's bright. He's a qualified accountant who did four years of college. How many professional golfers can say that?

"My only worry with him," he continued, "is that he makes it too complicated. There's genius in simplicity. Pádraig loves picking holes, and he was a very important sounding board for me. As we say in Ireland, he sees around corners. He can overthink it, and that's fine, that's what he's done all his life, but overcommunicating it, that's the problem. And he's a talker. Rory's a talker too. Does that help him all the time? I don't think so. You guys love it, you tell him how great he is because he gives you lots of content. But does it help?"

The "lateral thinking" issue came into my mind with his decision not to put pairs together in practice rounds because he wanted "intrigue," and again when he opted to take fewer captain's picks because he thought it put undue pressure on them, and again with the alternate shot issue. There was always the risk that Harrington could lose the bigger picture, and McGinley's other worry about his friend was that he hadn't included enough diversity of opinion on the team. It's why McGinley had included Harrington as his own vice captain, despite Sergio García being extremely against the move (McGinley had to negotiate with García for weeks to make it happen). And he wasn't sure that Harrington had surrounded himself with people who would challenge him, though he admitted he wasn't close enough to the team to know for sure.

As it was, both of Harrington's new partnerships lost on Friday and put the team in a big hole. The drama with Fitzpatrick wouldn't leak until after the Ryder Cup, and it's worth noting that Harrington's captaincy seemed quite competent, and his players liked and respected him and were disappointed that they couldn't ultimately win for him. Still, when he sat on stage Thursday night and said that he avoided having his partnerships practice together to preserve "intrigue," the suspicions that had been growing in my mind all week were solidified—he wasn't the same thorough captain that Stricker was, and when you factored in the advantages that the US team already enjoyed, the week ahead could be a very long one.

An inescapable truth of the Ryder Cup since 2008 is that the numbers show a massive advantage for the home team. This fact is often obscured by 2012 and the European comeback at Medinah, but as much as we look at history for patterns and trends, and as useful as that can be, we also have to understand when an anomaly is staring us in the face. Whatever quibbles you have with Davis Love III's strategy, his loss at Medinah was a fluke, built on a pyramid of absurd longshots coming through one after another, and if any one of them failed, Europe would have lost. This is the kind of thing that happens when you have a tournament with such a small sample size, but it's so anomalous that it doesn't happen more than once or twice in a generation.

In the last three home Ryder Cups, America has come out of the pairs sessions with leads of 9-7, 10-6, and 9.5-6.5. It works the other way too: in the last three Ryder Cups in Europe, the Europeans have held pre-singles leads of 9.5-6.5, 10-6, and 10-6. In pairs matches, the home team is 58-38 in the last six Ryder Cups. That's a 60 percent winning mark, and though things can get unpredictable in singles, it was possible to guess with great confidence that the United States would head into Sunday with a lead.

There are factors like course setup that are important, but even more important—probably by a lot—are the home crowds. They're loud, they're boisterous, and they occasionally cross the line. (Like clockwork, stories emerge from each Ryder Cup of the away team being mistreated by fans.) It creates a stressful, defensive atmosphere for the visiting team and provides endless waves of energy to the home side. To overcome that dynamic requires incredible fortitude and a lot of luck, and in 2021, because of COVID-19, Whistling Straits hosted fewer Europeans than ever before—much to Harrington's dismay. You could argue, not without evidence, that Europe's one chance of a win in Whistling Straits was if it had been held in 2020 without fans.

Then there are the players. The US team is always better than the European team on paper, and they were far better suited to the challenges of Whistling Straits. While there were players like Collin Morikawa, whose recent form had dipped, and others like Koepka with injury concerns, those were matched on Europe's side by players like Lee Westwood, Tyrrell Hatton, and Matthew Fitzpatrick, who were also struggling.

We were in the Blowout Era, though it wasn't always easy to recognize, and when you take a team like the United States with more depth and talent, throw in a captain that appeared to be somewhere between competent and very good, and put that team in front of forty thousand rabid home fans every day, there was only one sensible conclusion: America was going to win, and win big.

But only a few of us actually believed it.

One was McGinley himself. I happened to run across him Thursday night, just off duty from his job as a commentator at Sky Sports, and while he was always reserved in second-guessing anyone on Team Europe, including his friend Harrington, he was pessimistic about their chances. It was not because of Harrington, but because of how strong the Americans appeared, and how ably they were being led by Stricker. He wondered aloud if perhaps Harrington should revive the Mark James strategy by leaning on four good partnerships in a desperate bid to hide the weaker players and build up a lead before Sunday singles. He wasn't sure it was a great idea, but already it seemed like something radical was needed.

It's never wise to discount European magic, but as the sun set on Whistling Straits Thursday, it was already becoming very difficult to envision Europe's path to victory.

*   *   *

"People talk about that first tee shot of the Ryder Cup being very nervous . . . It wasn't for me. I let David Hall take it."
—Henrik Stenson

"I got another question. How the hell are we going to get European fans into Whistling Straits? We've got a serious issue."
—Paul Casey

On Friday morning, hordes of fans congregated in the stadium seating around the first tee while it was still dark. They wore Uncle Sam hats and Miracle on Ice hockey jerseys, and they waved flags of all shapes and sizes. All around, the media worked the crowd, mining the local color, and here and there a few chants rose: "U-S-A!" and "I believe that we will win!" A DJ played music, everything from "Jump Around" to "Sweet Caroline," and when the few scattered Europeans tried to start a chant of their own, they were booed into silence. Even the "Guardians of the Cup," the European group of singers who are a presence in every Ryder Cup, couldn't get much going, and they were regaled with chants of "Where's your vax card?" (Along with a few rogue shots from the worst America had to offer, like the one fan who took it on himself to shout that they "should be wearing turbans.")

Beyond the Guardians, there was a noticeable absence of European fans. Even in past US Cups, they could be seen traveling in packs, and when things went well, as at Medinah, they could make a lot of noise. Harrington himself had assumed that it would be 80/20 in favor of US fans, but it became clear that morning that the visiting team would have almost no support, much less anything close to 20 percent.

A blood orange sun rose over Lake Michigan, and a day that would turn out to be windy and pleasant began. Various American hype men came to the first tee, from Steve Stricker to Bryson DeChambeau to Tony Finau. Pádraig Harrington was booed roundly. When the European golfer Ross Fisher took to Twitter to call this "shocking etiquette," the time-honored tradition began—the away team decrying the behavior of the fans. Fisher had apparently forgotten how the fans in Paris booed Furyk, and all week the fans in Whistling Straits would be measurably better than the wild crowds at Hazeltine, but none of that mattered when it came time to stand on the soapbox.

A bridge led from the putting green by the clubhouse to the tunnel on the back side of the grandstands, and at 7:03 a.m., Justin Thomas and Jordan Spieth emerged together from the tunnel onto the tee. They received the first of many true Ryder Cup roars, and they were set to take on Sergio García and Jon Rahm in the opening match.

One of the great mysteries of the modern Ryder Cup stems from the fact that America always chooses to play foursomes (alternate shot) in the morning on Friday and Saturday, while the Europeans always opt to play it in the afternoon. It's practically a doctrine at this point, but when I asked Aquino, the stats guru, exactly why it was done this way—what advantage did it confer?—he was coy. I pressed, arguing that the order is no longer any great surprise, and he told me that because the statistics show that each side is more successful with their own order, this is how it's done. He claimed that nobody knows quite why it works that way— it could be that there's no advantage beyond home course advantage— but that the numbers tell a story, and everybody obeys them. I could not tell if this was true, or if he was just guarding the real secret, but since 2006, this is how it's gone on both sides of the Atlantic.

The sun was incredibly bright off Lake Michigan as the match began, and the US team struck first when Justin Thomas buried a seven-footer on the par-5 second hole. Alternate shot is a famously volatile format, though, and the Spaniards won the next two holes on long putts from Jon Rahm—the second one a fifty-eight-footer. Meanwhile, the most energy Justin Thomas could muster came when the Europeans wouldn't concede a two-foot putt on the sixth hole, and by way of complaint, he held his putter by the grip to show how short it had been.

This was the start of a spectacular Ryder Cup for Rahm, the world number one. His team needed him to be a hero in order to have any chance to upset the Americans, and that's exactly what he was. He followed up that torrid start with a twelve-footer and a fourteen-footer on holes seven and eight—Europe had wisely aligned them so that Rahm would be doing the majority of the putting on the front nine—and when Sergio hit his iron on the tenth hole to gimme range, the Spanish team was 3-up against one of America's toughest pairings.

The acumen of the two was wonderful to witness, in its way—the living embodiment of the Spanish duos who had lifted Europe for decades, from Ballesteros on down the line. The Americans scraped a hole back on thirteen, but on fifteen it was García's turn to hit a twenty-four-foot birdie and put his team 3-up with three to play—a situation called "dormie," when the worst the leading team can do is win a half point, and the trailing team must win all the remaining holes to avoid defeat. The Americans birdied sixteen to stay alive, but when García's tee shot on the long par-3 seventeenth reached the front of the green and Justin Thomas went left, the rest was formality; the Europeans won 3&1 to put the first point of the Ryder Cup on the board. (On that hole, Spieth still managed to hit one of the most memorable shots of the entire Ryder Cup—stuck at the base of a sheer grass wall below the hole, he hacked into the deep grass, popped the ball high in the air, and nearly fell over as his momentum forced him to run almost all the way down to the water. He never saw his ball land six feet from the hole. Thomas, who couldn't buy a putt all day, missed the six-footer for par, and the match was over.)

"They made about 150 feet of putts," Spieth said after the match, somewhat ruefully. "Sometimes you run into a buzzsaw."

On the course, the American fans were subdued in the morning. Even the songs by the Guardians and their opposite—a group of Americans in Viking helmets—felt tame. Lone cries were the most memorable shows of energy: "Put on a uniform!" someone yelled to Mickelson, and when Jena Sims walked past the ninth hole in Koepka's match, another fan yelled, "Jena, I follow you on social media!" Lee Westwood took some predictable heckles about never winning a major, Jordan Spieth had a fan kicked out for some infraction, and the media and fans were discovering together how difficult the hilly course was to walk if you weren't on the fairways.

"The good news is they're about to start selling beer," said one man behind the ninth green, moments before 10:00 a.m.

It's tempting to call this moment the high point of the Ryder Cup for Europe—fans relatively quiet, score at 1-0 to the visitors—and maybe there's truth to that, but by the time that first match concluded, the news was already bad for Europe.

In a metaphorical sense, the first point was already on the board, and had been hours earlier. In the final match of the morning session, Xander Schauffele and Patrick Cantlay had won the first five holes against one of the scariest European teams on the board, Rory McIlroy and Ian Poulter. Schauffele's approach on the first hole stopped five feet away, the Europeans made a mess of the second after a poor drive and weak approach from McIlroy, Cantlay's tee shot on the par-3 third came to rest less than nine feet away, and the Euros bogeyed again on four when Rory sprayed his drive left. With a chance to stop the bleeding on five, Poulter hit his approach to eight feet, while Cantlay hit a weak effort to thirty-six feet. Then, in a classic match play moment, Schauffele plunged a dagger into the Europeans by sinking his long putt, and Rory was sufficiently rattled to miss the short one. The Americans were 5-up after five holes.

They played the string out, and the match ended with a 5&3 win for the US, but it was essentially over the minute Schauffele made his putt on five. The result was a relief for Stricker and his vice captains. They saw how strong the Schauffele-Cantlay pairing could be in Melbourne, and they knew the two were good friends, but statistically they weren't a perfect match, and it had been a calculated risk to keep them together. In the aftermath, the partners praised each other and alluded to a text from Tiger Woods that had inspired them (the content of which would become one of the big mysteries of the Ryder Cup).

In the middle matches, Harrington's last-minute change of pairs came back to bite him, with Brooks Koepka and Daniel Berger taking down Westwood and Fitzpatrick in the third match. Berger was considered the team's alternate shot expert, able to pair with anybody, but it was Koepka who arguably played the more spectacular shots as the Americans birdied five of their first eleven holes. The odd couple pairing of Dustin Johnson and Collin Morikawa—a pair that was actually flagged as high-risk by the statistical models—completed the strong morning with a victory over Casey and Hovland.

Stricker had phoned Johnson and Morikawa separately more than a month before the Ryder Cup. He knew they were both shoo-ins for automatic qualification, and when he thought of pairing them together, it seemed like a potential superteam, despite what the statistics said ("We went against that," said Stricker, "because who doesn't pair well with those guys?"). Morikawa was thrilled about the idea of pairing with Johnson, and said that he had played pairs golf in college with a player of similar temperament, and it worked perfectly with his own personality. Johnson was similarly amenable; he probably would have said, "Sure, Strick," regardless of the partner, but being paired with the game's strongest iron and wedge player was a particularly easy sell.

"Statistically it doesn't make sense," Davis Love said of the pairing. "I'd write down Brooks and DJ every time, but they don't want to play together. They want to hang out, they ride to the hotel together, but they know they're just a little bit oil and water on the course. But somehow DJ and Morikawa just knew they were going to be great together. Just like I knew I was great with Fred Couples. Some captains split us up, and thought they'd take their two long drivers and make two good teams. But we're happy together!"

In their first match Friday morning, Morikawa's approaches were typically pristine, and signaled a piece of very bad news to Pádraig Harrington and Europe—his brief end-of-year slump was over. In the decisive moments, though, it was Johnson whose irons made the difference.

His approach to five feet on eleven, along with a tee shot inside five feet on the par-3 twelfth, led to birdies, and from there the Americans coasted to a 3&2 win.

And they were fully secure in their surroundings. After, Davis Love joked about how Austin Johnson, Dustin's brother and caddie, trusted Love so completely that when it became clear it wasn't going to rain on Friday morning, he threw his umbrella in the rough for Love to pick up. The rest of the morning, Love carried the umbrella, drawing endless heckles from the fans who kept reminding him that it wouldn't rain.

"I'll be honest," said Morikawa after, "I was more nervous at the Walker Cup."

It wasn't quite a perfect start for Stricker, but it was close—his team led 3-1 heading into four-ball. Still, nobody felt remotely comfortable. You didn't need a long memory to remember Paris, when the US team led by the exact same score after the morning session, only for the Europeans to sweep the afternoon matches and erase all American momentum. In fact, Europe had won the Friday-afternoon session by a score of 3-1 or more for the last three Ryder Cups.

When the lineups came out for the afternoon, there were murmurs of surprise in the media center. It was all but known that DeChambeau and Scheffler would make one four-ball pair and Finau and English another—Stricker, along with most modern captains, wanted everyone to play on the first day—but for the other two pairs, it seemed likely that he'd pick two of his winning teams from the morning. Instead, he split up Cantlay/Schauffele and Johnson/Morikawa, opting for Johnson/Schauffele in the first spot and Thomas/Cantlay anchoring the session. That was his scripted plan from early in the week, backed up by Scouts Consulting's statistical models, and he wasn't going to deviate now.

* * *

Like everything else he touched, it worked. The afternoon session was more tense and closer overall than the morning, with the wind reaching as high as 25 mph, but the situation on the ground was that Europe was struggling to find a lead, and the "sure thing" matches all leaned American from the start. Finau and English, who had become friends at the meetup two weeks earlier, traded pars with the all-Irish team of McIlroy and Shane Lowry for four holes, lost the fifth, and then rattled off four wins in five holes, punctuated by Finau driving the green on the short par-4 sixth and missing his eagle putt by inches. Finau would end up with six birdies in just fifteen holes, and his eleven-footer for birdie on thirteen was the final decisive blow in a 4&3 victory.

In the leadoff match, Xander Schauffele once again got off to a hot start, establishing a 3-up lead after five with Johnson over Wiesberger and Casey. The Europeans fought back to 1-down at the turn, but the uphill par-4 tenth, with its drive over the gully and uphill approach, usually into the wind, was proving to be a favorite battleground for the Americans, who would win it in three of the four matches that afternoon. This time it was Johnson who made birdie, which he followed up with a fifteen-footer to win the eleventh. That putt earned a massive cheer from Michael Jordan, who had set up behind the hole with a beer, a cigar, and what looked like two bodyguards. After Johnson's third straight birdie on 12, the US team was 3-up, and Schauffele's dad wore a big grin as his wild hair was blown by the gusts. (Schauffele would later joke that they'd had "all the seasons" during the round.) Time was running out. Casey gave them a prayer with a birdie on sixteen, and Weisberger followed up with one of his own a hole later, but when Schauffele lagged a sixty-two-foot putt to two feet, that match too was over.

At that moment, the Europeans were down 5-1, and Harrington was facing a reality no captain wants to face—the match was becoming dangerously lopsided on the first day.

"I know this," Azinger had told me the night before. "Pádraig Harrington is scared to *death* that they might lose."

"For his own legacy?"

"Of course! But he's freaking out, because he doesn't have control of it."

Now Harrington was starting to see the shape of things, and to stare down the barrel of his biggest fear.

Europe had its best highlight of the day in the second match out on the course, when Rahm, the hero of the morning, paired with Tyrrell Hatton, found himself in a grudge match with DeChambeau and Scheffler. On the fifth hole, DeChambeau put his name in for shot of the Ryder Cup when he made the choice to cut off the dogleg on the par-5 and go straight at the flag. The shot was downwind, which he'd been hoping for, and that morning on the range, he'd been achieving ball speeds over 200 mph. If the moment was ever going to be right, it was now. He aimed about one hundred yards right of the fairway, waggled his club, swung, and took a dramatic two-step as the ball soared away.

Comically, the Golf Channel cameras were panning back and forth looking for the shot on the fairway, but they were about one hundred yards too short. When they finally found the ball, it was rolling farther than any ball had the right to roll. While Rahm, Hatton, and Scheffler had between 243 and 274 yards left on their approach, DeChambeau was within 72 yards.

Nobody loved it more than Phil Mickelson, who was so energized by the shot that he shouted, in DeChambeau's words, "some things that cannot be repeated." DeChambeau made eagle and won the hole, which was lucky, because he told Scheffler after the drive landed that if he somehow made par, he was going to walk home.

"When you have Bryson do things like what he did on five," Rahm said later, "you know you're going to have a couple holes where a half is going to be a very good score."

A back-and-forth affair ensued, and on the twelfth hole, after Rahm hit his tee shot to twenty inches, DeChambeau responded by hitting his to nineteen. The fans went wild, and as the players approached the green, they conceded each other's putts, and the crowd began chanting DeChambeau's name. In that moment, it was possible to put aside all the complications and feel good for him after a miserable summer.

Michael Jordan, a fixture at American Ryder Cups, was still sipping his beer and smoking his stogie on eleven when the DeChambeau group rolled through, and Henrik Stenson made Jordan laugh when he told him he was going to come to his club and take all his money. Along the thirteenth hole, a half dozen boats were anchored in the green-brown water, and on fourteen, I found Phil Mickelson giving updates inside the ropes to none other than Steph Curry. Both of them were soon accosted by a man in a chicken costume screaming, "Caw! Caw!" at them. (Curry cawed back.)

On eighteen, the Europeans desperately needed a birdie to keep the US team from going up by the gaudy score of 6-1. Rahm's approach went to twenty feet, and Scheffler also reached safely, but Hatton gave his team a chance with a 202-yard approach that stopped seven feet from the pin. Scheffler and DeChambeau had short par putts, which meant the pressure was squarely on Hatton, who had not carded a birdie since the first hole. With all eyes on him—someone in the crowd yelled, "In case you didn't know it, this is kind of the definition of a must-make!"—he buried the putt to stave off disaster. A tribe of European staffers following the match cheered with a defiant kind of anger, clearly upset at the American crowd.

After the match, a strange scene occurred when an American fan came to the edge of the bleachers and shouted Jon Rahm's name until he reluctantly looked back.

"You suck!"

"As do you," Rahm shot back, and other American fans booed the heckler.

Standing with his team, DeChambeau was disappointed to halve the match. "Needed to get that one," he said.

In the anchor match, Stricker's surprise pairing of Thomas and Cantlay seemed not to be working out, as the duo lost four holes between three and eight to go 3-down. Thomas woke himself up with a thirty-two-foot birdie on the ninth, and in a case of terrible timing, the Europeans went completely cold. They'd only make one more birdie the entire match, and that came from Hovland on the par-5 sixteenth. The bad news for him was that Thomas smashed a 282-yard approach on that same hole, then sank the seventeen-footer for eagle. On eighteen, almost the entire American team gathered on the hillside behind the green to watch the conclusion. All four players gave themselves long birdie putts, but in what looked like a must-win match for the Europeans, pars from each team resulted in a disappointing half. After the match, Thomas was so hoarse from shouting his way through two grueling matches that he barely had a voice left to do his interviews.

By day's end, Stricker's side held a 6-2 lead. It was the biggest first-day advantage any team had held since 2004, and the biggest for the US team since 1975. The American goals shifted in the face of that reality—with one good session, one good day, they could get to the point where a comeback was all but impossible.

As for Harrington, he tried to talk himself into the idea that Hatton's putt might be a momentum swing, à la Poulter's Saturday heroics at Medinah. He submitted his pairings for Saturday before Stricker—in what would become a common theme, the Americans took the maximum allowed time to grind over their own lineups—and he did his best to defend Rory McIlroy after his 0-2 start.

Stricker took us through his own day. He arrived at the course at 5:30 a.m., planning to enjoy some golf in the morning, but instead hung out by the par-3s as each group came through, being present in case his players needed help or advice on how the hole was playing. The American team had decided over the years that that was the best use for a captain during actual play, until it was time to begin the long planning meetings for the next sessions.

"Davis and Jim told me you don't get to see a lot of golf," Stricker said. "And they were right."

The largest turnaround in Sunday singles history was a 5.5-point swing by the Europeans at Medinah, which meant that to keep outpacing history and prevent the Europeans from having a slight prayer of retaining the Cup, there was a clear target for Saturday: 11 points. Reach that, and the Cup was theirs before anyone even teed off on Sunday.

* * *

With such a massive lead, Stricker now had some built-in advantages. The biggest of these was that he didn't need to change anything—he knew exactly which teams were playing well (i.e., most of them), and he could load his lineup in such a way that Harrington, now more desperate for points, would potentially have to play into his hands.

That dynamic came to pass with the Saturday-morning foursomes lineups. Harrington had led with Rahm and García Friday morning, but as he explained it to me, the ultimate goal of winning a pairs session is to place your worst team against the other team's best—a four seed versus a one seed, to put it in college basketball terms—and then give yourself a small edge in all the other matches. This kind of "stacking" is easier said than done, because it's not at all predictable how the other captain will send out his lineup, and Harrington himself had made sure to play Rahm in the second spot on Friday afternoon to avoid the Americans pulling that tactic on him.

On Saturday morning, though, trailing 6-2, early momentum would be critical, and thus he led with Rahm and García once again.

"I just *had* to," Harrington said. "I couldn't avoid it. The fact of the matter is we had to get the points, and to get them as quick as we could." (Interestingly, he also opted to rest Rory McIlroy, who had been playing poorly. A logical decision, but noteworthy because it was the first time in twenty-seven Ryder Cup sessions that he'd ever been benched.)

As Harrington saw it, the Americans knew this was coming, and deliberately avoided putting their best team in the top spot against the Spaniards. I couldn't get Aquino or Stricker to admit it, but the lineups certainly seem to bear Harrington out. In the top spot, Stricker threw out Koepka and Berger. Not that they were sacrificial lambs—the stats showed that Berger was a particularly strong foursomes player, and the two had won the day before. Still, they hadn't played especially well, and the pairings that came next looked a lot like an intentional stack: Morikawa-Johnson, arguably their best team, playing second, followed by Thomas-Spieth and Schauffele-Cantlay. These were the same four pairs that had played Friday morning, but now the order was shifted around.

On paper, it looked like a massive advantage for the Americans in three matches, with Europe as favorites in match one, and that's exactly how it played out.

Every match was close—two reached the eighteenth green, and the others made it all the way to seventeen. Up top, the Americans put an enormous dent into the Spanish mystique—and the idea of European momentum—by winning the first three holes. It was Berger making the birdie putts after good approaches by Koepka on the first two, and on the third, Sergio's tee shot flew twenty yards left into the native area, and the best they could manage was bogey. With American red on the board early in match one, and the prospect of paper advantages in the rest of the matches, it was now incumbent on the Europeans to stage a comeback.

It started on six, with a nine-foot birdie putt for Rahm, and after the Americans made bogey on eight to see their lead shrink to just one hole, García came through with the shot of the match, a forty-foot chip-in, to square things at the turn. From then on, the momentum was all theirs. Rahm set up a birdie on twelve, which was turning out to be a very good hole for him, with a tee shot to seven feet that Sergio knocked in, and on thirteen, Koepka hit a miserable approach from just 108 yards, coming up short of the green in the right intermediate rough. That led to bogey, and on fifteen, Koepka got into a dustup with two rules officials when he sought relief from a metal drain. Both men refused, ruling that it wouldn't affect his swing, and Koepka lashed out: "If I break my wrist, it's on fucking both of you guys."

Though Sergio gave one back on fourteen when he flew the green, the Spaniards went dormie on sixteen when he hit a spectacular second shot on the par-5 244 yards—just after a fan in the crowd told him he would choke—stopping the ball less than five feet from the hole. Rahm made the eagle, Berger pushed his tee shot on seventeen into the right rough, and Europe had its second outright win of the Cup. With that win, Sergio García reached twenty-four Ryder Cup victories, breaking a tie with his nemesis Nick Faldo and becoming the all-time leader.

And once again, that was as good as it got. Johnson and Morikawa birdied four of their first five holes—DJ even outdid Sergio with a forty-seven-foot birdie on the third—and were 4-up at the turn. Casey and Hatton made a strong surge on the back nine, winning three holes to cut the deficit to one, but when Hatton missed a five-footer on fifteen, the lead was back to 2-up. Stricker was on hand to watch them split sixteen with pars, cutting a lonely figure as always, and two more pars on seventeen were good enough for the Americans to close out a 2&1 win.

Justin Thomas's difficult Ryder Cup seemed to be continuing in the third match, where he and Spieth fell 3-down to Hovland and Wiesberger after six holes, but a twelve-footer from Thomas on seven and a twenty-six-footer by Spieth erased that margin in short order, and a run of three straight wins on holes fourteen to sixteen, punctuated by Thomas's 240-yard 4-iron to set up a Spieth eagle on sixteen, forced the Europeans to the brink. Hovland holed a long birdie putt on seventeen to stay alive, but when his drive sailed far right on eighteen and Wiesberger hit the desperate approach into the water, Stricker had another point.

Finally, in the anchor match, it was almost inconceivable to believe that Westwood and Fitzpatrick could beat the young dream team of Cantlay and Schauffele, and after Cantlay buried a twenty-three-footer to go 1-up at nine, he was all intensity as he marched to the tenth tee.

"It's time to put our metal spikes down on their fucking necks," he said.

It was an intense quote, and a very specific one. It may also have solved the mystery of the Tiger Woods text that had been discussed for the past two days. It emerged after the Ryder Cup from Rex Hoggard at the Golf Channel that the content of the text had referred to stepping on Europe's necks—perhaps with some colorful language added in— and it seems possible, even likely, that Cantlay was quoting Tiger directly as he made the turn on Saturday morning.

Whatever the case, he was as good as his word. The Europeans started the back nine with two bogeys, and a 3-up margin was plenty for the two friends on the verge of yet another win. Schauffele hit his approach to two feet on fifteen, and a pair of pars on seventeen ended the match. Afterward, Schauffele explained the philosophy that had made them so successful.

"No weird faces, no apologies," he said. "We know we're trying our hardest on each shot. We have each other's back."

For the third straight session, the Americans had won 3-1, and now the overall lead had stretched to 9-3. It was agonizingly close to over—Stricker was just 2 points away from that 11-point threshold that would turn Sunday into a coronation.

The sky grew darker for the afternoon four-balls, the air was colder, and for the first time, the tension was mounting as it became clear that this could be the last meaningful golf of the whole event. Justin Thomas and Daniel Berger, both sitting for the afternoon, kicked things off on the first tee by chugging beers thrown from the crowd and spiking the empty cans on the ground. The fans loved it, but at least one European golfer, who didn't want to be named, thought it had crossed the line.

"Is that necessary?" he asked. "It's not a frat party. I take my hat off; we got well and truly pounded. However, my question would be, if Arnold Palmer and Jack Nicklaus were sitting on that first tee, would that have happened? It won't really get spoken about that much because the win was such a dominant win, but put it this way: if you're going to entice and create a hostile environment, it fuels the fire."

The intensity, and the fatigue of two days of pressure golf, began to tell in players' behavior. At least three—DeChambeau, Thomas, and Shane Lowry—griped about being forced to make short putts. Lowry was particularly animated throughout, spurred on by a group of Irish fans, and later made accusations that fans had shouted in his backswing. Vice captain Luke Donald yelled at a photographer who got in Viktor Hovland's eye-line. And for the first time, the Europeans managed not to lose a session.

It was Rahm and García who led the way again in match two, taking on the team of Koepka and Spieth that was one of Stricker's few forays out of the pods. They had intended to play Spieth and Thomas again, but were getting word that Thomas looked tired, and they wanted to make sure he was well rested for Sunday. The pairing shocked Spieth, and the one thing Stricker felt bad about after the Cup was that Spieth and Thomas hadn't been able to play a four-ball session together. When he apologized to Spieth when it was all over, Spieth had a quick comeback: "If you had played us, we could have won 20-8."

The highlight of the match came on the sixteenth, with the Americans threatening on the par-5, when Rahm, fresh off a birdie that put the Europeans 1-up, hit out of a miserable spot in the bunker to twenty-six feet and drilled the birdie putt to steal the hole away. The moment carried García away, and he raced to give his partner a hug.

"I was the number one spectator watching a great guy do great thing after great thing," García said after the match. "It was awesome to be a part of."

The elder Spaniard took the lead role with a par on the last, and the Spanish pair finished 3-0 together. In spite of the team loss, they etched their names in Ryder Cup history as the latest proud duo from their country to achieve Ryder Cup success. They earned their place in the Spanish lineage—a worthy continuation of the Armada. It was one of the very few points of pride for Europe that weekend, but it was a big one.

When Lowry and Hatton nipped English and Finau in the lead match—thanks to Lowry's ten-footer for par on the last hole, which produced an almost violent celebration—Europe had reduced the deficit to 9-5 with two matches out on the course. In theory, at least, a manageable 9-7 deficit still seemed possible.

But in the third match, DeChambeau and Scheffler, still smarting over a disappointing half point Friday, saved their best golf for the crunch. Trailing by a hole at the fourteenth, DeChambeau blasted a drive 340 yards over the dogleg, past the bunkers, and onto the fairway. With forty yards left to the hole, he pitched on to seven feet and finished the birdie to square the match. It was Scheffler's turn on fifteen, and when his sixteen-foot birdie putt went down, the Americans had the lead. With both teams beginning to congregate near the last few holes, Scheffler struck again on the par-5 sixteenth, pitching to inside three with his third shot and winning the hole. Finally, with the coup de grâce, it was DeChambeau attacking the long par-3 with a tee shot that stopped seven feet away. When his birdie putt was conceded, both players had secured their first ever Ryder Cup win. The feeling was so good between them that they even executed a chest bump—a potentially hazardous decision for Scheffler.

Theirs was not the anchor match, but as it happened, they were the last ones on the course. That's because the final pairing for the US team was the indomitable duo of Johnson and Morikawa—the two players who finished with the best strokes gained numbers of anyone in the field by the time the weekend was over—who were not the least bit afraid to see McIlroy and Poulter across from them. Stricker's intent heading into the week was that nobody would play all four pairs sessions, because it would wear them out for singles, and the great irony is that the only player who did was Johnson, the oldest man on the team. In fact, he was eager to go.

"Since 2010, Dustin Johnson has done every little thing we've asked of him," Love marveled. "It's incredible."

On the sixth, Morikawa drove the green with a 334-yard blast, converted the eagle, and followed up with a 227-yard dart to seven feet on the long par-3 seventh. Another birdie there, and a hole-winning par on nine, saw the Americans 3-up at the turn. Ian Poulter refused to die easily, making three birdies on the back nine, but at every step, Morikawa was right there to match him with birdies, and the Europeans couldn't put the slightest dent into the lead. It had turned into an incredible duel between the young American and the English Ryder Cup legend—McIlroy didn't make a single birdie the entire match—and it was Poulter who finally blinked on the fifteenth, settling for par as Morikawa drilled a twenty-two-footer to close out the American win.

That made 3 points in three matches for the American super pair, and 4 points total for Johnson, who would have a chance on Sunday to become just the second American ever to earn 5 points in five matches.

More importantly, Stricker had his 11 points before Sunday singles. Pádraig Harrington wouldn't dare admit it was over—he told his team that if each person took care of his 1 point, there was no telling what they could accomplish on Sunday, and he told me later that he really believed it. Stricker wouldn't admit it either, and once again he used the full hour to prepare his singles lineup, still afraid of a letdown. But for all neutral parties, the outcome was now clear—America would be favored in eleven of twelve matches come Sunday, and the last remaining bit of drama was not whether they would win, but exactly what kind of rout it would be.

The scene after the afternoon matches came close to resembling a victory party. Justin Thomas's girlfriend (now fiancée) pulled out an old cheerleader move, DeChambeau hugged his mom, Scheffler chatted with his own mother, Morikawa was all smiles in an interview with Jimmy Roberts, and Fred Couples put his arm around Cantlay and called him "my boy here." All that was missing was the alcohol.

"It's a long day tomorrow," said Lowry, fresh off his winning putt. "I was looking at stuff on my phone, and for some reason it popped up, and it said, 'If you've got a 1 percent chance, you have to have 100 percent faith.'"

The captains preached the same message, a message both thought their teams needed to hear:

The Europeans still have a chance.

* * *

Q. *No modern team since 1979 has reached nineteen points. Has that been discussed in the room, setting a record?*

STEVE STRICKER: *No, I didn't know of that point total at all.*

—Press conference, Saturday night

The Europeans did not have a chance. There were two defining moments very early on Sunday that quelled all hope, and they came from the unsung heroes of Whistling Straits, Scottie Scheffler and Bryson DeChambeau.

Stricker, so keen to learn lessons from the past, had Davis Love III by his side while he made lineups for Sunday singles, and there was nobody better to consult than Love, who to this day beats himself up for how he let the 10-6 lead at Medinah slip away.

"It still crushes me," Love said. "Not for me, but for the guys we put in a position not to succeed. We left them hanging . . . certainly Bubba and Webb. Bubba and Webb going first was just a complete air ball. And we should've sent Tiger Woods out first, just like we send the big guns out first since then. We learned a lot from it, but it's a tough lesson."

The night after, he was talking to Darren Clarke, and Clarke was still incredulous. "You know we're going to load the boat," he said. "Why weren't you loading the boat?"

In the book *Inverting the Pyramid*, author Jonathan Wilson traces the history of soccer tactics, and the title refers to how, over time, the original concept of playing more players in attacking positions was quite literally inverted as the game modernized, to the point now where the wide base of the pyramid is now on the defensive end. In Sunday singles at the Ryder Cup, the opposite phenomenon has happened. The old custom of playing the best players at the end—a custom Tony Jacklin first violated in 1983, to Jack Nicklaus's chagrin—has been inverted to where the team with the lead strategically puts its best players out first in order to deprive the trailing team of momentum, and the trailing team is almost forced to do likewise, because to backload the lineup would potentially cede the opening matches of the session and make it impossible to gain any traction. Medinah was likely the last straw for the old ways, with the best players toward the back or the middle; today, the biggest weapons always go first.

Davis Love referenced basketball to put it in perspective: "You don't get a forty-point lead at halftime and come out at halftime and go, 'Okay, we're going to play prevent defense the rest of the game.'"

On Sunday at Whistling Straits, Harrington led with McIlroy, Lowry, Rahm, and García, while Stricker—spoiled for depth—ran out three of his best pairs in order: Schauffele, Cantlay, Scheffler, DeChambeau, Morikawa, Johnson.

The first sign that there would be no Medinah-style miracle came from Scottie Scheffler, who drew Jon Rahm. The Vegas odds had America favored in every match except this one—a sign of the respect everyone had for the world number one who had been so heroic for the first four sessions. However, there was reason to believe he was ripe for a loss. From Rory McIlroy at Hazeltine to Justin Thomas at Melbourne, there's a rich vein of recent match play history indicating that players who play all four pairs sessions for a trailing team—especially a trailing *away* team, battling an unfriendly crowd—end up completely exhausted by Sunday.

In fact, the Scheffler matchup couldn't have worked out any better for the Americans, because he had been used as a four-ball specialist with DeChambeau, played only twice, and had fresh legs compared to Rahm, who had been marching across the difficult terrain of Whistling Straits for almost seventy-two holes already and whose mental state was approaching total exhaustion. When the pairings came out, the US team was excited to see that match in particular, and they urged him to bring down the Spanish giant.

"This was a different American team," Harrington lamented. "Scheffler comes in only having played twice, and *happy* that he's only played twice. No chip on the shoulder."

From the start, it was a bloodbath, and not the way Vegas expected. Scheffler made birdie on his first four holes, Rahm was staggered and unable to respond, and the scoreboard told the rest of the European team that their best hope, the fighting spirit of their side, was 4-down after four holes.

"It was amazing to see that," Dustin Johnson said later. Johnson is not prone to gushing about his fellow players, but he didn't hold back on Scheffler. "One thing that could really push the US team was Scottie going out and beating their best player."

Tony Finau called it "huge momentum," and Spieth concurred, saying, "We all saw it. We knew it was happening."

Scheffler would eventually win 4&3. There was some poetic payoff in the fact that Scheffler had impressed Stricker by beating Rahm at the

WGC Match Play that spring, and now he had rewarded the captain's faith by doing it again.

Scheffler told me he's still figuring out his match play style, but what he knows is that he hates losing, and playing against a stud like Rahm gets him more fired up than usual. In this, he shares his DNA with the other young Americans, and their collective brilliance at Whistling Straits earned the respect of another player Scheffler beat in Austin, Ian Poulter.

"The old brigade is gone," he said. "The old brigade of yesterday has passed the baton down to a younger crop of golfers who are a bit more ruthless, a bit more aggressive, and they have a lot of swagger about them."

"I think the most important thing for the US team is a lot of young guys that are great players have bought in to the Ryder Cup," McIlroy said. "I think that was probably missing in previous generations."

The next moment that put a stamp on the impending victory came one match later, when Bryson DeChambeau stepped up to the tee at the par-4 first hole. Sergio García, 3-0 to that point, was his opponent, but DeChambeau couldn't have cared less who he was playing. He ripped a 354-yard drive onto the green, and it set the crowd on fire. The sheer physical strength of the act imparted a thrill that traveled from spectator to spectator like electricity, and he cultivated the bedlam by holding his putter high over his head as he marched down the fairway. Sergio García hit his approach to twelve feet, showing admirable courage under the circumstances, but then DeChambeau stepped up and drilled his forty-one-foot eagle putt. The reaction went beyond bedlam.

"I thought we needed to lead with power," Love said afterward. "You don't save Bryson for the end. You bring the hammer. And Bryson drives the green. Then makes the putt. Well, okay, now it's over."

And he didn't just mean that the hole was over, or even that particular match. He meant the whole Ryder Cup.

In fact, DeChambeau's drive was a perfect representation of the week. As Harrington would tell me later, the US team ended up gaining a massive seventeen strokes over the Europeans off the tee, won thirty-four par-5 holes to Europe's fourteen (ending with a 46-under total score to Europe's 22-under), and excelled on the short par-4s.

By loading the boat, Stricker did exactly what he needed to do. The United States won five of the first seven matches and halved another, and DeChambeau clinched the tying point.

In the late morning, I stood next to Harrington near the contestant interview area overlooking the eighteenth green, where players had to walk through when making the turn. It wasn't hard to see the devastation on his face. He seemed unreachable, with a thousand-yard stare, and though he did his best to encourage Shane Lowry as he went through, Lowry—3-down to Patrick Cantlay at that moment—could only offer him a sad shrug. A common response from the European team after the last match had ended was their disappointment at having let Harrington down, and Lowry was clearly feeling it acutely then, especially as Harrington's countryman and a captain's pick.

Cantlay, coming after him, was all business, eyes dead ahead. Lowry made a gallant run on the back nine, buoyed on by an even larger pack of Irish fans than had showed up Saturday, but after getting the deficit down to 1, Cantlay crushed him with three straight birdies between fourteen and sixteen.

Morikawa clinched the Ryder Cup with an anticlimactic half point—only DeChambeau and Scheffler, fresh off sinking the Spanish Armada, were there to watch—and from there, the margin grew. Dustin Johnson got his historic fifth point with a 1-up win against Paul Casey, Koepka took down Wiesberger 2&1, and Justin Thomas isolated and pounded Tyrrell Hatton 4&3.

Remarkably, both Lee Westwood and Ian Poulter—who, even on this disastrous weekend, finished as the fourth best player on either team in terms of strokes gained—managed to beat back against the tide, winning their singles matches against Finau and English, respectively. Westwood had been in this position before, in 2006, as the second-to-last match out in a European drubbing, and he knew how hard it was to keep your focus when your team had already won. He also knew this was almost certainly his final Ryder Cup match, and he wanted badly to finish on a high note. He used that experience to his advantage and, by his own reckoning, "stole one" from English, overturning a 2-down deficit on the fifteenth tee.

As for Poulter, who beat Finau 3&2 to improve his Ryder Cup singles record to an absurd 6-0-1—there will never be anyone better—what he achieved against a tough American player was best summarized by the words of Viktor Hovland, who looked at him with awe when they met afterward behind the eighteenth green.

"*The fucking postman,*" he said.

Spieth and Fleetwood fought to a lackluster half, and in the final match, Matt Fitzpatrick, whose bad luck was unending, somehow managed to hit his approach into the stream on the eighteenth hole, handing the last match to Daniel Berger. With that win, the six US rookies completed their Ryder Cup with an astounding 14-4-3 record. Stricker had long maintained that he was happy to have so many first-timers because they came in with no Ryder Cup scar tissue. Once again, the results bore him out.

As the Americans began to celebrate—this time, Schauffele got in on the beer-chugging act, and Morikawa made the rounds with a giant bottle of Moët—the scoreboard told a story of carnage.

The reality settled in: it was the greatest blowout in the modern history of the Ryder Cup.

*   *   *

On Saturday night, a reporter asked Sergio García what he had said to Rory McIlroy, whose play had been far below his standard as he stumbled to an 0-3 mark in the pairs sessions.

"I told him the absolute truth," García said. "I told him that not only me but the whole team is proud of him if he goes 5-0 or 0-5, that we love him and that we are always proud of the effort that he makes and the heart that he puts into his golf and into the team."

On Sunday, McIlroy led his team in the number one singles spot and defeated Xander Schauffele 3&2. The original plan was to send him out eleventh, but the team wouldn't have it—he was Rory McIlroy, and he had to lead the way. It was too little, too late in terms of the team outcome, and he knew it, but it served to restore a dose of pride in what had otherwise been a disastrous week.

As he conducted his interview with Sky Sports on the sixteenth green, something remarkable happened: he broke down in tears.

"I love being a part of this team," he said. "I love my teammates so much. I should have done more for them this week . . . I just can't wait to get another shot at this."

After another long pause to collect himself, he said, "It is by far the best experience in golf. I hope little boys and girls watching this today aspire to play this event and the Solheim Cup because there is nothing better than being a part of a team, especially the bond we have in Europe."

A moment later, with the Golf Channel, he broke down again, saying, "They've always been the greatest experiences of my career. I've never really cried or got emotional over what I've done as an individual. I couldn't give a shit."

He was echoing something I'd heard from Henrik Stenson, who told me, "I've always said I'd rather be on the losing side of a Ryder Cup team than not to play on a Ryder Cup team."

"Rory's a young man," Harrington said, "and he takes a lot on. He has a lot weighing on his shoulders, and the reason he cried afterwards was because he takes on too much. He shouldn't have to have those responsibilities. And remember, probably the only other person you can put in that position would be Tiger, and Tiger would be famous for not giving like Rory gives."

Jon Rahm told reporters that the Ryder Cup felt better than his US Open win; Shane Lowry called it the best week of his golfing career, and said, "I'm having the time of my life, and we're six points behind. What's it going to be like when we're leading?"

In the hours following the American victory, Team USA proceeded to get very drunk—a time-honored tradition for the winners—but I saw six players from Team Europe cry. Different eyes, same tears.

"I hate this tournament," Westwood said in the team press conferences. "It makes you so emotional."

They laughed and joked, and sometimes the mood flipped drastically from one moment to the next. It became clear that Tommy Fleetwood had done something risqué in the team room, possibly involving partial or full nudity, and as the team teased him and Fleetwood stared daggers in return—particularly at McIlroy, who seemed to be on the verge of spilling the secret—the mood seemed almost lighthearted despite the loss. And then, not twenty seconds later, I looked back at Fleetwood, and he was crying.

Everything that made Team Europe special through the years was on display in that room, and the fact that it shone through after what looked on paper like an embarrassing loss only proved how enduring their bonds were. Nor was this a 2008 Faldo situation—they loved Pádraig Harrington, and they did everything they could to defend his captaincy.

"I'm quite a practical person," said Harrington. "But I know I needed to be more than that when you're the Ryder Cup captain. I do think I managed to bring these guys together. Okay, we didn't get the results we wanted, but I think we were a team. And that's the most important thing."

Harrington would be hit by regret in the days to come, but when it came to his team, everybody in that room knew he meant what he said.

* * *

When the drunken Americans took the stage—drunken except for Tony Finau, the Mormon, who nonetheless smiled and laughed with the others—it was a scene of barely restrained debauchery.

"I think we all as a team vote DJ as our emotional leader," said Justin Thomas, tongue firmly in cheek despite DJ's 5-0 record. "Poor guy went out there, tried to get six points, but all he could do was five. He is our leader. We're following Grandpa into the abyss."

When asked by one writer if he could still party with his teammates despite his advanced age, Johnson didn't hold back.

"Absof . . . lutely," he said, showing admirable restraint after the *f* sound escaped his lips.

In the midst of them all sat Steve Stricker, looking isolated as ever, shoulders hunched, almost retreating into himself. He adamantly refused to give any colorful answers, and returned again and again to the theme of preparation. The players openly campaigned for him to captain again in Rome, but if anything, the idea just made him more uncomfortable— above all else, in that moment, he was tired. He did, however, call the assembled players the greatest team in Ryder Cup history, and it was difficult to argue with him.

And I thought then of Jason Aquino's term, "institutional memory," and how Stricker embodied it. From Valhalla, he had learned the benefit of pods, and how to invest your team in winning the Ryder Cup. From Medinah, he had learned the importance of setting a proper singles lineup and setting up the course to your team's advantage. From Gleneagles, he had learned quite a lot, in particular the importance of being predictable for your players, letting them see the process unfold far in advance, and seeking their input and the input of vice captains at each step. From Hazeltine, he learned the value of statistics. From Paris, he learned what to seek in captain's picks—tailor them to the course— and the need to meet as a group ahead of time. From Melbourne, he learned which personalities fit best in the team room. From his own playing days, he learned to minimize the number of extracurricular commitments, to forgo videos and speeches, and to let the players be comfortably themselves.

In the era when Team USA was losing repeatedly, I often asked myself a question that I know others were asking too: What if these American teams, with their superior talent, were run with the wisdom and efficiency of the Europeans? If the European template is so good that it can lift them over better players, sometimes to dramatic degrees, what would happen if you implemented such a system on the side of the best golfing nation on the planet?

What happens when American power is no longer stifled by mismanagement, but elevated and ultimately unleashed by a superb captaincy?

Whistling Straits was the laboratory. As dusk fell on Sunday night, the answer could still be seen, faintly, on the towering scoreboards posted across the course:

19-9.

EPILOGUE
Visions of Rome

"I don't agree that it's just going to be fine, and that we can go on and do exactly the same thing in two years' time and expect to win. I think our competitors got a lot stronger. Our competitor is a lot smarter off the golf course. Our competitor will be coming here with a different mentality than they had in France. I don't think this should be brushed under the carpet. This was a serious defeat."

—Paul McGinley

"If I win, I'll be considered a great manager. If I lose, no matter how good a job I've done, there will be something said, something found out, to say, 'That's why you didn't win.' It's horribly black-and-white."

—Pádraig Harrington, two months before the Ryder Cup

As the Americans became drunker and drunker in the minutes following their victory, the talk turned to Rome and the 2023 Ryder Cup. They were riding high, and rightfully so, and almost immediately their minds leapt to the great challenge of breaking a thirty-year dry spell and winning in Europe. At that moment, they felt like nobody could beat them. "We're going to Rome!" they shouted, and Davis Love III hastened to remind them that no, first they were going to Charlotte—not quite as alluring a destination, but home to the 2022 Presidents Cup where Love would serve as captain.

In the hours and days and weeks that followed that Sunday at Whistling Straits, the obvious question came up in America and Europe: Does this represent a sea change in Ryder Cup fortunes? The same question had been asked in 2016 after the Hazeltine victory, but that American team hadn't been so comprehensively young and confident. It included key players like Jimmy Walker, Phil Mickelson, Brandt Snedeker, Zach Johnson, J. B. Holmes, Matt Kuchar, and Ryan Moore, and it was clear even then that most of those names would have perhaps one more Ryder Cup in them at most, either because of age or skill.

The Whistling Straits team, by contrast, represented a generational shift that had never been seen to quite the same degree at the Ryder Cup, at least since Jacklin's European teams of the mid-1980s. Inevitably, one or two of the names will drop out of the upper echelons by the time Rome arrives, but the nucleus is there, and it's easy to imagine players like Schauffele, Cantlay, Morikawa, Thomas, Spieth, Scheffler, Berger, and DeChambeau—none of whom have reached their thirtieth birthday—playing a vital role in US Ryder Cup fortunes for years to come. In fact, the same is true for the "older" players like Koepka and Tony Finau, who have barely hit thirty and could have another decade or more in their golfing prime.

And who matches them in Europe? Rory McIlroy, Jon Rahm, Viktor Hovland . . . and then it starts getting hazy. Was Tommy Fleetwood more than a Ryder Cup flash in the pan in Paris? Can Fitzpatrick show more grit as his career develops? And will any of the younger golfers on the European side who didn't make Whistling Straits, but whose names were bandied about afterward, rise to the levels of the Americans? Can we expect greatness of Robert MacIntyre, Rasmus Højgaard, or Guido Migliozzi? And even if Ryder Cup glory is in their future, can it happen as fast as two years, when at least some of the old guard like Poulter, Westwood, Casey, and García will finally have aged out?

* * *

I found Pádraig Harrington eager to talk after the Ryder Cup. He made the media rounds to get his perspective out, in part because he was finding it difficult to read some of the criticisms floating around—the Matthew Fitzpatrick ball incident, in particular—and in part because this was his way to go on the record without responding to every social media post.

I had found the criticisms of Harrington extremely mild by Ryder Cup standards, and his players totally supportive. The general perspective was that America had the more talented team, Stricker was an excellent captain, and home course advantage did the rest. But Harrington was the man in the spotlight; he was scared of losing a Ryder Cup from the start, and even the tamest critiques stung. Still, he dealt with it all with his usual good humor, and despite the evident pain, he didn't sound bitter or defensive.

"People ask, 'Do you regret anything about the Ryder Cup?'" he said. "And some of me says, What the hell was I doing taking a Ryder Cup in the US?"

That perspective came late. Before the Ryder Cup, unlike many outside observers, he was fully convinced Europe was going to win. He reiterated his point about the US team learning from the European template—he was particularly impressed with Stricker's pick of Scheffler as a specific partner for DeChambeau—about their good fortune in practicing in the tournament wind the week before Europe arrived, and about small management coups, like the fact that Stricker held his nightly team meetings in the clubhouse to give his players freedom at night, while Europe got a police escort to the hotel first and then had to reconvene.

And he knew that the pandemic didn't help—along with limiting the number of European fans, it made 2021 arguably the easiest Ryder Cup in terms of time management for the players, and he knew that Europe fared better when there was some kind of controversy or drama.

"Can I regret COVID?" he asked. "Is that allowed? COVID was bad. There you go."

On captain's picks, he admitted that he would have had other choices if Lee Westwood hadn't made the team, but he wouldn't budge on his original logic, even if the statistics refuted him.

"All I know is, if you pick somebody or the guy qualified, the guy qualified feels very comfortable being there, and the guy picked—especially if he's in any way a pivotal pick—feels a lot more pressure," he said.

He also reiterated that the most important thing to him was creating a lasting memory for his players, and that for a European team, the best way to do that was to involve all twelve players in a group setting, as opposed to the American separation tactics. In fact, it was Harrington who insisted that even if the losing team no longer had to stay to watch the winning team's trophy ceremony, he wanted all the players and vice captains to shake hands in a line on the eighteenth green. In the end, he felt that was one of the better moments for him, because he shook hands with Jim Furyk and Davis Love—former losing captains—and they knew his pain, and he knew theirs.

"When I was thinking about the job," he said, "I feared, Would I be able to give to the players what they need? In my career, I've been very focused on doing my thing. But now I have to work and understand twelve players and many other components in terms of caddies, wives, vice captains, everybody else. Could I give of myself? And I believe I did. Everything I feared, I overcame. I believe I gave everybody as good a Ryder Cup experience as they've ever had."

* * *

Even in an era when home course advantage is massive, it's clear that America is operating from a position of strength, and Europe from a position of hope. Pádraig Harrington was of the mindset that the European process was not broken, and there was no need to do anything different, while Paul McGinley was duly worried about the poor performance in Whistling Straits. While allowing that it was the best American team he'd ever seen, and the "strongest package we've ever faced there," the statistics didn't show that America played so incredibly well that they were unbeatable. Harrington backed this up—his stats people showed that six of the top twelve golfers in strokes gained for the weekend were European.

McGinley sits on a special four-person Ryder Cup advisory board that formed within the European Tour two years ago. It includes Sir Damon Buffini, a hugely successful businessman who chairs the board; Richard Scudamore, the former executive chairman of the English Premier League; and Ian Ritchie, the former chairman of Wimbledon and chief executive of the Rugby Football Union. Their joint goal is to "bring brand Ryder Cup to the next level," and while the others focus on the business and marketing side, McGinley's role is a strategic one—he'll advise the European Tour on all practical Ryder Cup matters, including the choosing of the next captain.

When he served as captain, one of the posters he hung in the team room read, "Passion has determined our past; attitude will determine our future." In his mind, even if winning at Whistling Straits was always going to be difficult, the team's attitude wasn't exactly in the right place.

"The Americans have matched us in the passion stakes," he said, "so now it becomes about attitude, about being the Rottweiler, of being inside that siege mentality of playing away from home and knowing it's going to be incredibly difficult. Where's the psychology? Where's the mentality? That was going to be critical to our success. And did we have that in place, or were we too focused on all the other things?"

By "all the other things," McGinley was referring to the team's decision to wear cheeseheads in homage to the home crowd on Wednesday, or the inspirational videos that circulated on social media. Those stories took on outsize importance early in the week, and ultimately none of it mattered. McGinley is fond of saying, "Always make the big thing the big thing"—it's a quote he thinks came from Bill Belichick, originally—and his job, and Europe's job as a whole, is to figure out what that big thing will be in Rome.

He spoke about creating an advisory board that could help the captain—he wondered who advised Harrington to take fewer captain's picks, for instance, and not to use the opportunity COVID presented to take more, the way Stricker had—but he also spoke more theoretically about concepts like "harnessing the underdog mentality" that has prevailed in Europe for decades.

Still, it's easy to see Whistling Straits as the moment when the United States erased the strategic advantage they'd held for years, learned how to play as the favorites, and saw the successful culmination of the process that had begun when the Ryder Cup task force was formed. McGinley might be the brightest Ryder Cup mind ever unleashed on this event, but in our talks after Whistling Straits, even his ideas about how to turn things around began to sound a little vague, a little hopeful.

The US has tasted blood, and is out for more. Just weeks after the Ryder Cup, Zach Johnson—the odds-on choice to be the American captain in Rome—approached Davis Love on a putting green near their homes in the barrier islands of Georgia with a list of Ryder Cup topics he wanted to discuss. It got so in-depth that they decided to schedule a time to meet to hash it all out.

Part of that discussion is analyzing what went *wrong* at Whistling Straits. When Love told me that, I couldn't help but scoff—how can you improve on the biggest victory ever? His response incorporated elements like food and transportation that were so granular they'd be too boring to recount here—at one point, it got down to what kind of water Dustin Johnson drinks—but that have a big impact on the players' experience, and will be improved in the future. Susan Martin, a manager at the PGA of America who works closely with all the captains and teams, has already sent out a questionnaire to everyone involved with the Ryder Cup to identify other areas of improvement.

If they've come so far as managers and planners that they're thinking in great depth about the food and the cars, it seems clear that absolutely no stone is being left unturned. And coupled with the quality of the players, it's a disheartening prospect for their enemies; it's America unleashed. Provided they don't blow it with bad captains or dysfunction or other avoidable mistakes, it's easy to read this as the sunset of the

European era of dominance. If the Americans can win in Rome, they'll have made the case.

At the start of the Whistling Straits Ryder Cup, when all evidence pointed to a US victory, so many fans and media members couldn't quite be convinced; such was the European aura. After three days of golf, the complete opposite mindset had set in, and the prevailing winds of belief were totally reversed. Invincibility has changed hands, and now the Americans look unbeatable.

The question is, Do you believe it?

* * *

It took a long time to reconnect with Stricker after it was over. He was his usual polite self in text exchanges, but the simple fact of the matter, as he explained when I finally got him on the phone in early November, is that he just didn't want to think about the Ryder Cup anymore. Speaking with a reporter about it, as you might imagine, was very low on his wish list. He fulfilled an obligation to play at the Furyk and Friends event in Jacksonville, but otherwise he spent the days and weeks after reconnecting with his family, enjoying home life, and bow hunting for deer in the woods of Wisconsin. There was a strangeness to the transition of going from total commitment for three years to just nothing, and he coped with that strangeness alone.

"And that's partly why it took me so long to call you," he said. "I was checked out of golf. I didn't even want to watch it. I was just . . . I was done."

(I learned much later that around this time, Stricker had been laid low by a mysterious virus, and not long after our last call, he'd have to spend eleven days at the University of Wisconsin Hospital, where he lost twenty-five pounds and suffered from jaundice and heart arrhythmia before recovering.)

We spoke about tactics and players and moments, but what I wanted to know the most was how he felt afterward. This, of course, is a tough thing to get out of Stricker, whose least favorite activity is talking about himself and his emotions.

"It's a good question," he said. "There was a ton of relief after it was over. You know, throwing that whole extra year on there just made it that way a little bit. You just couldn't wait for it to get there and be played. You don't think you're going to win by that kind of margin, but I had a lot of dreams. But definitely enjoyed it, definitely glad it was over."

If that sounded a bit ambiguous, he left no room for doubt in what came next.

"It was the highlight of my golfing career."

This jived with what he said immediately after the Ryder Cup, that as a golfer who had never won a major, the Ryder Cup captaincy was his major. Paul McGinley had said the same thing, but McGinley had also been very open about how much it hurt that he found something he was great at, and that he'd never be able to do it again. If he were allowed, I got the feeling he'd captain the Ryder Cup team for thirty years.

Not so for Stricker—he'll be there for the team when they need him, but the worst news you could ever give him, I sensed, was that he had been chosen again. And yet, he's found in the months after Whistling Straits that the captaincy doesn't leave you so easily.

"It's weird," he said. "I still catch myself thinking about it, you know? The pairings, and all that kind of stuff. We thought about it for so long."

*   *   *

When we talk about the Ryder Cup, we conceive of it as a continuous event from 1927 to the present, with short delays for 9/11 and COVID-19, but otherwise unbroken. In fact, after the 1937 event, it wasn't held for a decade. The reason is no secret—World War II. Like a lot of other sporting events across the globe, from domestic leagues to the Olympics, the Ryder Cup was not held for the duration.

Here in America, we have an idea of the sacrifices our country made in that war. They included 405,000 people killed and many more wounded in the effort to win that fight. It sounds like a lot, and it *is* a lot. But in history, there's always context. In that same war, for instance, the Soviet Union lost twenty-seven million people, including nineteen million civilians.

There are degrees of loss, and in the United Kingdom, the total dead was slightly higher than America at 450,000, but there are a couple important things to keep in mind. First, their population is smaller, so it was a bigger proportional blow. There's also the fact that 67,000 of those dead were civilians, most of them killed in the Blitz by the German bombing raids. The United States had its own domestic tragedy in Pearl Harbor, but do you know how many Americans were killed on the US mainland in the course of that war?

The answer is six. A family on a picnic in Oregon found a "fire balloon" the Japanese had flown over on wind currents. The fire balloons were a kind of ambitious but ill-fated attempt at civilian terrorism, and while the project failed overall, this particular balloon exploded and killed a pregnant woman named Elsye Mitchell and five children from her church group. That was the only civilian death toll to speak of in the continental United States.

Meanwhile, for years, the British people lived in fear. Imagine the psychological toll it takes when at a moment's notice, you may have to run to a shelter, praying desperately that you or your loved ones aren't killed by German bombs. And they had it better than continental Europe—at least the Germans never actually made it across the English Channel. The United States came out of that war, economically and militarily speaking, as a robust superpower about to step into its golden age. Not so for the United Kingdom, which lost unbelievable amounts of wealth, had to retool its entire infrastructure and production away from wartime needs, entered a period of austerity, and had to rely on the United States for billion-dollar loans—the dollar, by then, having become the world's foremost currency.

Professional golf felt the effects too. Starting after World War I, the sport that had been invented in the UK and that had been dominated by the UK for decades started going the other way, fast, and became a sport dominated by Americans. Despite a resurgence starting with Jacklin, the truth is that British golf has never quite recovered from those wars, just like the British empire never recovered. They haven't come close to their former status, and it's a safe bet that they never will.

In the midst of all that, in 1947, just two years after the end of World War II, the British PGA had nowhere near enough money to stage a Ryder Cup, much less to send twelve golfers to America to compete abroad. Even if it had, it's unlikely it would have been a priority. Viewed from that angle, 1947 looks like the moment when the Ryder Cup was no longer feasible, and when it should have died. But as we've seen, this event has a strange way of surviving against the odds, and the savior this time was an American named Robert Hudson.

Hudson was a grocery executive from Oregon who owned a food-processing company, introduced the Piggly Wiggly store to the Portland area, and became extremely wealthy. The parallels between him and Samuel Ryder, the man who founded the Ryder Cup, are interesting. Hudson was a grocer; Ryder was a seed merchant. Both of them came to golf late in life, and both became obsessed. Like Ryder, Hudson had an itch to give back to the game. At one point in the 1940s, with the Portland Open about to go bust, Hudson saved it by sponsoring it through his store. Then he brought the 1946 PGA Championship to Portland Golf Club, and a year later he did something even more incredible—this man, who was still new to the sport, and whose handicap would never get lower than 16, decided to bring back the Ryder Cup.

There's a good chance he didn't even know what the Ryder Cup was the last time it had been held, in 1937. It didn't matter—he learned, and something about it spoke to him. He decided that he would work with the PGA of America to resuscitate the event, and when he started, nothing would stop him.

Case in point: when he learned that the British were broke, he paid for everything himself. All expenses, from travel to food to lodging, were on his dime. He paid for a British team to reach the US aboard a ship called the *Queen Mary*, met them in New York, threw a party for them at the Waldorf-Astoria, and then traveled with them for four days to Portland by train.

Thanks to Robert Hudson, there was a Ryder Cup that year, and the next time, and the next time. It was a moment in history when exactly the right person entered the stage at exactly the right time. Though he didn't play and he didn't captain, Hudson's impact was fundamentally no different than Tony Jacklin's—without him, there would be no Ryder Cup.

That British team that came to Portland had one or two recognizable names to a modern fan, but not many. The American team, meanwhile, was a murderer's row: Ben Hogan, Jimmy Demaret, Byron Nelson, Sam Snead. It might sound like the beginning of the greatest David versus Goliath story ever told, but it wasn't. America had entered its prime in so many ways, and golf was one of them. They won 11-1, and that lone point for the British came in the very last match. It got so bad that Ben Hogan didn't even play the last day.

We don't know what those British players thought during that Ryder Cup, and there aren't many primary sources. We don't know if they thought they could win, if they were just happy for the adventure, or if they felt grateful or embarrassed at the end. With hindsight, though, you can see their real purpose: to keep something important from dying. They came from England and Scotland and Wales and Northern Ireland. Their names were Jimmy Adams, Fred Daly, Max Faulkner, Eric Green, Reg Horne, Sam King, Arthur Lees, Dai Rees, and Charlie Ward. Their playing captain was Henry Cotton.

We sometimes want to believe that sports matter more than they really do, and we're not above shoehorning in some extra meaning where it might not belong. Nevertheless, when learning about that 1947 team, my mind immediately went to 1985. When Sam Torrance made his winning putt on that seventeenth hole to break the long European victory drought, we can't go so far as to say it was for the redemption of Great Britain, or a renunciation of the war, or anything melodramatic like that. There are too many complications that spoil the metaphor.

But I can't separate that moment, the first European Ryder Cup victory, from the memory of the 1947 British team. They went to Portland because they understood that even something like a golf tournament, which may look trivial even at the best of times and probably looks even smaller in the aftermath of a global war, still mattered in the way that these institutions *do* matter, in that they mark our existence and our continuity. They didn't go to accomplish something great on the course; they went so that the Ryder Cup would survive down the years, and one day there *would* be people doing great and dramatic things on the course, and these things would be meaningful, at least to somebody.

And one day the players who triumphed would be English, and Scottish, and Welsh, and Irish, and to get to that point, the most important thing was for them to show up, to keep the dream of that future alive. In 1985, almost forty years later, the dream came true.

Everyone from that team has passed away now. Max Faulkner was the last to go in 2005, but seven of them were still living in 1985. And I catch myself wondering what they must have thought about that result. We'll never get to ask them, but I bet they remembered their trip to the West Coast of America, and I have a feeling they had a thought all their own, a thought that even Jacklin and Torrance and Ballesteros couldn't have had, because they simply weren't old enough to remember: we're back.

Which is a long way of saying this: these guys have gone through worse defeats than Whistling Straits, and they haven't gone away yet.

* * *

I spoke to Ian Poulter after the Ryder Cup. I wanted to clear my head of all strategic and theoretical talk, and just listen to the voice of the great man himself in the wake of a record-setting loss. Unlike so many others associated with this event, he tends to speak in simple sound bites, and to reduce things to their essence.

I wanted to speak with him about age, and time—of all the Ryder Cup stalwarts like him now in the twilight of their careers. But he had no interest in nostalgia; he ran down the familiar list of young European players who could be contributing in Rome.

"They're not there yet," he said. "But two years is a long cycle in the game of golf, and we'd be proud to hand the baton down to the boys. And to be honest with you, there's always been upsets in the Ryder Cup. It doesn't go by paper; it doesn't follow form."

I had my doubts about the younger players, that they could ever live up to the stature of living legends like him and Sergio García and others, or that they could translate the passion of decades of European heroes in quite the same way. He did not share my doubts.

"It's very easy to explain," he said. "When you put a shirt on, you have the responsibility of every player who has ever worn that shirt. That's how you need to treat it, and that's the level of passion that you need to go play with. And if you don't feel that sense of passion, then you should not tee it up."

I agreed with him, but it didn't seem like he was answering the question about the new Europeans. I pressed the issue.

"Do you think it matters to the younger generation as much as it does to you?" I asked.

The famous light came into his eyes.

"Don't you worry about that," he said. "I'll make it my fucking job to let them know."

If you had heard him—if you had *seen* him—you'd have believed it too.

ACKNOWLEDGMENTS

To study the Ryder Cup is to study history, and because the golden age of the Ryder Cup began in the 1980s, it's my good luck that much of that history is living history. As such, I want to thank first and foremost the people who shared their wisdom and experience with me firsthand. It will be clear to readers that Paul McGinley and Tony Jacklin gave extensively of their time, and I'm heavily in their debt for all they taught me about the European juggernaut and Ryder Cup strategy. Of all the interviews I've done in my time as a journalist, these are two of the best, and that has nothing to do with me. Paul Azinger and Davis Love III were notably generous and compelling on the American side and equally critical to the goals of this book. Pádraig Harrington deserves a special mention, not just for his openness and good humor, but for his willingness to speak with vulnerability after a difficult loss. Talking with the media has never been Steve Stricker's favorite activity, but he was kind to give me his time and insight, and to let me see inside the mind that was cleverer and more thorough than many expected when the road to Whistling Straits began.

To all the players who spoke with me over the course of this project, and to the agents who were helpful in facilitating it, I also give my thanks. It's easy enough to say no, and many do, but I believe personal legacies live on in books long after commercials have stopped airing, and no player has ever been poorer for agreeing to give a little of his valuable time to a project like this one. There are too many to mention by name, but I'd like to single out the Ryder Cup legend Ian Poulter, who was fully, consummately himself in our post-Cup talk—defiant, unbowed, hilarious, and a little bit frightening. There will never be another Poulter, and that is a major sigh of relief for Team USA.

To everyone in and around Whistling Straits who helped me on this journey, from Brian Gabriel to Stephen Maliszewski to Mike O'Reilly to Chris Zugel to Jason Mengel to Dirk Willis to David Kohler and Herb Kohler, your help and wisdom were invaluable, and your golf courses are beautiful. To Julius Mason at the PGA of America, for helping me with logistics when it wasn't always easy; I am beyond grateful.

It has been an honor to exist for these last few years on the periphery of the media room at golf tournaments, and once again I owe a massive debt of gratitude to all my fellow journalists who have helped me in the process of writing this book. Sean Martin deserves special mention for his help in reading the manuscript and correcting more than a few mistakes. Doug Ferguson of the Associated Press merits top billing, as always, for his intelligence, wit, superb storytelling ability, consummate professionalism, and the significant help he gave me along the way, often in ways that I wasn't smart enough to ask for. It will be a sad day when men like him, and Bob Harig, and Ron Green Jr., and Steve DiMeglio, and too many others to name eventually leave this sport. That day is hopefully far into the future, but with the changing nature of journalism, there will be something irrevocably lost when they're gone. I consider myself very lucky to have shared the tent with them.

I also owe massive thanks to these fine journalists and podcasters and bloggers and jacks-of-all-golf-trades: Dave Shedloski, Chris Solomon, D. J. Piehowski, Kevin Van Valkenburg, Dan Rapaport, Chris Powers, Alex Myers, Steve Hennessey, Joel Beall, Adam Schupak, Ben Everill, Brendan Porath, Andy Johnson, Kyle Porter, Peter Santo, Garrett Johnston, Rex Hoggard, Brentley Romine, Ryan Lavner, Luke Kerr-Dineen, Stephanie Wei . . . We're all in the same business, and some of us work at rival publications, but I've found that there's a sense of camaraderie and even friendship that outweighs any sense of competition, and I'm always thrilled to see them at events. I've benefited from their acquaintance in concrete, material ways, but also simply from the association, simply from tagging along, simply from absorbing their expertise.

To my brilliant editors at *Golf Digest*, Sam Weinman, Ryan Herrington, Tod Leonard, and John Strege, for their constant help and understanding and patience and deft skill, I thank you sincerely. When it comes to patience, Josh Jackson and Allison Keene at *Paste* magazine also deserve a big thank you.

There are saints at the PGA Tour whose job descriptions include helping annoying askers like me, and they also happen to be extremely nice people. To Tracey Veal, Joel Schuchmann, Jack Ryan, Amanda Herrington, John Bush, Doug Milne, Rachel Noble, Stewart Moore, Michael Balicker, and others I'm shamefully forgetting . . . You were endlessly helpful, and believe me, I needed it.

To Todd Lewis at the Golf Channel—thanks for delivering that note.

There are various others affiliated in some way with the Ryder Cup or Whistling Straits or Steve Stricker whose assistance was massive, some of whom made the pages of this book and others who didn't. They include Jason Aquino and Chandler Withington, two of the smartest Ryder Cup minds in the known universe; Justin Ray; Dan Zelezinski; Jon Miller at NBC; Gary D'Amato; Richard Forsythe at Royal Melbourne; Dennis Tiziani; Mario Tiziani; Bob Samuelson; Bob and Carolyn Stricker; and Mike Hesselman.

Along with my own interviews, I relied on many written sources for my research, many of them digital, but foremost among the books were the phenomenal oral history *Us Against Them* by Robin McMillan, Paul McGinley's *Landscape of Success*, Paul Azinger's *Cracking the Code*, *How We Won the Ryder Cup: The Caddies' Stories* by Norman Dabell, *The Ryder Cup: The Complete Story of Golf's Greatest Competition* by Nick Callow, *The First Major* by John Feinstein, and the wonderfully British-centric *The Ryder Cup 1927–2014: A History of Golf's Greatest Match* by Peter Pugh and Henry Lord. I occasionally found David Feherty's *Totally Subjective History of the Ryder Cup* helpful, though I still have no idea which parts are true. Outside of the world of books, it's worth tipping my cap to John Hopkins for his excellent profiles of Seve Ballesteros.

To my agent, Byrd Leavell, the man who makes it all happen, and to my editor, Brant Rumble, for his friendliness, encouragement, and most of all his critical improvements to this text: thank you.

To Mom, Dad, Tom, my grandparents, my brothers, and my sister: you are my foundation. Harold Ryan, you won't be forgotten. And last, to Emily, Sutton, and Alden—without you, there's nothing.

INDEX